HOW WE RECOVERED
THE ASHES

"THE ASHES"

It was in 1882, after the famous seven runs victory of the Australians, that the *Sporting Times* first used the term which has now become familiar to everyone. In that paper appeared the following epitaph:–

In Affectionate Remembrance

of

ENGLISH CRICKET

Which Died at the Oval on

29th AUGUST, 1882,

Deeply Lamented by a Large Circle of
Sorrowing Friends and
Acquaintances.

R.I.P.

N.B.—The Body will be Cremated and the
Ashes taken to Australia.

TO

THE MEMBERS OF THE

MARYLEBONE CRICKET CLUB

AS WHOSE REPRESENTATIVES WE FOUGHT
OUR BATTLES ON AUSTRALIAN WICKETS
AND FOR WHOSE CREDIT WE ARE
PROUD TO HAVE BROUGHT HOME
THE ASHES OF VICTORY

P. F. Warner

HOW WE
RECOVERED
THE ASHES

BY

P. F. WARNER

Captain of the M.C.C. Team

The MCC

CRICKET
LIBRARY

This centenary edition is published by

Methuen

1 3 5 7 9 10 8 6 4 2

Published by Methuen Publishing Limited
215 Vauxhall Bridge Road, London SW1V 1EJ

Methuen Publishing Limited Reg. No. 3543167

© 1963, 2003 The Estate of Sir Pelham Warner

Preface © 2003, Marina Walker
Foreword © 2003, Gerald Howat

A CIP catalogue record for this book is available
from the British Library

ISBN 0 413 77346 9 and 0 413 77399 X

Printed and bound in Great Britain by
St Edmundsbury Press, Bury St Edmunds, Suffolk

CONTENTS

CHAPTER I

CHAPTER II

CHAPTER III

CHAPTER IV

CHAPTER V

CHAPTER VI

LIST OF ILLUSTRATIONS

LIST OF ILLUSTRATIONS

PREFACE TO THE CENTENARY EDITION

Plum lived for cricket: in 1945, when my mother, very young and Italian, arrived in England for the first time, on one of the first passenger flights to land at Heathrow after the war, she was taken to meet her father-in-law, and he immediately began the urgent business of teaching her how to play cricket. He showed her how to bat on the Persian rug in the sitting room of the South Kensington mansion block flat where he then lived, which, when I came to know it around five years later, smelled of Quality Street toffees and the cabbagey stews of post-war London.

Since then, being Plum Warner's eldest grandchild has made strong men scrutinise my face to see if they can catch a glimpse of the great man. Famous playwrights, city brokers, literary biographers, professors of Latin will engage me in discussion, nearly fifty years since Plum's death and nearly a century since he was playing cricket. They talk of his prowess, his decisions and the difficult passages of his career (Bodyline above all), as if it was all still happening now and remained a matter of some urgency. Recently, in Barbados, I met the historian Hilary Beckles, author of the two-volume work *The Development of West Indies Cricket*: he greeted me warmly too because, he said, my grandfather had played an important part in desegregating the West Indies team. (I have to say I wasn't only proud, but also relieved to hear this.)

When my sister Laura and I were children, Plum was a distant, heroic figure who lived and breathed the mysterious essence of cricket: his brown eyes were legendary (we were told he never needed glasses), while his prolific fluency as the game's historian also inspired awe (he had written almost twenty books about cricket and never needed to look up a single score). Numbers of all kinds grew to huge proportions in his ambit: there were the famous scores and centuries, and when I knew Plum, he seemed very old – in those days ninety, as he was in 1963, was a very great age. But, above all, he was the youngest of twentyone children, and Laura and I used to tease him by asking him to tell us all their names. We crowed with delight when he faltered.

Plum was an exotic, too. He had come from far away, from the Caribbean, where he was born to an English family that had been there since the early days of colonial settlement. In the French islands of the archipelago and in the former Spanish territories, such families are Creoles, and see themselves as part of a local, complex, multifarious culture. By contrast, this is a designation the British never adopted in their Empire: home remained England; in their imaginations they saw themselves as belonging nowhere else. Nevertheless, for all his perfect English-gentleman mien, Plum was born in Trinidad with a Spanish mother called Rosa Cadiz, educated in Barbados first, and later at Rugby and Oxford.

Soon after leaving Oxford Plum returned to the West Indies as a member of Lord Hawke's touring team in 1897. In a match against Trinidad, his brother Aucher was in the opposing side.

Three years later, in 1900, Aucher captained the first West
Indian team to tour England. Aucher persuaded Plum to help
them out, after several defeats. Plum did so with a vengeance,
scoring a century for the West Indies against Leicestershire.

He always had vivid memories of Trinidad and felt an
attachment to its people and its history, which comes through
strongly in his various memoirs. Plum first learned to play
cricket "in the marble gallery" of his father's house from "the
bowling of a black boy who rejoiced in the name of Killebree"
(which means hummingbird), as he describes in the opening of
his book, *My Cricketing Life*. That house was burned down a
long time ago, but in Port of Spain, in 1996, I was shown where
the family lived afterwards, and I looked over the fence (it is
now a school) through luxuriant light-flecked foliage and the
tall tangle of tropical trees at a quiet, painted and shuttered
wooden house with a veranda, a privileged enclave but otherwise typical of the tropics.

Plum had also travelled farther afield. Cricket had taken him
all over the globe, and in the days before air travel, these desti-
nations seemed immeasurably distant and strange. My father
used to tell the story of how, when he was about three years old
(this must have been the M.C.C. tour of Australia in 1911–12),
they had sailed through the Suez Canal. He woke up one
morning, and going up on deck found the whole ship and the
crew completely blackened by the dust from the coal that was
being taken on for the next leg of the journey. Days of scrub-
bing and repainting followed, as the ship was restored to her
former state.

Soon after those first lessons in the South Kensington flat,
our mother was to be introduced to the King at a garden party.
She made herself a beautiful and dramatic black and white

dress in the New Look fashion, trimmed a magnificent picture hat for the occasion, and was photographed walking in with Plum. Later, when I looked at the photograph published in the *Illustrated London News*, it seemed that the sphere of cricket and the power of England existed in some deep relation to each other, and made Plum at the M.C.C. the King's sporting counterpart. An aura of patriotic romance of history and nation hung around Plum's slight, courteous figure, and though it was absurd to think like this, I might as well own up to it now.

By the time I knew him in the Fifties, Plum was living with our granny in the South Kensington flat, which was reached by a fascinating lift manned by an ex-soldier with one arm. To raise us to the second floor, he hauled on a rope in the corner running free through a hole in the lift floor and roof. Their sitting room was filled with memorabilia: the daffodil yellow of a run of Wisden, of course, a clock in the shape of a wicket, a clothes brush in the shape of a bat, biscuit tins with pictures, a cigarette box in the shape of a ball, the huge silver cup that was stolen later from our parents' house, Grandpa's caps and hats with different-coloured ribbons, his umbrella with the gold band and his watch-chain in his pinstripe waistcoat, all inscribed PFW. Caricatures hung on the walls, Spy cartoons and photographs of Plum with Queen Mary, of Plum carried off the ground by the crowd, as well as drawings of kangaroos with captions utterly mysterious to me as a child, such as 'Plum brings back the Ashes'. Most excitingly for us children, our grandparents bought a television set. Like so many of my generation, the first programme we watched was the Coronation and we were given a miniature state coach and horses in celebration.

Perhaps Plum's most surprising quality was his light build.

He had suffered from all kinds of ill health as a young man and he never became a giant of brawn of arm and breadth of shoulder, as most athletes are these days. He was also celebrated in our family for the smallness of his appetite: one evening at dinner, when he was asked if he would like a second helping, he replied, "One pea, please."

We spent a great deal of our childhood abroad, and did not see much of our grandparents, but Plum's self-effacing yet poised, slender yet impressive figure embodied history for me, not only a chapter of cricketing history, but many loops and knots to do with England and abroad, with ideas about where one belongs and who one is: he was the pattern of an English gentleman, and everything about him was indeed absolutely cricket. Yet his life shows wonderfully that what that meant was very complicated, and this too was like the game.

MARINA WARNER

KENTISH TOWN, LONDON
July 2003

FOREWORD

The departure of the first official M.C.C. touring party to Australia in September 1903 heralded a significant change from some forty years of private ventures overseas by teams from England. Ever since H. H. Stephenson had led the pioneering visit to Australia in 1861, there had been a two-way traffic between sides from each country. Tours were undertaken as entrepreneurial enterprises organised by businessmen and professional cricketers. The frequency with which they happened is testimony to their financial success. History confers the status of the first Test match on that between James Lilleywhite's team and a combined Australian side in 1877. By 1903 there had been sixty-six such contests between the two countries of which Australia had won twenty-six and England twenty-eight, but the Ashes (to which reference is made below) were then in Australian hands.

The assumption of responsibility for the tour by the Marylebone Cricket Club was the culmination of four years of negotiations between Lord's and Melbourne besides internal discussions within the Australian colonies themselves. One Australian in particular, Major Ben Wardill, believed that future teams from England should be under the aegis of M.C.C. while

English opinion believed this would make it easier to raise stronger teams in that the counties would be more prepared to release their professionals for official tours. That the initiative came from Melbourne lay in the fact that the 'other' M.C.C., Melbourne Cricket Club, was the most powerful influence in Australian circles, especially after the disbanding, in 1900, of the Australasian Cricket Council. Major Wardill had been the Melbourne C.C. secretary since 1879 (his rank came to him as a member of the Harbour Trust Garrison Battery). He was an experienced administrator who had managed three Australian visits to England and he was the one person with appropriate *de facto* authority to negotiate on equal terms with the M.C.C. secretary, (Sir) Francis Lacey. The two men had first exchanged cables on the subject in 1899 but the idea had been set aside with the outbreak of the Boer War. Yet before the war was over, a dialogue was resumed. In a political sense Wardill could speak with a more authoritative voice after the formation of the federated Commonwealth of Australia in 1901. Nevertheless, in cricketing terms, there remained antipathy between officialdom at Melbourne and at Sydney. As we shall see, it would be a New South Welshman (not a Victorian) in Francis Iredale, a professional journalist and former Test player, who wrote independently to the British *Daily Mail,* during July 1903 on issues affecting the M.C.C. visit only weeks before the departure for Australia.

By May 1901 Lacey was able to send Wardill a letter which showed both the seriousness of M.C.C.'s intentions and his care for its authority. "I now enumerate the conditions subject to which the M.C.C. will endeavour to send out an English team". As those conditions (with one significant difference – the fifth) were substantially the ones which would apply two years later, they deserve to be identified. Lacey wrote:

1. All matches to be played under laws passed by the M.C.C. for the time in force.

2. English team to go out under same conditions with regard to gate money as the Australian team arranged on visiting this country.

3. Programme of fixtures to be submitted for approval of the M.C.C. who shall have complete control of the tour and the team.

4. The English team to receive cordial invitations from the Australian Cricket Associations.

5. M.C.C. feel it advisable to send out an umpire.

There matters stood for virtually two years (May 1901 to April 1903) though within that time A. C. MacLaren would take a side to Australia in 1901–02 (which lost the Tests, 4–1) and the Australians would come to England in the summer of 1902 and win by two matches to one. Indeed, only a few weeks in 1902 separated Test matches at Melbourne in March and Edgbaston in May. Politically, the Boer War had ended in 1902 and Australia was tentatively adjusting to the constitutional settlement which gave only certain defined powers to the new Federal Government. Wardill deemed the time was right and his cable to Lacey on April 29 1903 asked: "Can you revive scheme abandoned 1901?" Lacey's immediate reply was scarcely encouraging: "Unlikely but will consult committee". Having done so, he sent a much more positive letter on June 5:

My dear Major Wardill,
I am writing to you to report progress and to let you know

that the M.C.C. are doing their best to meet your wishes.
The Committee first asked the Hon F. S. Jackson to captain a side. He was unfortunately unable to do so and
reluctantly declined. The Committee have now asked Mr
P. F. Warner to undertake the management of a team pro-
vided they can secure one which they would like to
represent the Club.

Lacey went on to say that Warner had asked for a fortnight's
grace "to sound certain amateurs on the subject" and he concluded that a cable would follow to "explain my action in the
matter." On June 24 Lacey cabled Wardill confirming what
he had said in the letter yet to reach Australia. He must have
realised this because he followed it with a long, and therefore,
expensive cable, reiterating the five conditions originally set
down and adding: "Phillips to accompany as umpire". All so
far had been plain sailing – even if the steam-ships which
bore the letters took some five weeks. But with the mention
of 'Phillips' shoals lay ahead. A cable was immediately sent
by Wardill to Lacey "cordially" (to use Lacey's original word)
inviting M.C.C. to come out to Australia but two weeks later
another cable was sent, not to the M.C.C. but to the *Daily Mail*
and not by Wardill but by Frank Iredale from Sydney. The gist
of it was that the Victorian Cricket Association were "adverse
(sic) to the English team bringing their own umpire", adding,
"in view of the letter which Phillips had recently written to
the Victorian Cricket Association, questioning the fairness of
Saunders' deliveries, they strongly objected to him coming out
as umpire."

James Phillips was a colourful character, born in the colony
of Victoria, and one of those players of the Victorian era for-

ever criss-crossing the cricketing world. For ten years from
1888 he commuted between Australia and England, playing for
Victoria and Middlesex. But it is as an umpire that he has a
greater claim to fame. He did more than any other person to
stamp out "throwing" at the turn of the century. He had no-
balled no less a personality than C. B. Fry in 1898 and it was his
influence which led to a famous meeting of county captains on
the subject at Lord's in 1900. In the following summer he had
no-balled the Lancashire fast bowler, Arthur Mold, sixteen
times. He had, as the cable to the *Daily Mail* indicated, criticised
the Australian left-arm spinner Jack Saunders in the third Test
against England at Sheffield in 1902. His letter to the Victorian
Cricket Association may not have been very tactful but at least
it showed how matters stood and gave reasonable grounds for
opposition to his coming to umpire.

Lacey, on seeing the letter in the press, cabled to Wardill (as
the instigator of the proposed tour) that the M.C.C. committee
believed that "Phillips had entirely won the confidence of all
Australian cricketers." Wardill, perhaps seeking an acceptable
compromise, cabled on July 8 that "the Associations [note the
plural] do not favour any visiting umpires" and that umpires for
the big matches be "selected here same conditions last team."
The abbreviated style indicated that the policy pursued should
be as in 1901–02 with MacLaren's team. M.C.C. deemed it
sensible not to take Phillips (or anyone else) and cabled to
that effect three days after seeing Iredale's letter. It was a wise
decision in the light of later knowledge of a meeting of the
Victorian Cricket Association which had bitterly criticised
Phillips and which was given wide publicity in the Australian
press. Nevertheless, there would – as Warner's book shows –
be umpiring issues during the tour. As for Saunders, he played

in only two Tests in 1903–04 and was not picked to go to England in 1905. Some time afterwards, it was disclosed that the Australian selectors had left him out because they feared Phillips (who umpired in four of the five Tests in 1905) would no-ball him.

Iredale's letter also asked for the follow-on rule of 150 runs not to be applied as "it was not applicable to Australian matches which are played to a finish." Lacey, correctly dealing with Wardill, agreed in a cable on July 10 that "big matches should be played out." He accepted a proposed fixture list which would include playing at Perth (which did not happen) and in the Goldfields and visiting Tasmania. Iredale, as a paid overseas correspondent, continued to cable his views to the *Daily Mail*, writing critically, for example, of the selected M.C.C. party to go to Australia. *Cricket* commented on July 30 that Iredale continued to "point out to the M.C.C. what they ought to do about their team." He had also written that Australian preparations "were very much advanced" and that "the prestige of Marylebone was very much at stake" if the tour should not happen for any reason. M.C.C. were learning far more about the proposed tour through his newspaper reports than from Wardill.

Such a non-event as the cancellation of the tour seemed, by late July unlikely, although the English papers, on an almost daily basis, speculated on who had been invited, who had declined and who would finally be in the team. More immediate, from the M.C.C. point of view, had been the appointment of the captain. Warner, as we have seen, had been offered the captaincy on Thursday June 4. After he had been dismissed for thirty-nine against Yorkshire at Lord's he was summoned to the committee room "feeling a bit nervous and wondering what I had done!" Warner, having asked for a few days' grace to make his decision, sounded out some possible players. When the announcement of his appointment was made public in the press there was, in his own words, "a storm of criticism." We may examine the case for and against Warner as captain of M.C.C. in Australia.

He was a few weeks under the age of thirty with the experience of having led three sides overseas in the preceding six years. He had taken teams to the United States twice (1897 and 1898) and had assumed the captaincy of Lord Hawke's side to New Zealand and Australia in 1902–03 when at the last moment the latter was unable to go. He was acknowledged as a natural leader of men. When captaining Hawke's XI against Victoria as recently as March 1903 he was approached by Wardill about bringing a side across in a few months. He had agreed with him that "the proper body was the M.C.C." and promised to make the case when he got home. As a player he had made twenty centuries in first-class cricket, including a double century against Otago. The *Westminster Gazette* in 1900 had described him as "not only a great batsman but a great traveller and a successful organiser". The *Daily Telegraph* a year later declared that, in making 197 not out against Somerset, "he scored with equal facility from all bowlers."

Yet this was the Golden Age of batting and Warner ranked low in the hierarchy of men such as G. L. Jessop, MacLaren, Jackson and Fry. Nor had he ever played for England although his century at Johannesburg in 1899 would acquire retrospective Test match status The 'popular' press wished MacLaren to lead England as he had done, indeed, on fourteen previous encounters with Australia (he succeeded W. G. Grace in 1899). The assumption was made, not without reason, that Lord Hawke, the chairman of the M.C.C. selectors, had a 'personality clash' with MacLaren though *The Times* challenged MacLaren's "prescriptive right to command." But there is more to be said. MacLaren had himself written to Wardill offering to bring out a side in 1903 along the accepted pattern of a private venture. When he followed this up with another letter saying he would come instead in 1904–05, Wardill decided to pursue the direct approach he had made to Warner at Melbourne. Of that the press knew nothing and a section of it continued to "savage" Warner. W. A. Bettesworth, writing in *Cricket* in August, took Warner's side, asserting that he was "the most abused man of the day, condemned as an interloper and nonentity." In contemporary politics he was seen to have taken the place of Joseph Chamberlain "as the man at whom it (was) thought convenient and even praiseworthy to throw as many stones as possible." In a long article, Bettesworth called Warner "a cricketer in the front rank (whose) cheerfulness under all kinds of conditions is proverbial" and only uttered the caveat that he must not allow his fascination with journalism and book-writing to interfere with "his cricket or his duties as captain".

Warner's first task was to secure some top amateurs. The papers made much of a supposed private conversation between him and MacLaren as to whether either would serve under the other. Warner, however, had no intention of declining the M.C.C.'s invitation while MacLaren felt he could not go to Australia again under the leadership of another, finally deciding not to go for what he publicly said were reasons of cricket etiquette but which privately was linked to his personal finances. Jackson, having declined the invitation to captain the side, still remained unavailable, as was Fry – again, for financial reasons. The possibility of journalism work for him on the tour did not materialise. There was some irony in the Gentlemen *v.*

Players match at Lord's in July. Fry (232) and MacLaren (168) shared an unbroken third-wicket partnership while MacLaren captained the Gentlemen with Warner in his side. Australia would never see MacLaren again, nor Fry nor Jackson, while five other leading amateurs also declined to join the M.C.C. party.

Coinciding with the public discussion of Warner's suitability to captain M.C.C. was a private one on his suitability to marry a fairly wealthy heiress. Within the society circles in which Agnes Blyth moved, Pelham Warner would have been seen as no great 'catch'. He was a young man with no money who had abandoned plans to make a career at the Bar. But the romance found favour with Agnes' family and she (accompanied by a chaperone) would sail to Australia with him.

In the three months between his appointment and the departure of the M.C.C. party Warner, in conjunction with the selectors, gathered a team of which he wrote in the *Sportsman* just before departure that it was "far from representing our best amateur strength but I very much doubt if the professional element could have been bettered." As late as September 3, there was a chance that the Lancashire amateur, R. H. Spooner, would tour, but a few days later he declined. In the end, Warner had only two other amateurs besides himself. R. E. Foster and B. J. T. Bosanquet would prove their worth while his professionals included several whose names belong to the folklore of cricket – Tom Hayward, J. T. Tyldesley, George Hirst, Wilfred Rhodes, A. A. Lilley and Herbert Strudwick. Warner, in the opening chapter of his book, analyses the abilities of the tourists, believing them to be as "good as any side which has left for Australia in recent years and, in one essential, bowling, distinctly superior." But *Cricket*, undoubtedly sympathetic to Warner and his men, commented "as far as appearances go there will have to be a good deal of luck if (the team) is to pull through".

Gradually, as the time for departure approached, all sections of the press swung round to support Warner. Fry, in the *Daily Express,* wrote a notice of encouragement which Warner quotes at length in Chapter 2. So, with the goodwill of the public and from a St Pancras Station crammed with people, he and seven of his party left London on September 25 on the boat train for Tilbury. The remainder crossed overland to Marseilles and the tourists came together a week later on the R.M.S. *Orontes.*

*   *   *   *   *   *

Warner's account of the tour itself bore the hallmarks of the experienced and able writer which he already was. All the major matches – whether against the Colonies (or States, as they had become after the Commonwealth had been formed) or against Australia – were treated in depth and he gave an impartial and analytical record of what happened. He tackled squarely the two umpiring 'issues' which arose during the first Test and in the preliminaries to the fourth, finding himself attacked in the Australian press in a manner prophetic of the events of 1932–33.

In choosing the title *How We Recovered the Ashes* he gave formality to a word which one reviewer of his book called "slang and of only very temporary significance." Yet the Ashes already had a twenty-year history. When Ivo Bligh's team beat Australia at Sydney in 1883, the *Sydney Morning Herald* reported that "Mr Bligh now has in his custody the revered ashes of English cricket". The urn had come to stay and to remain a prize of mythical substance and elusive value. Indeed, in the centenary year of M.C.C.'s 1903–04 tour, the issue of whether or not it might for ever reside at Lord's had become a matter of some controversy. Warner, always a man with a sense of history, had chosen an appropriate, not to say evocative, title and his book would prove the first of a sequence bearing titles such as *The Fight for the Ashes*. It established a pattern in its detailed account, full scores and statistical summaries. The *Westminster Gazette* praised his volume for "its bright and manly narrative", calling it a book "genuinely worth writing and written genuinely well". If he already had some status as an author, it was enhanced. In the years to come he would be very much the cricketer-journalist, even writing for *The Times* anonymous reports on Middlesex matches in which he was playing.

How We Recovered the Ashes had appeared surprisingly soon after Warner had returned to England. It was a measure of its success that the public were still prepared to read about the tour after the barrage of information they had had in the press. Of all the newspapers who reported the tour, perhaps the most enterprising was the *Sheffield Daily Telegraph*. With both George Hirst and Wilfred Rhodes, the illustrious Yorkshire pair, in the M.C.C. party, the paper had a captive readership. Arrangements had been made with Albert Knight, the Leicestershire batsman who played in three of the Tests, to send a letter back to the paper from time to time.

After the tour was over, the long-serving sporting editor of the paper, James Stainton, published *Bringing Back the Ashes* in a ninety-six-page, fully-illustrated booklet. For the reader who might find it hard to pay eighteen shillings and sixpence for Warner's book, Stainton's represented an excellent three-penny-worth.

Some comment is called for on the nomenclature used in various publications. In Australia souvenir booklets were published in the three major cities. That produced in Sydney for the first Test, for example, was called *Warner's English Cricket Team in Australia* and its sixty-four pages make no reference to the M.C.C. at all. Even Warner, in his own book, styled his team in every match 'England' rather than M.C.C. Not for another seventy years would 'England' rather than 'M.C.C. *v.* (say) New South Wales' be seen as correct. The souvenir booklet on sale at Melbourne in time for the second match of the tour was called *My Guide to the Tour of the English Cricketers*, but it did indicate that the Marylebone Cricket Club was managing the tour. With no doubt unconscious irony, the front page stated "Fry's cocoa was the very best", followed later by the name of C. B. Fry in a list of prominent players left behind in England.

The British press seldom used 'M.C.C.' as the name of the team. *The Times* regularly reported the doings of "Mr Warner's team in Australia" and would put "Mr Warner's team" at the head of match scores. Its first reference to 'M.C.C.' came in January 1904 with the comment, on January 6, that "the M.C.C. in Australia, at the half-way point, have not yet tasted the bitterness of a single defeat". When victory came to England on March 3, after the fourth Test, it was 'the rubber' rather than 'the Ashes' which was won. Even the fifth Test was described in that paper as "Mr Warner's team against an XI representing All-Australia." A correspondent writing in *Cricket* in December 1903 took the press to task for not calling the team in Australia 'the M.C.C.', even suggesting that the papers would continue to regard it as Warner's team if 'we' lost. Indeed, he had a point. When the tour was over *The Times,* on March 9 1904, reported that the team "selected by the M.C.C. (had) exceeded all expectations". It was left to *Wisden* in 1905 (not to the *Sheffield Daily Telegraph*) to endorse the authority of the M.C.C. though even that source stuttered between 'M.C.C.'s team' for the first four match reports and 'M.C.C.' thereafter.

There is some interest in how all this plethora of information found its way from Australia to England. It was in 1894, when A. E. Stoddart's team toured, that the first report of a match in Australia appeared in an evening paper in England the same day – play having ended in Australia some five hours before the first editions were on the news-stands. This was achieved by the *Pall Mall Gazette*, a quality paper enjoying a high reputation and which combined news with literary features. With the cost of cables at press rate, barely more than the close-of-play scores were given and, as often as not, they arrived too late for the last evening edition. But a start had been made. Soon longer reports were being received, though at public-rate which took the price per word from two shillings to five shillings, but still there was no guarantee of same-day publication. MacLaren's tour of 1897 saw some news agencies prepared to pay a cable company fifteen shillings a word for messages classified as 'urgent', which sometimes reached England in two hours.

By the time Warner's team left for Australia in 1903 there were two competing cable companies aware that whichever was the faster would secure the business of the English Press. Indeed, by the second match of the tour, when M.C.C. played Victoria at Melbourne, the Central News Agency was sending information from Australia by both the Pacific Cable Company and the Eastern Telegraph Company. Rather like the historic railway 'races' from London to Aberdeen in the 1890s between two rival companies, so did the telegraph companies compete in 1903. Racing against each other, they brought times down, minute by minute, until the Pacific Company transmitted from the first Test at Sydney in December to the Central News Agency in London in three and a half minutes! A contemporary wrote: "Puck's 'girdle round the earth in forty minutes' was a funeral procession to this". Such information, sent at urgent rate, was re-transmitted ten times entirely through links established at points within the British Empire, the longest link being from a Pacific island to Vancouver. Even the public-rate was conveying messages in thirty minutes so that the British public, as never before, were fully informed – if not on the same day, certainly at their breakfast tables next morning – on the day's play. We may use *The Times,* reporting the first Test, as an example. That paper, on the very morning of the first day's play at Sydney, carried the sensational news that Australia were twelve for three wickets in the match against "Mr Warner's team" together with a hundred words of text. On the next day (Saturday, December 12) 1,600 words were devoted to that first day's play and just over a hundred (quoted as supplied by Special Service) to the first hour's play on the second day.

All this was expensive and a complicated system of code words was devised with pre-arranged words, meaningless in themselves, which were indicators of what had happened. We may take an illustration from the first two words of a cable sent during the second Test at Melbourne: "saddest, canakin." 'Saddest' meant that England's numbers 4 and 5 were bowling (Hirst and Rhodes); 'canakin' that Australia's Duff was stumped Lilley bowled Rhodes. Later the word 'valiant' indicated that a brilliant catch had been taken in the slips. This was the style for messages at the public-rate. For urgent (and therefore more expensive) messages figures were used in combinations of five (counting as one word), so that '12504' meant that England were 125 for four while '04125' meant that Australia had achieved a similar score.

Such were the tools with which journalists in England crafted their prose. Warner, on his return home, said that such papers as he had seen had often contained errors of interpretation. To these press reports might be added, if the reader took the *Daily Mail*, cables giving an Australian point of view from Frank Iredale and, as we have seen, Knight's letters to the *Sheffield Daily Telegraph*. Knight had been asked to write on places and people as well as matches. He proved to be (said his editor, Stainton), "a charming raconteur and descriptive writer" who talked about cities, gold mines, ships, Tasmania and the Hobart Cup. A paragraph must suffice:

> The young and foolish members of our party went down for the first and last time one of the richest gold mines. The drive passing by orchards of apricot, cherry and peach was very pleasant. We exchanged our garments for dirty rags and with some perturbation descended a slimy, wet, oblong shaft ... Our guides pecked and pecked away but no auriferous quartz could they show us ... (We) breathed a grateful sigh when at the top we landed and all resolved if ever tempted to study gold-mining to do so within the walls of some museum.

Two other players who each wrote an unpublished diary were R. E. Foster and Albert Relf. Their recollections are in the archives, respectively, of the M.C.C. at Lord's and Sussex County Cricket Club at Hove. Foster's is primarily about the cricket itself with comments on the hospitality and welcome given to the tourists, the weather and the gate money. His own score of 287, in the first Test, was the outstanding individual performance of the tour and it remained unbeaten until Donald Bradman scored 334 at Leeds in 1930. This is what he wrote:

> Braund and I kept plugging away and were together at close of play, 73 (self) and (67) Braund. The attendance was grand being 37,000. Sunday, went to church. Very hot day. Called on Walter Allen [G. O. (Gubby) Allen's father]. Monday, I got my 100 an over before Braund did. We were both playing well when he was bowled. After lunch Lilley came in but played the fool and was caught. This left us at 332 for 8, which was chucking our position away. Relf came in and played beautifully till he was caught. Meanwhile I had got to 203. After tea Rhodes and I went on and in an hour and ten minutes put on 130 for the last wicket before I was caught at cover.

On the following day there was trouble with the crowd over an umpiring decision (on which Warner writes at length). Foster added in his diary:

> He (Hill) was undoubtedly out as I was standing at short leg and could see. The members started booing and hissing which, of course, was taken up by the rest of the ground and a most disgraceful scene ensued. Though many members tried to excuse it, nothing could make up for the scene.

Relf's diary has far the more evocative appeal of the two. It is written on a Lett's desk diary with daily entries of varying length so that some are compressed tightly into the day's allocation of space. Relf relished all he saw and did, quite apart from the cricket. His entries for the same two days in the first Test on which Foster wrote have their own interest:

> A glorious day. Had a walk round the town in the morning then drove to the ground. A rare, good day's cricket. Mr Foster played magnificently also Braund. Mr Foster made record score got in a Test match, viz 287. Myself and Rhodes gave very useful assistance, one of the best day's cricket I ever saw. All treated to wine at dinner and Lady Darnley came to our table and congratulated us. Spent the evening writing letters home for tomorrow's mail.

On the next day he wrote:

> A lovely, cool day. Received cable from home to say that all is going well and I have another daughter. Some very good cricket again; a very bad crowd, not in numbers but barrackers just because Crockett gave Hill out. Had some pretty shells given me from the Fiji islands. Spent the evening talking about the unsportsmanlike manner in which the members behaved.

Relf's Diary ended after his non-selection for the third Test (and subsequent ones.) We may conjecture there may have been some sadness compounded by home-sickness. He would make several more tours abroad including three seasons playing domestic cricket in New Zealand but some thirty years later would commit suicide in a fit of depression over the state of his wife's health.

Another of the team, Bosanquet, who had bowled so effectively, was asked to give his impressions in the 1905 *Wisden*. He had some interesting things to say on the Sydney soil known as 'Bulli' and the speed at which rain-affected wickets dried. It was to Warner, as a captain, that he gave the highest accolades, calling him "a wise and most successful captain", a man of "tact and kindly influence" and of "distinction" as an orator. This was a judgement with which both the Australian and English press were in accord. Many papers conceded that the M.C.C. had not been expected to win, although Jessop writing in the *Daily Mail* believed his judgement was vindicated. MacLaren was generous, writing in the *Daily Chronicle* of Warner's "pluck and determined nature". "Bravo, Warner and Co!" hailed the *Sportsman* while *The Times* attributed victory to the ability of the team to adapt itself to Australian conditions. Even *Punch* joined in with a limerick:

> There once was a skipper named Plum
> Whose team made the prophets all glum;
> "It's bad through and through",
> They declared "it won't do",
> But today all those prophets are dumb.

"How Warner can smile at his critics now!" commented *The Australasian* while the Melbourne *Truth* devoted a whole column to Warner's qualities of leadership, welding together "fourteen men of varying temperaments, and social qualities for thousands of miles, without jealousies, frictions and heartburnings". Such men, it concluded, "are rare in any sport".

So 'Plum' Warner and his M.C.C. team left for home. A vast crowd saw them off from Melbourne with a display of good humour and goodwill which they would show again in 1912 but which would contrast so sadly with Warner's own departure from Australia in 1933. Back in England there was a heroes' welcome from the cricketing world and a dinner given by M.C.C. Images of a military campaign always came easily to Warner: "I tried to convert that strip of twenty-two yards into a battlefield on which no quarter was to be given," he told his audience.

For the man himself, three months later in June 1904, came marriage to Agnes Blyth. She knew well enough what the pattern of her future life would be. Her time in Australia, when not with him, had been punctuated with telegrams of the scores of the matches and of her fiancé's performance. Their marriage was called by one paper "the wedding of the year", and vast crowds thronged Marylebone Parish Church. Play was stopped at Lord's so that those participating in a match could attend. Among the guests were Lord Roberts, back from the Boer War, and Sir Henry Irving, the actor. It was all a century ago and the splendour of the occasion belongs to a vanished age. Cricketers of every ilk wished him well. Those on the perimeters of luck and fortune in the many-sided scene which was Edwardian Britain shared for a moment the colour and gaiety of the romance. Warner might be forgiven if he felt that many concentric circles revolved around him. To the public at large he offered in *How We Recovered the Ashes* his account of a cricket tour which would have its own distinctive place in the history of the game.

GERALD HOWAT

NORTH MORETON, OXFORDSHIRE
July 2003

HOW WE RECOVERED THE ASHES

BY
P. F. WARNER
Captain of the M.C.C. Team

WITH AN INTRODUCTION BY BISHOP WELLDON

AND NEARLY ONE HUNDRED ILLUSTRATIONS

London :
CHAPMAN AND HALL, Ltd.
1904

PREFACE

THE difficulty of writing the account of a cricket tour, in which one has had the privilege of acting as Captain, is that one is almost invariably obliged to adopt the personal note. The capital " I " must needs crop up incessantly ; for how can one describe one's own experiences without doing so in one's own unworthy person ?

I do greatly hope, however, that there is not too much of the Everlasting Ego about this plain, unliterary narrative. No one felt more than myself how great was my responsibility in carrying the credit of English cricket to Australian fields ; no one appreciates more than myself that that credit reposed, not in the hands of the Captain alone, but more particularly in those of every single member of that fortunate Team which worked and fought side by side for the recovery of the historic ashes. And, if the personal note crops up now and again in these reminiscences, it is only because a man must speak of the things he saw and learnt for himself, and to do otherwise is mere affectation and false modesty.

I owe special thanks to many helpers, and in particular to Bishop Welldon for his breezy and genial introduction, and to B. J. T. Bosanquet, who has contributed the valuable chapter on " Australian Wickets." The list of illustrations contains a formal acknowledgment of the many sources to which I am indebted for what I think may claim to be an exceptionally complete series of pictures ; but I must add a word of especial gratitude to the proprietors of *The Australasian*, and to Mr. H. Krischock and Mr. J. Gazard of Adelaide, who, with the utmost generosity, placed all the riches of their negative-cases at my disposal.

Since one cannot always say the same thing equally well in two sets of phrases, I have here and there drawn upon my contributions to *The Sportsman* and *The Westminster Gazette*, to whose editors I am indebted for the kind permission to quote from my special articles.

P. F. WARNER.

LORD'S CRICKET GROUND,
May, 1904.

INTRODUCTION

BY BISHOP WELLDON

THIS chapter, as an introduction to Mr. Warner's narrative of his cricket tour in Australia, will, I hope, be regarded as no more than the humble porch of a stately edifice. It will be enough if it serves to evince my genuine interest in the doings of the English Eleven, whose fellow-traveller I was from Europe to Australia. We sailed on the good ship *Orontes*:—vessel of 10,000 tons burden—the finest in the Orient-Pacific fleet. Her commander, Captain Ruthven, is commodore of the fleet. The sum of her officers, crew, and passengers of all classes cannot have fallen much below a thousand souls. She left Tilbury on Friday, September 25th, and she reached Adelaide, where the first match was played, on Monday, November 2nd. Some of the cricketers embarked upon her at Tilbury; they were Mr. Warner, the Captain, Mr. Foster, Mr. Murdoch, Knight, Braund, Fielder, Relf, and Strudwick. The others, viz., Mr. Bosanquet, Hirst, &c., joined her at Marseilles. I myself came on board at Gibraltar; for I had been spending a fortnight in Portugal at "Cintra, glorious Eden," as the guest of Sir Frederick Cook, M.P., at Montserrat. Thus, although it had been no part of my project in visiting Australia to enjoy the society of the

English Cricket Eleven, it so happened that I was with them all the time that they were on the sea. We parted on the well-known Adelaide Oval, and I saw but little of them afterwards. The story of the cricket tour will be told by Mr. Warner. It is only of the voyage that I can write. Yet I hope I may claim to have made a friendship with the cricketers in the weeks we spent on

BISHOP WELLDON.

the same ship. I stood by them in health, and with one or two of them (if the truth must be told) in sea-sickness. I umpired for them (as will presently appear) in the great cricket match against the ladies of the ship, when the ladies, I regret to say, did not always obey my decisions with the unhesitating loyalty characteristic of true sportswomen. I was bowled out on one occasion by so good a ball that I said to Rhodes, who bowled it, that it seemed a pity to waste such a ball on a bishop.

Few greater compliments have been paid me in life than when Mr. Warner conferred upon me towards the end of the voyage the honourable and honorary title of Chaplain of the Team : for there were sad hours, as well as many bright hours, on our journey : and they too helped to knit us together. But now I have done with myself and my qualifications for contributing a chapter to my friend Mr. Warner's book.

The cricketers who sailed on the *Orontes* from Tilbury were the recipients of a hearty demonstration. Nearly two thousand spectators had assembled at St. Pancras Station to bid them God-speed. Mr. Bosanquet, who himself travelled *viâ* Marseilles, had intended to see his comrades off at St. Pancras : but for once in his life (if for once only) he was late : the cheers which followed his departing comrades might have been taken as greeting his arrival, and it was immediately telegraphed to Australia that he had been left behind for good. At Tilbury Lord Alverstone, the Chief Justice of England, whose daughter-in-law was a passenger on the *Orontes*, came, as President of the M. C. C., to offer the cricketers his good wishes. Mr. Green, one of the directors of the Orient Pacific Co., proposed their health, not without a happy reference to the good omen which Mr. Warner's recent engagement to Miss Blyth afforded for the prosperity of his Team. It was then, in replying to the toast, that Mr. Warner gave the first indication of the facile and graceful eloquence which has since charmed so many audiences in the Southern Hemisphere. It was remarked more than once that so polished a brain as Mr. Warner's has seldom been seen beneath the Southern Cross! The visits of English cricket teams to Australia and of Australian teams to England have been always more than mere athletic pleasure-parties. Cricket, indeed, is the greatest of all games—the greatest because it presents a unique combination of skill and luck. Nowhere, perhaps, does proficiency count for so much, yet nowhere is proficiency so easily defeated by the accidents of weather, or the state of the ground, or even the winning or losing of the toss : in no game is it so easy to make a mistake ; in no game is the cost of a single mistake so dear. It is no wonder, then, that the memories of cricket awaken infinite discussion. Old cricketers become heroes to others and sometimes to themselves. To have achieved a century of runs in a match between England and the greatest of her colonies—the one colony which has proved equal, and often, I am afraid I ought to say, superior, to the Mother Country in the famous national game—is itself a title to immortality. For one of the striking features of cricket is its localisation—it flourishes in some counties of England but not in others. It flourishes to a much higher degree in some parts of the Empire than in others : out of England it is carried to greater perfection in Australia than anywhere else.

Hence a special interest has always attached to a Test Match between England and Australia. But international cricket matches are not only cricket matches. They tend as well to excite and promote a kindly feeling between the nations which take part in them. They have brought Englishmen to Australia and Australians to England. They have associated them as members of the same great national family : they have given them the sense of a common "home": they have in some measure at least inspired a generous rivalry of devotion to the same throne. It would not be wrong to say that the strong patriotic feeling displayed by the colonies, and by none more than by Australia and New Zealand, towards the Mother Country in the late South African War, has largely sprung from the interchange of courtesies, and the fostering of mutual respect through international athletic competitions at home and in the colonies.

Mr. Warner's Cricket Eleven, therefore, takes its place in the list of Elevens which have visited Australia. But in one important aspect it was unique ; it was the first Eleven whose Australian tour was organised by the Committee of the M.C.C. Hitherto some distinguished cricketer has been invited, or has elected to take an Eleven to Australia ; he has chosen his own team ; he has made his own agreement with them ; some players he has chosen, others of equal or higher repute he has passed over ; but although his Eleven represented nothing but his own judgment or his power of attracting cricketers to go with him, they have been regarded in Australia, and perhaps, too, in England, as the English Eleven. Their victories have been accounted the triumphs, and their defeats the humiliation, of England. But no Eleven can be representative of English cricket unless they are appointed by the supreme authority in the English cricket world. To the M.C.C. belongs the duty of choosing the cricketers for a match against the Australians. It is probable that the day of private adventurers in international cricket is past. Whatever Elevens sail for Australia in the future will probably be chosen, as Mr. Warner's has been, by the Committee of the M.C.C. This is one condition necessary for a satisfactory representation of English cricket ; the other is that cricketers upon whom the official choice has fallen should

not, except for grave personal reasons, decline to obey
it. Mr. Warner's Eleven, before they left England, were
exposed to a good deal of criticism : that they were as
good a bowling team as could have sailed from their
native shores was hardly denied : but they were said to
be weak in batting. There can be no doubt that the

THE AMATEURS OF THE TEAM.

absence of such batsmen as Mr. Jackson, Mr. Fry, and
Mr. MacLaren was regretted, as it was certainly regret-
table : all that can be said is that, if any one of them had
been willing or able to accompany the tour, he would
have received a hearty welcome from all cricketers, and
not least from their comrades in Mr. Warner's Eleven.
The Eleven as they sailed for Australia were the best

Eleven which the highest authority in cricket could get together.

One element of success they possessed in the happy relations existing between Mr. Warner as Captain and his fellow men. They liked and respected each other. Such was Mr. Warner's popularity that when the time came for awarding prizes during the voyage to the most elegantly attired figures in the fancy-dress ball, he and Miss Blyth received an unusual number of votes, and although the ballot was (as in political elections) absolutely secret, some suspicious and jealous persons, who had failed to get prizes, accused the amateur and professional cricketers of having voted, not according to their consciences, but *en masse* for their Captain and his *fiancée*. It is enough to say that a captain who is popular with his cricket team is worth a hundred runs in any match.

English cricket died, according to *Punch's* famous cartoon, on August 10, 1882, and its "ashes" were carried to Australia. Since then, to recover these ashes has been .the ambition of all English cricketers. Mr. Warner, under whose Joint-Captaincy with Mr. MacGregor the Middlesex Eleven had attained for the first time in many years the championship of County Cricket, was fired with ambition to retrieve the honour of his country. He had visited Australia before, as the Captain of Lord Hawke's team, which played a number of matches in New Zealand and Australia during the winter of 1902–1903. Thus it was his fortune to play cricket in Australia twice within a year. It was thought to be a happy omen of success that among his fellow-passengers was the Countess of Darnley, who had made the voyage to Australia with

Mr. Stoddart's triumphant team in 1894, and who had herself been, as a bride, the supreme triumph of the Hon. Ivo Bligh, now Earl of Darnley, when he took an English Eleven to Australia in 1882. Mr. Warner, indeed, could hope for no such triumph ; but Miss Blyth was on board the *Orontes*, and was to see the matches in Australia—and defeat (he felt) was impossible in her presence. When Mr. Warner embarked on the *Orontes* he had already won his prize.

The voyage of a Cricket Eleven to the Antipodes cannot widely differ from any other voyage. The pleasures and terrors of the ocean do not depend upon particular ships or passengers. The *Orontes*, I have already said, is a splendid vessel. She is as steady as a bishop. Her officers believe or declare that a special good fortune attends her. But I was told, when I came on board, that she had experienced what some of the ladies called "half a gale" in the Bay of Biscay, and there was certainly a time between Colombo and Fremantle when a spirit of gloomy meditation settled upon the better half of her passengers. Still, the most suffering invalid will, I think, admit that the Melbourne Race Course and Sydney Harbour make amends for much rough weather ; and were there not compensations for the Indian Ocean in the records of not a few Australian scoring-boards ? A long voyage is always a test of human nature. Persons who have never heard one another's names find themselves set down in a position where they cannot help knowing one another's business. Their tastes, their habits, their dispositions do not accord. Some of them, it may happen, are in love ; others disapprove of other people being in love. Some want to read in peace ; others want to play games ; some go to bed early, others get up late ; some feel well, and others ill; some prefer dances, others prefer prayer meetings. If two persons cannot agree perhaps they quarrel ; but if they quarrel they cannot as on land keep out of each other's way ; they must rub shoulders every day on the quarter-deck. Above all, the love for gossip, which is so strong in human nature, leads one person to invent and then to tell and at last to believe an amazing but rather ill-natured story of somebody else. If the captain or the purser of an ocean liner were at liberty to reveal all the difficulties or differences in which he has been called to play the part of mediator or arbitrator, it would be found that he deserves to rank with a Confessor in the Roman Catholic Church.

But who would dream of putting Captain Ruthven or Mr. Murdoch into the witness-box ? If they could a tale unfold they would not unfold it. But whatever their inmost feelings may have been, they preserved an unruffled demeanour ; nobody ever saw either of them out of temper. There were ladies, perhaps, who would now and then call one or the other an unfeeling wretch, if they asked for some wholly unreasonable privilege and it was refused them. But even these ladies, when the voyage was over, were in their hearts grateful to the sympathetic serenity of both. The passengers were an interesting body. If it were not personal it would be tempting to describe the eminent barrister who presided over the sports with an authority never questioned upon any matter except a point of law ; the experienced traveller, whose opinion was generally asked and always given upon such matter as the probable run of the ship or the chance of seeing a whale ; the wrong lady who was always wanting to sleep in some other cabin than her own; the other young lady who, in a moment of abstraction, mysteriously disappeared down an air-shoot; the adventurer who had gone home in search of a fortune and had failed to get it, and was returning sadly to end his days in Australia; or the omnipresent boy, aged four years and a half, who was never happy but in collecting ice-plates or ringing the bell at the sports, pacing the deck in company with the

THE PROFESSIONALS OF THE TEAM.

quartermaster and asserting that he himself and not the Captain was the "boss" of the ship. There were momentous occasions in the course of the voyage; it will be enough, perhaps, to mention two of them as specially affecting Mr. Warner's Eleven. The great cricket match between his Eleven and an Eleven of ladies, the Eleven using only their left hands or whichever hand they were not accustomed to use, and the ladies not only playing right-handed but making full defensive use of their skirts, ended in a victory for the side which would naturally be called the fairer, if they had paid a proper regard to the umpire's decisions. As things were, it was impossible to help feeling an acute pain at the spectacle of the Captain of the English Eleven leading back to the wickets a young lady— his own *fiancée* too—who had been given out l.b.w. after a flagrant breach of the rules of cricket in stopping a straight ball with her dress. The ladies won the match by three runs principally owing to the number of no-balls and wides, which the Yorkshire professionals bowled by hitting the roof with the ball. It was in honour of the victory that Lady Darnley gave a tea-party to both Elevens. Captain Ruthven, in proposing success to the cricketers, told them that this was the sixth time that he had taken an English Eleven to and from Australia. But the honours of oratory were divided between Lady Darnley herself and Mr. Warner, and an old classical scholar was heard to remark that he should have thought either of their speeches quite perfect if he had not listened to the other.

We were a mixed party, but we got on well together ; we called each other names at least occasionally, but we thought each other " jolly good fellows " ; we played our games with patience and fairness ; we tried to fight against the cliqueism which is nowhere so great a curse as on board ship. Even the sweeps were not as black as they are painted. We did not wholly forget that we were Englishmen and Englishwomen representative of the greatest Empire under heaven. And Sunday by Sunday we met on the quarter-deck or in the saloon for Divine Service as a consecration of our voyage in the sight of the Most High.

We are parted now ; we shall never all meet again ; the cricketers, whose " honest chronicler " on the first stage of their journey I am permitted to be, have played their matches with the success which Mr. Warner will relate. Mr. Warner himself has taken a step so happy that no century on the cricket field can equal it. But if this book, and with it this chapter, chances to fall into the hands of anyone whom the writer of the chapter knew so well on the long voyage to Australia, and has never seen since, or even heard of, may it remind him or her of his grateful feeling for his fellow-passengers in the far-off days of the *Orontes*.

EN ROUTE.

HOW WE RECOVERED THE ASHES

CHAPTER I

THE TEAM

THIS book sets out to give a plain, unvarnished narrative of the exploits of the M.C.C. Team in Australia during the season of 1903–1904. So much has been written in the papers about the Team and its recovery of " the ashes " that perhaps it may seem at first sight as though there were scarcely need for a full-sized book upon the subject. And yet there are still many things to relate. The inner history of the tour, naturally enough, never got into the papers, and a great deal that did get into the papers, more especially in the way of criticism and comment, was so distinctly incorrect and misleading that I believe most lovers of cricket will like to have the true story set before them clearly and simply. And I hope I need not say at the beginning that, if I set down anything with favour, at least I shall write nothing in malice. I only want to tell the plain truth in the plainest possible way.

Let me begin at the beginning, and say how it came about that I was invited to take a team to Australia at all. At the time when I was chosen by the M.C.C. for the proud position of Captain of their Team, I did not escape a great deal of criticism from the daily papers, some of whose critics maintained that I had neither the experience nor the qualifications necessary to captaincy. And yet as a matter of fact the idea had been suggested long before it was first mooted officially. I had held my tongue about it, but I had already been invited from the other side. After the tour of MacLaren's last Team, he was at once asked to bring out another in the winter of 1903. However, he was unwilling to make the experiment again. He said that he felt pretty certain that Hirst and Rhodes would not be allowed by the Yorkshire Committee to join any possible combination ; and apart from them he maintained that there were practically no bowlers in England. I believe that I was the next man to be invited. When I was in New Zealand with Lord Hawke's Team in March, 1903, Major Wardill wrote to me and asked me definitely whether I would not bring over an Eleven. I put the question aside at the time, but a few weeks later at Melbourne I was approached by both the Sydney and the Melbourne authorities. To all these kind suggestions I always made one reply :—" Ask the M.C.C. They are the proper people to send out a team." The Melbourne Cricket Club then urged me to undertake that on my return home I would at least approach the M.C.C. in the matter, and use my influence to get them to send out a representative team. I said I would ; and directly I got home I suggested to the Committee at Lord's that F. S. Jackson should be asked to act as captain. He was invited to do so, but declined. The Club then asked me if I would not undertake the captaincy myself. I well remember the day when the invitation was first proposed to me. It was on the first afternoon of the Middlesex and Yorkshire Match at Lord's, June 4th. I had just got out, and was going to change, when W. H. Patterson came up into our dressing-room and said the Committee wished to speak to me. I went down at once, and was then asked whether I would captain a side in the event of the Club undertaking a tour in Australia.

It was not to be supposed that one could accept so flattering but responsible an invitation off-hand, and I asked for some little time to consider. About June 20th I made up my mind to accept. I thought that I could get the right men, and I hoped that I could lead them ; altogether it seemed a duty that ought not to be shirked. The M.C.C. then cabled to Australia, saying that they had made up their minds to send out a team under certain conditions, the principal of which were :—(1) That all games should be played under the M.C.C. Rules. (2) That they should have half the gate money—an arrangement which excluded their having any share in the money taken on the stands. They also said that they hoped it would be understood that they were welcomed by all the Cricket Associations in Australia ; that is, by the New South Wales, Victoria, South Australia, and West Australia Associations. In the meantime they asked me to approach some of the principal amateurs, and in the first instance Fry, Martyn, and Palairet were invited. At the same time the announcement that I was to captain the team appeared in the papers.

This announcement was received with a storm of criticism, and several papers, with volcanic energy, proceeded at once to publish what claimed to be authoritative lists of the Team long before any invitations had been sent out.   This was naturally a little unfortunate, since it caused names to be bandied about freely before the Committee had even begun to consider the claims of the players mentioned.   I may say that the Committee who chose the Team consisted of Mr. A. G. Steel, Lord Harris, Mr. A. J. Webbe, Mr. W. H. Patterson, and myself.   Mr. Steel insisted that no man should be chosen who was not personally approved by myself. I do not want at this time of day to recur to the various newspaper reports that were circulated, more especially to the very mischievous one which endeavoured, quite without success, to embroil Mr. MacLaren and myself. Mr. MacLaren's claims to captain an International Eleven were of course obvious to every man of judgment, and to no one more than myself.   Like every one else in the cricket world, I could not help feeling of what immense value his presence would be to any English team touring in Australia, and during the course of the Lancashire and Middlesex Match in July I had a few words with him on the subject, and asked him whether it was not possible for the difficulty to be got over, and for him to join the Team.   He said that unfortunately it was impossible for him to go in any capacity but captain, having regard to the fact that he had already captained England in the field on so many occasions ; and, as the M.C.C. had already made their selection for a skipper, matters were clearly at a deadlock.   It was a most unfortunate incident,—deeply regretted by both of us, I am sure,—that this conversation should have been twisted by certain newspapers into a statement that I had gone behind the M.C.C. and expressed my willing-

THE ENGLISH TEAM ON THE FIELD.

Knight.   Hirst.   Hayward.   Rhodes.   Arnold.   Lilley.   Warner.   Foster.
Tyldesley.   Bosanquet.   Braund.

ness to give up the conduct of the Team. That, of course, I should never under any circumstances have done, and the mere suggestion naturally made me appear disloyal to the Club that had done me so high an honour.

It may perhaps interest the general reader to reflect upon the considerations which influence an English Captain in choosing a touring team for Australia. The difficulties are very considerable. In the first place, the team is so far from its base ; and in the second, for a long tour of this kind, one needs above all things a set of men who are loyal, keen, good-tempered, and " triers," men, in short, who will pull well together and put cricket first, keeping out of the way of the many temptations of a great Australian city.

The first two men to be picked were naturally Rhodes and Hirst, the two best bowlers of the present day in this country. I cannot help remembering with a smile of satisfaction what that excellent critic of the game, K. S. Ranjitsinhji, said to me when he heard that Rhodes had decided to go. " Well, no doubt he will make a good many runs for you," said Ranji, " but in first class cricket in Australia he will not take a dozen wickets." There were not wanting also those who thought that Hirst would fail with the ball, pointing to the fact that his first visit to Australia was not very successful from the bowler's point of view. However, there is no need now to insist upon the fallacy of both these prophecies. Rhodes was the mainstay of the Team ; and Hirst, to say nothing of his batting, bowled excellently throughout the tour, and was of much more value as a bowler than his average would suggest. Then came Braund, next to Hirst the best all-round man in

England. For a wicket-keeper there could be no choice but Lilley ; and Strudwick, who had had a splendid season, was clearly the right man for second string. One now needed a bat or two, and I had no hesitation in plumping for Hayward, whose record in Australia was in itself his own testimonial. Several sapient critics maintained that he was a " back number," with how much justice the story of the tour has proved. The same question of past record made Tyldesley an inevitable choice ; but R. E. Foster's selection was received with some criticism. It was urged that he had fallen out of first class cricket, and would not be in form. I maintained, however, that at twenty-five a man can lay aside the game for a few months without forgetting it, and his performances in 1900 and 1901 alone were enough to prove that he was absolutely in the front rank of batsmen.

Arnold was not a difficult choice as an all-round man, but Bosanquet's selection was followed by a hail of criticism and disapprobation. It was suggested that because he happened to be a member of the same county team as myself, I must have chosen him out of favouritism ; as though a man who has played with another week-in, week-out, on all sorts of wickets, is not far more likely to know every point in his play and in his temperament than the occasional pavilion critic or newspaper reporter ! Knight is such a fine hard-wicket batsman, that he seemed precisely the right man for Australian wickets, and, had we had a typical Australian summer, I expect he would have been one of the best and most consistent scorers in the Team. The choice of Relf was chiefly due to C. B. Fry. I wrote to Fry asking him what he thought of my taking Relf, and

HIRST AND RHODES.

received such an enthusiastic testimonial to Relf's many abilities that it seemed absurd to leave him out. Fielder was suggested by MacLaren. I asked him to advise me in picking a fast bowler, and MacLaren replied that though Barnes was undoubtedly the best man, if present form were considered, he was nevertheless temperamentally unsuited to a long tour, and almost certain to break down in health. "Take Fielder," said MacLaren, and I am very glad I did. When you are travelling with fourteen men, somebody must be left out, and Fielder had not as many opportunities as some of the others. Nevertheless, he bowled excellently, more particularly in the second innings of the third Test Match at Adelaide, and against Victoria in November. He will train on into a great bowler, for he has pace and strength, and bowls a fine ball which swings away from the bat at the last moment.

We have now the Team complete, and it may be interesting to consider them individually before they embark. A better set of men I never hope to see upon a cricket field.

It must be many years since England was so rich in all-round players of the highest class, but the best of a brilliant group is George Hirst, the Agamemnon of Yorkshire; indeed, it may well be questioned whether the present generation has seen a better. Noble, the Australian Captain, I consider the best all-round cricketer in the world on Australian wickets and under Australian conditions; but in England George Hirst is, at any rate, his equal. The averages speak with no uncertain voice of his worth as a batsman and bowler, but they do not tell what an inimitable field he is at mid-off, where no catch is too hot for him, and where he is wonderfully

quick on his feet. The tighter the match the better he
plays.

In the early part of the last English summer Rhodes
was, for him, comparatively unsuccessful, but he came on
again at the end of the season, and finished up with a
" bag " of 193 wickets for fourteen runs apiece. There is
a very prevalent idea that Rhodes is quite easy to play
on a hard, true wicket. I venture to question this.
At any rate, his performances prove quite the contrary,
and in bowling, even more than in batting, one can only
judge by performances. Rhodes first came out in 1898,
so that 1903 was his sixth season of first-class cricket.
The summer of 1898 was fairly good—there were many
sticky wickets in May and June, but in July and
August the conditions favoured the batsman ; yet
Rhodes took 154 wickets for fourteen runs each—an
altogether remarkable achievement on the part of a boy
who was then not yet twenty-one. The summers of
1899, 1900, and 1901 were among the driest we have
ever had, yet in those three seasons Rhodes took 691
wickets at an average of, roughly, fourteen runs a wicket.
Whence, then, comes this notion that he cannot be
successful except when the turf is false ? It was freely
predicted that Rhodes would be quite ineffective on the
hard Australian wickets; but the sequel showed how
very wrong the critics were.

Cricket history has written that Somerset are no
respecters of the reputations of their opponents. In the
days when Surrey were at the height of their fame, it was
no unusual thing for them to meet with a Paardeberg at
the hands of S. M. J. Woods' Eleven, and Yorkshire
have again and again gone down in sensational fashion
on the Taunton ground. Braund was originally a Surrey

man, but, finding that his abilities were not appreciated at their true value at the Oval, he migrated to Somerset, and it may with truth be said that the Westerners number no better fighting man in their ranks than this admirable cricketer. He is the most efficient of the new type of leg-break bowlers ; he can play a forcing or defensive game as circumstances demand ; and he is reckoned amongst the great slips of the day. He is all enthusiasm, and would willingly bowl one end and field long-off at the other. It is hard to imagine a side which includes Braund becoming slack in the field.

Hayward's reputation as one of the soundest and most reliable batsmen is so well established that it is scarcely necessary to enumerate his many great performances not only in county cricket but in Gentlemen *v.* Players and England and Australia matches both here and in Australia. Indeed, his record in test matches will bear comparison with that of almost any other player. As far back as 1896 Hayward was playing for England, and he had twice visited Australia—in 1897–1898 with A. E. Stoddart's Team, and in 1901–1902 with A. C. MacLaren's Eleven. On both of these tours he was highly successful, while in the five test matches in 1899 he scored 413 runs in seven innings, including 130 at Manchester and 137 at the Oval. The memory of his past deeds must assuredly stand him in good stead when he goes in to bat against the Australians.

Tyldesley's right to a place in the Team no one could question. He is, and has been for some years, one of the best batsmen in England and a grand field.

R. E. Foster had played so little first class cricket last season that his selection was received with some surprise; but let the public carry their memory back to the Gentlemen and Players match at Lord's in 1900, and recall those two superb innings of his which beat all previous records. No cricketer—not even W. G. Grace—had ever before made a double century in Gentlemen v. Players. In that year Foster would have been one of the first men chosen to represent England had the Australians been in this country. Nor was Foster—though, curiously enough, failing entirely in the Gentlemen v. Players match—a less great batsmen in 1901, for during that summer he scored over 2,000 runs, with an average of fifty. In 1902 Foster did not play cricket until August, but in eleven innings for Worcestershire he again averaged fifty.

Another cricketer who achieved great fame during the season of 1903 was B. J. T. Bosanquet, of the Middlesex Eleven. I claim credit for having introduced him to the notice of the Middlesex authorities, and therefore I naturally feel interested in all he does on the cricket field. It was in August of 1898 that Bosanquet made his *début* in county cricket, but his first appearances were scarcely successful, as in two innings he made only seventeen runs, did not take a wicket, and missed an easy catch at cover-point. In 1899 he proved himself almost the best all-round man in a strong Oxford Eleven, but it was not until the following season that he really began to assert himself. In that summer he did very well indeed for Oxford, and in one of the not very many Middlesex matches in which he was able to take part hit a double century. In 1901 he was one of the three most reliable batsmen in the Middlesex team, and though the season of 1902 was a bad one for him, he played so finely all last summer that if

BRAUND.   B. J. T. BOSANQUET.

LILLEY,   STRUDWICK.

an England Eleven had been chosen his claims to a place would have been very strong.

He, like myself, was a member of the team which at the commencement of the winter of 1902 sailed away to the sunny skies and warm climate of Australasia, and the tour was for him a great success. In Australia especially he did particularly well, scoring over fifty runs against each of the States, while his peculiar slow bowling caused quite a sensation on the Sydney ground. In their second innings the powerful New South Wales Team made over 400 runs, and in such a big total seven wickets for something like 150 runs was no mean feat. Many of the Australian critics were much impressed with the possibilities of his bowling on hard, true wickets.

In his Oxford days Bosanquet was a fast bowler pure and simple, but nowadays he has almost entirely discarded his former style, the majority of his wickets last year having been taken with very slow and, from the ring, harmless-looking bowling. But Bosanquet is likely to puzzle the best batsman in the world, for he sends down an apparent leg breaker which breaks back very quickly, and which, if it happens to pitch anything like a good length, nearly always causes trouble to the batsman's peace of mind.

But Bosanquet's usefulness to his side does not end with the innings of his opponents, for he is liable to make fifty or a hundred runs at any time against any bowling on any kind of wicket. No one that I have ever seen bats quite like him. Bosanquet learnt his cricket at Eton, but he has none of the grace of style of the typical Eton batsman, and indeed, to tell the truth, he is at first sight a decidedly stiff and awkward-looking player. He does not seem to play at the ball in a free, unconstrained way, but rather stabs at it, and gives one the impression of making his stroke at the very last moment. It may seem a strange thing to say, but Bosanquet is generally seen to greater advantage if the ball is turning a little than on an absolutely perfect pitch, the manner in which on this type of wicket he will flick the breaking ball round on the on-side being surpassed by scarcely any other batsman. He possesses one attribute which the great Napoleon said was the only one he envied our nation, and that is that he never knows when he is beaten. Unkind people have called this attribute by a harder name before now, but confidence in one's own abilities founded on past performances is a very different thing from conceit—and on the cricket field confidence plus skill is half the battle. Bosanquet has both.

Amongst the more recently promoted counties, none shows greater promise for the future than Worcestershire ; and to Arnold they owe a great deal for their present position. Last summer was the second time in his career that Arnold has made a thousand runs and taken a hundred wickets in a season, and he is, moreover, the only Worcestershire man who has accomplished the feat, though this, perhaps, is scarcely surprising, seeing that it is but four years ago since the county were promoted to first class rank.

Arnold is a batsman with a thoroughly sound style, but I am inclined to think that he is an even better bowler than he is a batsman. With a high, easy action, he keeps a good length, and seems able to make the ball jump up awkwardly even on the best of wickets, while, should the pitch help him at all, he can get on a good deal of off-break. A thousand and eighty runs, with an

TYLDESLEY.
KNIGHT.

RELF.
FIELDER.

average of thirty, and a hundred and thirty wickets for seventeen runs apiece bear ample evidence of his ability.

Knight has for four or five years past been by far the most reliable batsman in the Leicestershire eleven, but he surpassed all his previous achievements last season, and there are few harder men to get rid of when once he has taken root. He is just the man to stay in all day on a perfect wicket, for he has a splendid defence and leaves nothing to chance. He is not perhaps quite so strong in his on-side play as many other batsmen, but he is a master of all the off-strokes, being especially strong at a sort of half-drive half-cut, which he uses with great success.

As Knight is only in his thirtieth year, he is certain to do even better in the future than he has in the past.

Not much in the way of adverse criticism could be advanced against the names of those I have mentioned, but the selection of Fielder and Relf occasioned a good deal of surprise. Until last summer no one had ever heard of Fielder, but everyone who has played against him has been impressed with his bowling. With an easy stride up to the wicket and a nice swinging action, Fielder sends down a very fast ball which goes away, as a rule, with his arm, thereby affording an opportunity to the men in the slips to distinguish themselves. He was admittedly an experiment, but I was much struck with his abilities in the Kent and Middlesex match at Tunbridge Wells, and as I have already said, he did thoroughly well in Australia, all things considered.

Relf has been one of the most valuable men in the strong Sussex eleven for two or three years past, but last season he was a better cricketer than ever and a glance at the averages will give a good idea of the capital all-round work he has done. With a short run Relf bowls a fast medium ball, which is very apt to swing away from the bat at the last moment, and on perfect wickets always bowls well and steadily, for he keeps a good length and comes quickly off the pitch. He is apt to make fifty runs at any time, is a keen, hard-working field, and a thorough trier.

These rough remarks must suffice as dealing with the Team individually, and taking them as a composite body, since it is always pleasant to look back upon prophecy fulfilled, I may perhaps refer to my own forecast of the Team's possibilities which was published in the *Sportsman* just before we sailed. I do so, of course, in no spirit of " stiffed-necked pride "; but, as the Captain has to justify the faith that is in him, it is just as well that people should understand the grounds of his sturdy conviction !

This, then, was what I wrote at the time. " The Team is far from representing our best amateur strength, but I very much doubt if the professional element could have been strengthened. Barnes, of Lancashire, is possibly the best bowler in England on his day, but there was, I believe, a fear of his breaking down, and Hargreave is scarcely strong enough for the hard work which a tour in Australia involves. The bowling ought to be good enough, for though the perfect wickets are apt to try the best men, it cannot be said that the attacking force of the side is lacking in variety with Hirst and Rhodes left hand—one fast and the other slow ; Arnold, medium right ; Braund, slow right, breaking from leg ; Fielder, fast right ; Relf, medium right, and Bosanquet, slow. Here, at any rate, is plenty of change ; and as there are only two batsmen on the side who are not capable of making a hundred runs, the batting, though far from the best we can show, can scarcely be called weak. In the field there is little fault to find, and Lilley and Strudwick are probably better than any other two wicket-keepers in England. Playing day after day together, as they will do, the Team must gain in strength, and I believe, as a combination, they will work better together than is generally supposed. I venture to think that it is as good a side as any which has left for Australia in recent years, and in one essential, viz., bowling, distinctly superior."

Finally, the following figures will be of interest. They give the performances of every member of the Team from his first introduction to first class cricket up to the start of the present tour, and, so far as statistics teach anything, may be considered eloquent evidence of industrious and successful careers!

P. F. WARNER.
Batting.

	Rns.	H.S.	Av.
1895 ...	658	90	23·14
1896 ...	562	77	26·16
1897 ...	1,137	176	29·60
1898 ...	848	88	31·40
1899 ...	1,140	150	29·23
1900 ...	1,727	170	45·44
1901 ...	1,680	197*	45·40
1902 ...	832	139	30·81
1903 ...	1,141	149	39·34

J. T. TYLDESLEY.
Batting.

	Rns.	H.S.	Av.
1895 ...	339	152*	24·30
1896 ...	571	68	23·19
1897 ...	1,017	174	30·27
1898 ...	1,918	200	37·60
1899 ...	1,882	240	39·20
1900 ...	1,593	142	37·92
1901 ...	3,041	221	55·29
1902 ...	1,934	165	40·29
1903 ...	1,955	248	44·43

A. E. KNIGHT.
Batting.

	Rns.	H.S.	Av.
1895 ...	413	81	19·14
1896 ...	676	96	23·90
1897 ...	527	110	19·14
1898 ...	625	93	22·32
1899 ...	1,246	131	34·61
1900 ...	1,124	182	30·37
1901 ...	1,086	99	26·48
1902 ...	1,278	190*	32·76
1903 ...	1,834	229*	45·85

R. E. FOSTER.
Batting.

	Rns.	H.S.	Av.
1897 ...	228	53	19·00
1898 ...	272	65	22·66
1899 ...	1,173	134	32·58
1900 ...	1,807	171	51·62
1901 ...	2,128	136	50·66
1902 ...	551	109	36·73
1903 ...	—	—	—

* Not out.

T. HAYWARD.
Batting.

		Rns.	H.S.	Av.
1893	...	400	112	18·40
1894	...	884	142	26·26
1895	...	1,169	123	29·90
1896	...	1,595	229*	34·31
1897	...	1,368	130	38·00
1898	...	1,523	315*	42·30
1899	...	2,647	273	58·82
1900	...	2,693	193	53·86
1901	...	2,535	181	50·70
1902	...	1,737	177	32·77
1903	...	2,177	156*	35·68

Bowling.

		Wkts.	Rns.	Av.
1893	...	10	322	32·20
1894	...	11	206	18·80
1895	...	41	663	16·70
1896	...	91	1,541	16·85
1897	...	114	2,073	18·21
1898	...	30	1,028	34·26
1899	...	67	1,534	22·89
1900	...	21	687	32·71
1901	...	30	613	20·43
1902	...	20	844	42·20
1903	...	—	—	—

G. H. HIRST.
Batting.

		Rns.	H.S.	Av.
1892	...	177	43	14·90
1893	...	376	43	15·10
1894	...	564	115*	16·20
1895	...	710	64	19·70
1896	..	1,122	107	28·20
1897	...	1,535	134	35·30
1898	...	567	130	17·71
1899	...	1,630	186	35·43
1900	...	1,960	155	40·83
1901	...	1,950	214	42·39
1902	...	1,413	134	32·11
1903	...	1,844	153	47·28

Bowling.

		Wkts.	Rns.	Av.
1892	...	27	527	19·14
1893	...	99	1,425	14·39
1894	..	98	1,567	15·97
1895	...	150	2,560	17·10
1896	...	104	2,248	21·64
1897	...	101	2,346	23·23
1898	...	36	922	25·61
1899	...	82	2,031	24·76
1900	...	62	1,668	26·90
1901	...	183	2,999	16·38
1902	...	83	1,688	20·33
1903	...	128	1,913	14·94

L. C. BRAUND.
Batting.

		Rns.	H.S.	Av.
1896	...	170	51	12·20
1899	...	302	125	43·14
1900	...	562	107	24·43
1901	...	1,587	115*	36·06
1902	...	1,432	141	27·53
1903	...	1,425	132	32·28

Bowling.

		Wkts.	Rns.	Av.
1896	...	0	79	—
1899	...	4	178	44·50
1900	...	49	1,224	24·97
1901	...	120	3,675	30·62
1902	...	172	3,407	19·80
1903	...	134	2,816	21·01

E. ARNOLD.
Batting.

		Rns.	H.S.	Av.
1899	...	857	125*	34·28
1900	...	1,212	113	26·34
1901	...	781	83	20·63
1902	...	1,067	92	26·02
1903	...	1,157	128	30·44

Bowling.

		Wkts.	Rns.	Av.
1899	...	55	1,388	25·23
1900	...	90	2,372	26·35
1901	...	3	62	20·66
1902	...	113	2,134	18·88
1903	...	143	2,494	17·44

A. E. RELF.
Batting.

		Rns.	H.S.	Av.
1900	...	1,059	96	23·53
1901	...	694	53	19·27
1902	...	1,100	94	25·58
1903	...	863	120	21·04

* Not out.

Bowling.

		Wkts.	Rns.	Av.
1900	...	26	651	25·03
1901	...	66	1,827	27·68
1902	...	70	1,945	27·78
1903	...	124	2,335	18·83

B. J. T. BOSANQUET.

Batting.

		Rns.	H.S.	Av.
1898	...	168	54*	14·00
1899	...	419	71	29·73
1900	...	1,026	139	34·20
1901	...	1,240	127	32·63
1902	...	749	103	24·96
1903	...	1,083	108	34·90

Bowling.

		Wkts.	Rns.	Av.
1898	...	30	561	18·70
1899	...	55	1,250	22·72
1900	...	50	1,160	23·20
1901	...	36	1,351	37·52
1902	...	40	847	21·17
1903	...	63	1,323	21·00

W. R. RHODES.

Batting.

		Rns.	H.S.	Av.
1898	...	557	78	17·40
1899	...	432	81*	11·36
1900	...	655	79	21·12
1901	...	854	105	26·88
1902	...	490	92*	15·31
1903	...	1,137	98*	27·07

Bowling.

		Wkts.	Rns.	Av.
1898	...	154	2,249	14·60
1899	...	179	3,062	17·10
1900	...	261	3,606	13·81
1901	...	251	3,797	15·12
1902	...	213	2,801	13·15
1903	...	193	2,813	14·57

A. A. LILLEY.

Batting.

		Rns.	H.S.	Av.
1894	...	276	74	15·60
1895	...	1,399	158*	34·39
1896	...	979	132	24·19
1897	...	945	82	35·00
1898	...	934	112	31·13
1899	...	1,111	73	29·23
1900	...	892	112	25·48
1901	...	1,054	124	30·03
1902	...	639	72*	18·25
1903	...	675	59	25·96

Bowling.

		Wkts.	Rns.	Av.
1894	...	—	—	—
1895	...	—	—	—
1896	...	12	226	18·10
1897	...	13	441	33·12
1898	...	6	257	42 82
1899	...	4	212	53·
1900	...	1	57	57·
1901	...	4	127	31·75
1902	...	—	—	—
1903	...	—	—	—

* Not out.

CHAPTER II

DEPARTURE AND VOYAGE

WHEN I was driving to St. Pancras to catch the
10.50 on that memorable 25th of September, 1903,
it occurred to me that, besides the old friends who had
promised to see us off, there might, perhaps, be a few of
the general public to give us a good word, but at the
most I expected a mere handful of men around the
entrance. When I arrived at the station I was simply
amazed at the sight that greeted me. Every corner was
occupied, the platform crammed. There were any
number of ladies ; and as for the men, it was well said at
the time that every class in the community was represented, from the Lord Chief Justice of England,
President of the M.C.C., to " Master Bones, the butcher's
boy," who on Saturday afternoons plays for the third
Eleven of the Pinner Peripatetics !

Never shall I forget the glorious enthusiasm of that
send-off. Many of the best-known cricketers of the day
were on the platform ; and, whatever newspaper criticism
had had to say about us at the start, the reporters were
certainly energetic enough on our behalf that morning.
And, brilliantly verbose in the midst of them all, the
inimitable Craig, poet of poets, skipped from side to side
of the station, greeting old acquaintances, and doing

immense business with a noble poem in my honour—a
poem quite in Craig's most inspired vein! Who could
resist the tender appeal of this eloquent finale?

> " We'll stand by Warner as we ought,
>   The honour was by him unsought,
> We've faith in him, and nothing shall remove it.
>   We English love fair play,
>   At least, that's what we say,
> If 'tis so, by our actions let us prove it."

Was ever Captain in the days of old more sincerely
welcomed to the fray by his tame bard than we were by
the Surrey Poet?

Piles of luggage on the platform! Struggling porters!
Everywhere rush and riot. Bosanquet, Hirst, Rhodes,
Tyldesley, Arnold, Hayward, and Lilley being anxious
(for various reasons) to avoid the Bay, were coming
overland, but Bosanquet had promised to see us off,
and had sworn to be in time. The train was late in
starting, but still he put in no appearance: and at last
we steamed slowly out of the station, and, as he had
been inquired for at every corner, some enterprising
journalist at once cabled to Australia that we were
off without him. It was a great send-off, and among
the many kind wishes that speeded us on our way,
none gave me greater pleasure than C. B. Fry's excellent open letter in the *Daily Express*, full of good
advice, good criticism, and good fellowship. May I
indulge myself by quoting the final passages? Coming
from such a judge of the game, they might well give one
a little helpful confidence. I have read them many
times since with gratitude and delight:—

"Pelham, yours is a powerful Team, and should do
well if it plays as a team of brothers, and if you can

persuade your men to scorn delights—minor delights—
and to live laborious—pleasantly laborious—days
throughout the tour. Surely the seasoned cricketers
with you know that the prime condition of success in
the game is unadulterated physical fitness. So we need
not fear but that they will take the field like 'trained'
men.

"This is a bigger job than you've had as yet, this
captaincy of an English side in test matches. But with
your knowledge of the game, your accommodating
temper, your tactful touch, and your sanguine view of
things, you should do very well in this job, too. Then,
too, Pelham, they say you have luck—that you are a
lucky Captain. They say that of Lord Roberts also. It
is difficult to find the dividing-line between luck and
management in war and cricket. When a cricketer
talks of the luck of the game he knows what he means
—and he means much. For my part, I cannot see any
reason why your Team, given as much cricket-luck
as fell to the lot of the last Australian Team here,
should not return next spring with those wished-for
'ashes.'

"Much will depend on how you work your bowlers.
I wonder which of your 'swervers' will swerve best in
Australia? I wonder which will have most chances
with the new ball? George Hirst likes a new ball, and
so does Arnold, and so does Relf. Mind you do not
judge Relf on his Sussex average and leave him out;
mind you give him a thorough good trial; he might
turn out your best bowler. And if he does—well, remember he is a mettlesome, 'nervy' bowler, who should
not be kept on too long at a stretch. He pays for nurs-
ing. He can use a new ball, and he will be on the learn

all the time. But I fancy Arnold will prove your bowling mainstay—I know he ought to.

"About Fielder I am wondering. You seem to have chosen him chiefly owing to a performance of his against Middlesex on a very fiery wicket. I have seen our Bland bowl like an English bowler at Tonbridge. At Brighton it is different; and at Sydney, too, I guess. I only played Fielder once, and found him a good trier, but quite easy. On that day's form there are several much better fast bowlers in England—Tom Richardson, for instance. But he is young, this Fielder, and keen and strong. You can never tell. When Blythe went to Australia with Archie MacLaren I thought he would get more runs than wickets out there. But he proved a pronounced success. So may it be with Fielder.

"You must persuade that Bosanquet of yours to practise, practise, practise those funny 'googlies' of his till he is automatically certain of his length. That leg-break of his which breaks from the off might win a test match!

"And now, Pelham, farewell for a season, and the best of luck to you! I shall think of you as I dig with my niblick in the furze bushes, and, likely enough, regret I am not with you hitting at a bigger ball with a simpler instrument. Good luck, 'Plum'! If you win your first test match every hand at home will stretch out to you across the sea; and, if you do not, every real cricketer's hand will stretch out all the same.

"C. B. FRY."

But I must go on with my story, though there is not very much to relate of the journey itself. At Tilbury we boarded the *Orontes*, and were heartily welcomed by

Mr. Fred Green of the Orient Line, whose tables were flowing with champagne and hospitality, and who made a little speech of God-speed, full of spirit and kindliness to all. And then we were off, and the wind began to blow, with customary results.

Between Plymouth and Gibraltar we met a head-wind—"half a gale" the ladies insisted on calling it—and there were those who wished in their souls that they had chosen the better part, with Hayward, Tyldesley, and the others, and gone across country. For the *Orontes* dipped her substantial nose into the crested waves, and reeled with an energy that recalled the similitudes of the Psalmist. By the time we picked up our friends at Marseilles, however, things had quieted down, and we were able to enjoy the Mediterranean. We only stayed an hour or so at Marseilles, but a whole day was spent at beautiful Naples, and thence on to Port Said, and so through the Canal—that monument of engineering genius of the great nation across the Channel. At Suez we bade farewell to Europe ; but sorrow had been following in our wake, for here it was that Tom Hayward received the sad news of his mother's death. At such times as these mere words can do little enough to alleviate, but the sympathy of the whole ship went out to the great Surrey cricketer in his trouble.

After leaving Marseilles a sports committee was formed, with Mr. J. H. Want, a former Attorney-General in the New South Wales Ministry, as chairman, R. E. Foster as Secretary, and Bishop Welldon, H. E. Murray Anderson, the secretary of the Somerset Cricket Club (who was travelling as far as Colombo), and myself on the committee. Soon we were busy with bull and quoits, and all the various games which help to relieve the

tedium of a long voyage, and every afternoon after tea
we played cricket for an hour or two—capital exercise
with the thermometer standing at 90 deg. in the shade.

DECK CRICKET.

The photograph on this page will give some idea of the
pitch.   It will be seen that the roof was very low, and if
the bowler hit it in delivering the ball, it was a " no-ball."
Extras figured conspicuously in the score, by the bye!

The Red Sea was hot, but not unbearably so. At Colombo there was some talk of a match, but, as Braund was resting his side and Lilley's and Strudwick's hands were both rather sore after their hard season's work, it was thought wiser to run no risk, and so a cable was sent from Port Said declining the invitation of the Colombo Club.

We spent our days in reading and playing bridge, and taking our part in the deck tournaments, and after dinner there was generally a dance or a concert or some sort of amusement. The fancy dress ball was a great success, nearly everyone donning some costume or other, and the cricket Team emerging triumphant, for I carried off the first prize as " The Rajah of Bhong," and R. E. Foster as " A Gondolier " the second.

An Eleven got up amongst the second-class passengers challenged us at deck cricket, but we routed them at every point and returned victorious by 165 to 31. A limit of twenty runs per man was agreed on, and Hayward, Hirst, Rhodes, Relf, Fielder, and Lilley all reached the limit, while Rhodes and Fielder did the most successful bowling. On October 17th we passed the *Omrah*, homeward bound, and as she steamed by the signal went up " Success to Warner."

When we got to Colombo we found that a good deal of disappointment had been caused by our non-acceptance of the offer of the Colombo Cricket Club to play a match, but our refusal was readily understood when the special circumstances of the case were explained. The Marylebone Club are ever ready to encourage cricket, and we would most willingly have met the Colombo Team had it been in the best interests of this side to do so. As it was, we spent the day at the

Mount Lavinia Hotel, which is beautifully situated on the verge of the ocean, in a spot happily free (unlike Colombo itself) from the plague of mosquitoes. The amateurs went out to Mount Lavinia by train, and the professionals, drawn each in a rickshaw by a docile native at full speed, created a keen enthusiasm among the Cingalese population, as they were generally acknowledged to exhibit the characteristic qualities of the ruling race.

From Colombo to Fremantle there was something of a sea, and a good many of the ladies showed a chastened spirit, either keeping in their cabins or lying outstretched in silence on their chairs. Fremantle was reached in the very early hours of October 29. The punctuality of the ocean steamer was extraordinary, for Commander Ruthven reckoned on being off the harbour of Fremantle at 5 a.m., and it was just one minute later when he gave the signal for stopping the engines. In the days of sailing vessels, the Australian mail was not seldom a month late ; now it arrives not only on the day but to the minute.

Mr. Gardiner, the Colonial Treasurer, the President of the W.A. Cricket Association ; Mr. F. D. North, an old Rugbeian ; and several of the local cricket committee came on board the *Orontes* to welcome the Team, and in the course of the morning we went up to Perth, some twelve miles from the port, returning again in time to sail at mid-day. Rigid punctuality was the rule on the ship, and, in getting away to the very minute, we left five third-class passengers behind.

In the afternoon of the same day we had a most amusing cricket match between ladies and gentlemen, the ladies winning by three runs. Bishop Welldon and

D

Lilley acted as umpires, and the decisions at one end, at least, were given with a clearness and precision which left nothing to be desired. We had to use the un-accustomed left-hand, except in the case of genuine left-handers, but Rhodes quite failed to get a length with his right arm, and the score was chiefly made up of wides and no-balls. After the match Lady Darnley entertained both Elevens at tea in the saloon. Lady Darnley's presence was thought to be a good omen for the fortunes of the Team, for not only did her husband, at that time the Hon. Ivo Bligh, bring back "the ashes" from Australia, but she also went out on the same boat as Stoddart's very successful 1894-1895 combination.

The Australian Bight has a bad reputation, but nothing could have been better than the weather between Fremantle and Adelaide. The last few days of our long voyage across the seas were spent in playing off the finals of the various deck games, sports, &c., Tyldesley winning two events in the games and Strudwick carrying off the obstacle race. As we neared South Australia the desire of the Team to get as fit as possible was very obvious, for cricket on deck, slip-catching, and various forms of exercise were taken to more keenly than ever. The slip-catching gave us excellent practice, one of the Team taking the bat and tipping catches in every possible direction. This helped us to get our eyes in, after the rest of several weeks.

On Saturday, the 31st of October, Lady Darnley gave another tea-party, the whole of the Team and J. A. Murdoch being invited, in addition to several ladies. The M.C.C. flag, which we were carrying with us, was brought out for the occasion, and the table was decorated with flowers and the colours of the Team

THE FIRST TEAM TO DEFEAT THE ENGLISH.

R.M.S. *Orontes.*   October 29, 1903.

Lady Darnley, with an eloquence which the most accomplished orator might envy, proposed success to the Englishmen. Her good wishes were seconded by Captain Ruthven, who remarked that this was the seventh time he had carried an English Team to or from Australia. I replied in what is humorously called my "most finished style," expressing my gratitude for the good wishes conveyed to us and my confidence that

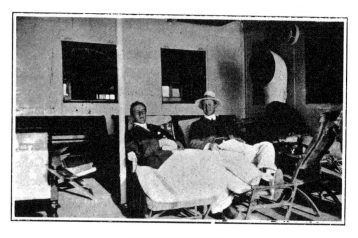

ON THE VOYAGE OUT.

the Team would acquit itself in a manner not unworthy of the best traditions of English sport.

At ten o'clock on Monday morning, November 2, the *Orontes* cast anchor in Largs Bay, and shortly afterwards a launch, flying the South Australian colours, was seen making its way towards us. On board were Major Morkham, of the Melbourne Club, Messrs. J. Cresswell and J. Hill, father of the cricketer, who was himself there to give us a hearty welcome. Without much delay we went on shore, a special train conveying us from the port to Adelaide, a distance of fifteen miles. On the railway station platform Sir Edwin Smith (President of the Cricket Association) was awaiting us, and by midday we were comfortably settled in the South Australian Hotel, which had been gaily decorated in our honour.

It was rather late in the afternoon before our baggage arrived, and our cricket on the Oval was limited to about an hour. The wicket was bad—one might almost say dangerous—but our practice served to give us some much-needed exercise. A small charge was made for admission, the proceeds being handed over to charities.

In the evening the Mayor (Mr. Cohen, M.P.) publicly welcomed the Team at the Town Hall. We marshalled our forces in the Mayor's private room, and as we marched in procession into the hall we received a magnificent reception from fully 2,000 people, every seat in the building being occupied. In front of the platform, on which were seated the Team, the members of the City Council, and the South Australian Cricket Association, were hung the Union Jack, the red and yellow flag of the M.C.C., and the red, yellow, and black colours of the South Australian Cricket Association.

I was indeed as much surprised by the welcome given to us as I had been by the send-off from England. As the Team entered the room we were most cordially greeted, everyone rising and applauding. Cricketers are, I hope, modest, and the cheers that were given us by the enormous crowd assembled in the Town Hall were not a little embarrassing. The Mayor made a long speech, in which he eulogised Englishmen, and English cricketers in particular ; and then, for the first time in my life, I addressed an audience from a platform. I have spoken on cricket in various parts of the world, but never have I addressed so large an audience from such an exalted pinnacle as the platform of a Town Hall in a great Australian city. I hope I shall not be accused of suspecting myself of eloquence if I give the substance of what I said that evening. As an exercise in oratory my remarks were insignificant; but they have some interest now, as one looks back, and recalls the hopes with which we set out on our difficult task. As a mere footnote to cricket history I venture to add them here.

"When we left London six weeks ago," I said, "a magnificent send-off was given us. Indeed, as one of the evening papers remarked at the time, it was like some famous general going out to fight, or a victorious army returning from the wars. But if the welcome we received on that occasion was hearty and spontaneous to a degree, the way in which you have received us to-night is no less hearty. In coming to Adelaide I feel that I am amongst old friends, and the six or seven months which have elapsed since I was last here have in no way obliterated the memory of those pleasant days. And it seems to me that Adelaide is a very fitting place for an English Eleven to commence a tour, for your cricket is full of splendid traditions, seeing that you can boast of having given to the world such names as Lyons, Hill, Jones, Jarvis, and George Giffen. Major Morkham has just remarked that George Giffen is the greatest all-round cricketer the world has ever seen. Well, we in England think that W. G. Grace is the Grand Old Man of cricket—but we too in England are the first to acknowledge that George Giffen is the Grace of Australia.

"Much has been said about this M.C.C. Team. You

have all heard of the *Daily Mail.* Now the *Daily Mail* is a paper that I have the greatest respect for—but I do not think I am very wrong in saying that sometimes it borders on the sensational. The *Daily Mail* (and others) tried to make out that Mr. MacLaren and myself were at daggers drawn. I assure you there is no truth in that. Mr. MacLaren and I are friends, and I would gladly have brought him with me, for his unrivalled abilities as a batsman and his knowledge of the game would have been invaluable. It is my great regret that neither Mr. MacLaren, Mr. Fry, nor Mr. Jackson are with us, but I have brought you on last season's form about the best eleven professionals in England, and the very best bowlers in England. There are, as you know, only three amateurs, and they, I am the first to admit, do not represent the cream of English amateur talent, though I ought to make an exception in favour of Mr. Foster, who, when he was playing cricket regularly two years ago, was one of the most brilliant batsmen England ever had.

" The success of a team, as it seems to me, does not depend on individual brilliancy, but on combination, and, as a side, I feel confident we shall work well together. This Team has been most carefully chosen, for on a long tour like this it is most necessary to have not only good cricketers but good fellows, and the professionals you will find not only great on the field of play but a credit to themselves and their profession off it.

" And so I think we have a great chance in the test matches. Indeed, I should be a craven if I did not. But if we do go down, we shall do so fighting gamely to the very last ball.

" A great deal has been said about me as a Captain. I

do not mind these criticisms—if one accepts the position
of Captain one must expect to be criticised, but I have
been captaining Elevens since I was fifteen years old,
and I am not aware that a great deal of fault has
been found with me. We appreciate your welcome
immensely, and I believe that the splendid march we
have just heard so ably played is a good augury for our
triumphal march through Australia."

Entertainment was followed at once by hard work,
and we began by practising for four or five hours every

PRACTISING AT ADELAIDE.

day on the splendid wickets of the Adelaide Oval—
wickets so perfect that to get any work on the ball
seemed almost an impossibility, while to find a delivery
getting up higher than the top of the stumps is the
exception indeed. We had taken, as I have said, great
care to keep ourselves in condition during the voyage
by deck cricket and various sports, with the result that
nearly all the Team got into something like form even
after but a couple of days' practice-work. Hayward
and Tyldesley both shaped particularly well, while
Lilley gave the impression of being likely to get a
great many more runs than he was credited with in

England last season, and Bosanquet was full of confidence and energy.

At first Arnold seemed a long way our best bowler, for he occasionally managed to get a little off-spin on the ball, while he can always bowl one which jumps up sharply from the pitch, and he has, too, an uncommonly good yorker. Relf did some very creditable work, and Rhodes, on a very slightly worn wicket, made a great impression on the many critics who daily gathered round the nets to take stock of us.

Nor did we neglect to practise fielding, for every day we gave an hour to practising catching, and a high catch requires a great deal of judging in the bright sunlight of Australia.

Meanwhile we were furnished with something like a sensation by the refusal of the veteran George Giffen to play against us except under special financial arrangements. He considered the terms offered him by the South Australian Association inadequate, and said that, if he accepted them, he would only do so on the condition that the money was handed over to the Children's Hospital instead of to himself. Giffen was curtly informed that the association declined to make any such arrangement, and they gave him a fixed time within which he was to say whether he would play or not on the original terms, viz., £5 for expenses. He promptly said he would play, but stated that he should give the money to the Children's Hospital himself, and send the association the hospital secretary's acknowledgment. This seems a small matter, and a personal one at that, but in Australia, where, it must be confessed, newspaper comment is much freer and less discreet than in England, an immense amount was made of the incident. One of the leading Australian papers, for example, pointed the moral in the following uncompromising phrases: "The whole episode has, of course, excited ridicule, but the best friends of the once peerless champion must regret that by this latest unreasonable outburst he has completely forfeited public sympathy. Giffen holds a Government appointment in Adelaide, and as the match is to be played on the Adelaide Oval an allowance of £5, when others were getting nothing, was sufficiently liberal. There is a very strong local feeling against the ex-champion's action, which is generally deprecated as a display of very poor feeling on the part of such a prominent representative Australian cricketer towards the Marylebone Club, which has in many ways shown marked courtesy to Australians visiting England. It is certainly very much to be regretted that such a player should be tempted to so ingloriously mark the latter days of a great cricketing career by repeating follies for the commission of which in the past he had been perhaps too generously forgiven."

Fortunately the matter blew over, and Giffen consented to play against us in the end. And this brings me to the South Australia match and the beginning of the serious business of the tour.

Before proceeding to cricket, I may perhaps be allowed to record that throughout the tour the amateurs and professionals stayed at the same hotel. This was quite a departure from precedent, and I am glad to say that it was a tremendous success. It keeps the team much better together, and promotes a much keener mutual understanding and a feeling that you are all one side, working together to a common end.

CHAPTER III

THE OPENING MATCH OF THE TOUR AT ADELAIDE

FIRST MATCH—v. SOUTH AUSTRALIA

THE first match of a tour, and especially so important a tour as this was, is generally a somewhat anxious one. So much depends on a good start, and a good performance at once spells confidence, whereas a poor one, however much extenuating circumstances—such as a lack of practice, unfamiliarity with strange surroundings, change of climate, &c.—may be pleaded, does not tend to put an eleven on terms with itself. Moreover, a captain has under his command eleven men who have never played together before. I won the toss —an omen of good luck for the future—the first duty of a captain, and as it turned out Hayward and myself were destined to give the side a good start. The cricket before lunch was very slow, only forty-five runs being made in an hour and a quarter, but we played, I think, the right game, in not taking any risks. The wicket was a good deal faster than those on which we had been practising, and neither Hayward nor myself timed the ball quite accurately, though, excepting for a difficult chance which Hayward gave to the wicket-keeper off Travers, we made no mistake. Travers, a left-handed

OPENING MATCH OF THE TOUR.

Warner jumps out to drive Travers.

bowler about Rhodes' pace, kept a splendid length, and, though unchanged, only ten runs had been scored off him at the interval. On resuming, both of us seemed to get the pace of the wicket at once, and runs came merrily. A four to long-leg by Hayward sent up the hundred, but twenty-two runs later I was caught at third man for sixty-five. Tyldesley was not in form, and Foster was run out in attempting a short run from a hit of Hayward's, and at the tea interval, at 4 o'clock, the score was 149 for three wickets. Hayward not out seventy-nine. The last hour and three-quarters of the day saw another ninety-eight runs added, without further loss—Hayward not out 126, Braund not out forty-seven. The Surrey batsman played magnificently. Most of his runs were made by off-drives and strokes in front of the wicket, and he lifted but one ball off the ground, and that only just failed to reach the boundary. His innings was a masterpiece of sound, scientific, and stylish batting. Nothing could have been more satisfactory for our future prospects than that Hayward should have been in form from the very start, for one looked to him more, perhaps, than to any other individual member of the side to get runs. Braund was a trifle "scratchy" to begin with, but improved as he progressed, and made several powerful drives. Our first day's cricket was, therefore, extremely satisfactory. Excepting just after luncheon runs never came fast, the average rate throughout being scarcely sixty an hour. But nothing is gained in Australia by rushing matters, and soundness rather than brilliancy tells in the long run. A day's cricket in Australia is infinitely shorter than with us at home. As a rule play does not begin until twelve o'clock—it was fifteen minutes later before the first ball was bowled on this occasion—there is a tea interval of a quarter of an hour during the afternoon, and stumps are drawn at six o'clock. In fact, four days' cricket in Australia is just about equal to three in England.

Monday, November 9, was a most disagreeable day. The strong north wind brought along clouds of dust, and the heat was uncomfortably oppressive. Play commenced at 11.30, but the crowd, owing no doubt to the state of the weather, was disappointing, for at no time during the day did it number more than 6,000. Hayward added thirty runs to his overnight score, and was then caught at mid-off. His innings of 157 lasted nearly six hours, and during all that time he was beaten but once, and the only mistake that could be set down against him was the difficult chance to the wicket-keeper which I mentioned. On the second morning he carried steadiness to an extreme, but it was a magnificent effort of skilful and stylish batting. Nearly all his runs were obtained in front of the wicket by drives and hard pushes ; very rarely did he attempt a late cut.

The rest of the innings was chiefly remarkable for a very spirited display by Lilley, who drove splendidly on both sides and hit up ninety-one in a couple of hours. Hirst found that he could not make his best stroke—the pull— so easily as he does in England, but he cut capitally. At tea-time the innings was declared closed, but my action in so doing was much commented on, as many held that there was no rule which enabled a captain to close his innings in a four-day match. However, Hill read the rule as I did, in that the closure applies to three and anything more than three-day cricket. At the end of the ordinary interval between the innings we took the

THE OPENING MATCH OF THE TOUR.

122—1—65.

E

field, but the umpires did not appear for at least another five minutes. It subsequently transpired they had been arguing as to whether we had the power to declare. Hill told them we had, and there the matter ended quite amicably, but the whole thing served as a good illustration of the difficulty which arises when one country adopts one set of laws and another another. It is a matter which demands the immediate attention of the M.C.C., for if you have one law applying to one country and another to another nothing but confusion can arise. As I have said before, one of the conditions under which Marylebone undertook this tour was that their rule should govern all matches. The Australians agreed to this. Yet a certain section—though an unimportant one—were disposed to cavil at those conditions.

Though the South Australian bowling is not now as strong as in the days when George Giffen and Jones were in their prime, it was, one may fairly say, a great performance to score 483 runs for eight wickets within five days of landing from a five weeks' voyage. I had omitted Knight, Fielder, and Strudwick from the fourteen I had to make my selection from, and with Arnold and Rhodes in ten and eleven every man of the side had made a hundred at some time or another in first class cricket. This total of 483 was compiled in seven hours and three-quarters. Throughout their long spell in the field the South Australians stuck to their task well, Gehrs at extra cover, Hill at mid-off, Travers at mid-on, and Jennings at third man and in the country being especially excellent. Claxton was the most successful bowler. With a high action he bowls rather over medium pace, and often made the ball go away quickly with his arm.

Travers kept a splendid length, and Giffen, though but a shadow of his once incomparable self, bowled a great deal better than his analysis might lead one to suppose. Hay, who had done such execution against Lord Hawke's Eleven six months previously, did not fulfil the promise he showed on that occasion, though when he went on a second time he sent down five or six decidedly good overs. A little over an hour and a half remained for play when South Australia went in, and, at the drawing of stumps, ninety-three runs had been made for three wickets. Our bowling was excellent, Bosanquet especially puzzling everyone with his slows, which were of excellent length and came quickly off the pitch. All our bowlers had a turn, and Rhodes received quite an ovation when, with his first ball, he caused Hack to play on. Hill was in very good form, but, just as he was looking dangerous, Lilley stumped him very smartly. Gehrs went for a short run, and had his wicket thrown down from cover-point.

On the third day the South Australians once more demonstrated how much they depend on Clem Hill, for, with the sole exception of Jennings, the rest of the batsmen curled up completely. I had been well pleased with our batting, and it was with much interest that I watched our bowlers at work during this innings ; and here, again, one had every reason to be satisfied, for everyone who went on did well. Perhaps the best were Arnold and Hirst, who at one time bowled unchanged for an hour. The Worcestershire cricketer kept a fine length—if anything a bit on the short side—while every now and then one got up sharply, and then there was that uncommonly good yorker of his. Mr. Pycroft has told us that the swerving of a ball in the air is caused

C. B. JENNINGS.

by the resistance it meets with from the atmosphere—
the thicker the atmosphere the more swerve will
the bowler be able to impart to his deliveries.
Well, George Hirst found that the Australian atmosphere was thinner than that of his own country, and did
not greatly encourage the swerve—but though he was
on that account forced to rely less than usual on what
the ball did before striking the ground he bowled admirably, and wanted a good deal of playing. I pur-
posely did not bowl Braund much, as he had not quite
got rid of the strain to his side which he sustained
shortly before leaving England, but he got a couple of
wickets at the end of the innings. The fielding was
crisp and clean for the most part, but the Adelaide
ground is rather rough in the outfield, and occasionally
a run was given away.

Lilley's wicket-keeping was of the highest order, and
this form, except on one or two very rare occasions, he
kept up until the end of the tour. He is, indeed, in my
opinion, one of the best stumpers that ever lived. On a
hard, true wicket one cannot imagine a better—on a
sticky pitch he surpasses anyone that I have ever seen,
for he takes the breaking ball from a right-hander which
just misses the leg-stump safely and cleanly, and how
many great wicket-keepers has one seen let that ball go,
thinking it must hit the stumps !

Clement Hill played a great innings when South
Australia followed on. He got more runs than usual on
the off-side, driving very strongly in the direction of
cover and extra cover. From the first ball he was quite
at home, and never gave the slightest chance. Hack
played an invaluable, if slow innings, but in spite of his
and Hill's effort we should have won easily had not

Jennings batted splendidly. Jennings is quite young ; he cannot be more than two- or three-and-twenty, and his cricketing future is bright with promise. There had

RELF.

been a shower of rain in the night previous to the fourth and final day's play, and when Jennings came in Rhodes was making the ball "bite" a bit. The pitch was not

sticky—very far from it—but the surface had lifted a
little, and for a time both Rhodes and Relf were not
easy.   But Jennings faced them bravely, and every
minute the wicket improved.   After lunch it was perfect
again, and as it had been arranged to draw stumps at
3.15 in order that we might catch the express to Melbourne, the match was eventually left unfinished, though
decidedly in our favour.   Jennings in the whole game
scored 103 runs without losing his wicket, and for him I
anticipate a place in the next Australian Eleven which
visits England.   With almost a model style, his defence
seemed excellent, and he is particularly good on that
half-drive, half-cut which sends the ball between point
and cover.   Rhodes had bowled well in the first innings,
but he did even better this time.   His analysis—two
wickets for seventy-eight runs—is misleading, as analyses
very often are, and gives no idea of how excellent was
his work, for with ordinary luck he might easily have
had five or six wickets.   Relf bowled very well indeed,
and showed in this match promise which was not subsequently fulfilled.

ENGLAND.

First Innings.

P. F. Warner, c. Jennings, b. Claxton	65
Hayward, c. Hill, b. Travers	157
Tyldesley, c. Giffen, b. Claxton	1
R. E. Foster, run out	2
Braund, b. Giffen	58
Hirst, c. Evans, b. Claxton	37
B. J. T. Bosanquet, b. Hay	19
Lilley, not out	91
Relf, c. Travers, b. Claxton	30
Arnold, not out	7
Byes, 8 ; leg-byes, 7 ; wide, 1	16
Total (for 8 wickets)	483

Innings declared closed.

Bowling Analysis.

	O.	M.	R.	W.		O.	M.	R.	W.
J. Travers ...	50	20	95	1	N. Claxton ...	26	2	76	4
G. Giffen ...	46	7	129	1	A. E. H. Evans	10	2	37	0
H. Hay	30	11	67	1	F. Hack	6	1	13	0
J. Reedman ...	13	1	41	0	C. Hill	1	0	9	0

Hay bowled 1 wide.

SOUTH AUSTRALIA.

First Innings.

F. T. Hack, b. Rhodes	16
A. R. Gehrs, run out...	31
C. Hill, st. Lilley, b. Bosanquet	18
G. Giffen, c. Lilley, b. Arnold...	22
J. F. Travers, b. Hirst	18
N. Claxton, b. Arnold	11
C. B. Jennings, not out	26
A. E. H. Evans, l.b.w., b. Hirst	0
J. C. Reedman, c. Lilley, b. Arnold	1
P. M. Newland, c. Rhodes, b. Braund	10
H. Hay, b. Braund	0
Byes, 6 ; leg-byes, 8 ; no-balls, 5	19

Total... 172

Bowling Analysis.

	O.	M.	R.	W.		O.	M.	R.	W.
Hirst	17	8	19	2	Bosanquet ...	13	0	38	1
Arnold	20	6	49	3	Rhodes	11	2	27	1
Braund	9	2	15	2	Relf	2	1	5	0

Arnold bowled 3 no-balls.

Second Innings.

A. R. Gehrs, b. Arnold	7
F. T. Hack, c. Hayward, b. Rhodes	54
C. Hill, c. Braund, b. Relf	116
G. Giffen, c. Braund, b. Relf	18
N. Claxton, l.b.w., b. Relf	14
C. B. Jennings, not out	77
J. C. Reedman, c. Braund, b. Rhodes	1
A. E. H. Evans, c. Hirst, b. Braund	22
P. Newland, not out	13
Sundries	21

Total (for 7 wickets) 343

Bowling Analysis.

	O.	M.	R.	W.		O.	M.	R.	W.
Arnold	22	4	63	1	Rhodes	41	11	78	2
Hirst	17	5	32	0	Relf	27	10	48	3
Bosanquet ...	21	4	62	0	Braund	12	1	39	1

Hirst bowled 2 no-balls and 1 wide ; Arnold, Rhodes, and Relf, 1 no-ball each.

FALL OF WICKETS.

First Innings of England.

1	2	3	4	5	6	7	8	9	10
122	134	149	266	322	336	367	446	Innings declared.	

First Innings of South Australia.

1	2	3	4	5	6	7	8	9	10
37	66	85	104	123	133	144	147	171	172

Second Innings of South Australia.

1	2	3	4	5	6	7
14	156	207	208	243	244	288

CHAPTER IV

THE FIRST MATCH v. VICTORIA

LEAVING Adelaide at 4.30 on the afternoon of Wednesday, November 11, we reached Melbourne at ten o'clock the next morning.

Here a warm welcome awaited us, hundreds of people, including the Countess of Darnley, Lord Richard Nevill, representing his Excellency the Governor-General of Australia, Lord Tennyson, Mr. R. Murchison, the President of the Melbourne C.C., Mr. James McLaughlin, Major Wardill, and several members of the Victorian Eleven, being on the platform. After lunching with the Lord Mayor of Melbourne at the Town Hall, we had some practice, and the next day began a match against Victoria, who were captained by Frank Laver.

The Melbourne Cricket Ground, with its lovely turf, fine stands, and huge scoring-board, or rather building, for it is of stone and red brick, on which every run, with the bowler's analysis, and the manner of the batsman's dismissal is shown, is far superior to anything we have at home. The Sydney and Adelaide grounds both have a cycling track round the edge of the field of play, but there is nothing of the kind at Melbourne, and for this reason the Melbourne ground is, perhaps, preferable to

PAVILION AND MEMBERS' STAND, MELBOURNE.

either of the other two, though the huge stands and trees make the light very bad for catching.

The members' pavilion is adorned with portraits of famous players and grounds, panelled with the teams that have figured for Victoria in past inter-State games, and has quite a museum of old-time cricket implements ; but the accommodation in the way of dressing and luncheon-rooms is not quite in keeping with the rest of the building. A new pavilion is, I was told, to be erected before next season.

Victoria may not be as strong on the cricket-field as they were some five or six years ago, but in meeting them we were opposing an Eleven who eighteen months ago had twice defeated South Australia, and had run New South Wales—the winners of the inter-State Competition—to a hard finish, while at Christmas time they succeeded in actually defeating New South Wales, though it is only fair to say that the New South Wales men had the worst of the wicket.

On this occasion my luck in the toss deserted me, and the Australians went in to bat on a beautiful wicket —on the slow side, the critics said, for Melbourne, but from an Englishman's point of view an absolutely ideal pitch, neither too fast nor too slow, and with all the fire out of it, very much like that at Trent Bridge, Nottingham.

That our opponents would make at least 250 runs we never doubted, but our bowling was so consistently excellent, and our fielding so keen and accurate, that by ten minutes past five the last wicket had been disposed of for 164 runs. All our bowlers—except Bosanquet, who could not find his length—did well, and Rhodes especially did wonderfully. He kept a beautiful length, made the ball spin quickly off the pitch, and continually deceived the batsman in the flight. Curiously enough, no one seemed to find him difficult so long as they were content to play him ; it was only when the batsman tried to score that his length and deceptive flight, which was helped by a slight breeze blowing from the direction of short-leg, told. Constant changes of bowling pay in Australia, as, I, for my part, believe they do anywhere, especially when one can call on so many bowlers of such widely different styles as Relf, Hirst, Fielder, Rhodes, and Bosanquet. Strudwick behind the wicket was in brilliant form, and the whole Team worked so well together that I do not think the Melbourne Press exaggerated when they described our fielding as near perfection as possible.

A feature of the game was the reappearance in first class cricket of Harry Trott, who showed that he still retained much of that skill which made him some seven or eight years back one of the great batsmen Australia has given to the world, while another interesting personality in the Victorian Team was J. Horan, a son of T. Horan, so well known as a member of the famous 1882 Australian Eleven, and as " Felix " of the Australasian.

When our turn came to bat, the wicket had become appreciably faster, and nearly every one who went in showed to advantage.

Tyldesley and Foster put on 160 runs for the third wicket, their cricket being as attractive as it was skilful. It was particularly gratifying to see Foster in such good form—for even for so great a player a prolonged absence from regular participation in first class cricket must make a difference. Tyldesley was Tyldesley at his best

—full of life and dash ; and I do not think I have ever
seen George Hirst bat better. At Adelaide he rather
overdid that famous pull stroke of his, but here he had
it under full control, and used it with constant and
disconcerting effect on the bowlers. A ball wide of the
off stump and on the short side he would sweep round
to leg ; the next minute an apparently similar delivery
would be cut most brilliantly past third man. Bosanquet
had a little luck at starting, but once he had got going,
his hitting was splendid in its power and placing. No
one would accuse him of being a pretty batsman, but he
uses his forearm with rare vigour, and he has that
inestimable virtue of always thinking he is going to
make runs.

Armstrong bowled wonderfully well. His leg break,
it is true, is much more leg than break, but he dropped
the ball either on the half volley or a good length just
outside the leg stump, and with eight men on the
on-side it was difficult to score from him.

Collins is a fast bowler, with an extra fast yorker
and a good slow ball, and Laver, like every other
Australian bowler, mixes his pace admirably, and
without apparent effort. The wide, corkscrew delivery
of Saunders, who starts his run from beyond the mid-on
fieldsman, rendered him, I think, rather difficult to judge,
and one was never quite sure of the distance of the ball
from the off stump.

The Victorian fielding was not good, and Monfries
seemed to me to have fallen away from the form he
showed when I was previously in Melbourne.

There had been a great deal of rain in Melbourne on
the Saturday night, and on Monday—the third day
of the match—the wicket was slightly affected at the

F

start, Saunders making one or two balls turn rather quickly.

After Bosanquet's dismissal I declared our innings closed—my idea being that in the forty minutes before lunch Rhodes might make the ball turn, and possibly get one or two wickets. Besides, with Fielder and Strudwick to bat, it was scarcely likely that our total would receive any material addition. As it happened, the wicket rolled out hard and true, and though Rhodes did get one or two past Bruce, he did not quite succeed in hitting the wicket.

For a long while the Victorians made a good stand, Bruce and McAlister hitting up eighty-eight runs for the first wicket, and Laver and Armstrong subsequently playing well; but at no time did the batsman gain the upper hand, runs coming very slowly all day.

Bruce played very well indeed, his style being beautifully easy and attractive, and McAlister was in for two hours and a half before Bosanquet bowled him round his legs.

At the tea interval only two wickets were down, but by six o'clock the match was all over, and we had won our first victory of the tour by an innings and 71 runs.

This win of ours was a really fine one, especially when one remembers that neither Lilley, Braund, nor Arnold were playing, and was achieved by all-round cricket of a high class. In this second innings our fielding was again very good, Relf and Foster bringing off splendid catches in the slips, and the work generally being of almost machine-like precision.

Rhodes again bowled well, and I was much struck with the excellence of Fielder, for he maintained a fine length and pace, and occasionally made the ball swing

away with his arm. Relf is nearly always a good bowler
with the new ball ; and, going on for the third time with
the score at 200, he quickly obtained the last two
wickets.

VICTORIA.

First Innings.		Second Innings.	
P. McAlister, b. Hirst	0	b. Bosanquet	45
W. Bruce, c. Bosanquet, b. Relf	4	c. Bosanquet, b. Rhodes	51
G. H. S. Trott, st. Strudwick, b. Rhodes	20	c. and b. Rhodes	16
W. W. Armstrong, b. Rhodes	28	c. Hayward, b. Rhodes..	35
M. Ellis, c. Relf, b. Hirst	1	run out	8
F. Laver (capt.), b. Fielder	26	c. Relf, b. Fielder	23
J. Horan, c. Strudwick, b. Fielder	25	c. Strudwick, b. Fielder.	1
B. Tuckwell, c. Bosanquet, b. Rhodes...	3	b. Relf	11
F. Collins, l.b.w., b. Rhodes	0	not out	0
E. Monfries, not out	41	c. Relf, b. Fielder	4
J. V. Saunders, c. Bosanquet, b. Rhodes	9	b. Relf	2
Extras	5	B. 5 ; l-b. 4 ; w. 1 ; n-b. 4	14
Total	162	Total	210

Bowling Analysis.

First Innings.		O.	M.	R.	W.	Second Innings.		O.	M.	R.	W.
Hirst		17	7	33	2	Hirst		17	4	34	0
Relf		23	8	39	1	Relf		17.3	6	26	2
Rhodes		20.2	8	26	5	Rhodes		20	5	58	3
Bosanquet		7	0	31	0	Bosanquet		13	1	43	1
Fielder		10	5	28	2	Fielder		12	2	35	3

Fielder bowled 4 no-balls and 1 wide.

ENGLAND.

P. F. Warner, c. Armstrong, b. Saunders	22
Hayward, c. Armstrong, b. Saunders	6
Tyldesley, c. Laver, b. Armstrong	90
R. E. Foster, c. Collins, b. Laver	71
Knight, c. Trott, b. Ellis	47
Hirst, c. Armstrong, b. Saunders	92
B. J. T. Bosanquet, b. Laver	79
Relf, c. Collins, b. Laver	8
Rhodes, not out	2
Byes, 11 ; leg-byes, 10 ; no-balls, 5	26
Total (for 8 wickets)	443

Innings declared closed.

Fielder and Strudwick did not bat.

Bowling Analysis.

	O.	M.	R.	W.				O.	M.	R.	W.
Saunders ...	45	13	126	3	Laver	...	...	21	3	76	3
Armstrong ...	44	11	73	1	Ellis	...	...	6	0	33	1
Collins	18	3	58	0	Bruce	...	...	1	0	5	0
Trott	8	0	46	0							

FALL OF WICKETS.

First Innings of Victoria.

1	2	3	4	5	6	7	8	9	10
0	10	33	34	81	81	84	84	145	162

Second Innings of Victoria.

1	2	3	4	5	6	7	8	9	10
88	116	116	172	188	188	191	204	208	210

First Innings of England.

1	2	3	4	5	6	7	8	9	10
11	36	196	196	292	396	441	443	Innings declared.	

CHAPTER V

THE FIRST MATCH *v.* NEW SOUTH WALES

NEW South Wales have deservedly won the reputation of being the strongest of the three great cricketing States of Australia, and it was, therefore, with no little interest that we looked forward to our meeting with them. Victoria and South Australia have each one or two individuals good enough to play in any representative Eleven, but the stronghold of Australian cricket lies indisputably in Sydney, for is not Sydney the home of Trumper, of Duff, of Noble, of Hopkins, and of Gregory?

There had been a great deal of rain in and around Sydney during the early part of the week; so much, in fact, that at one time it seemed quite possible that there would be no play on the Friday, November 20. However, a strong, drying wind sprang up late on Thursday afternoon, and the ground recovered rapidly.

It has, I believe, been said of me that I am a lucky Captain, and indeed fortune stood by me when I beat Noble in the toss, for I was thereby enabled to put our opponents in on a wicket which was certain to help the bowlers for an hour or two, and which, with the weather set fair, would roll out beautifully next day. Trumper and Duff, of course, were the first pair. Hirst, with the

wind just right for him, began, with Rhodes as his
vis-à-vis ; but the two great Australian batsmen opened
in that style which has so often knocked the best
bowlers in England off their length. Hirst once very
nearly bowled Trumper with a ball which pitched on the
leg stump and just went over the middle and off; but it
was Arnold who separated the batsmen, for, going on
instead of Rhodes, he at once got Duff splendidly
caught at the wicket.

The previous ball Duff had played into the stumps
without removing the bails. Noble was missed at slip
almost immediately he came in, but a minute or two
later Lilley brought off another superb catch. Trumper
played with all that dash and charm of style which he
almost invariably showed against us. Trumper stands
alone ; he is like no one, and no one is like him. In
repose he is not exactly a stylist, for as he faces the
bowler there is a rather ungainly bending of his right
knee ; but the moment he gets into position to make his
stroke he becomes the most brilliant, the most fascinating,
and the most attractive bat I have seen. He was
eventually stumped by yards. In the hope that the
wicket would improve during lunch Noble altered his
order, putting in Kelly and Howell, and keeping back
some of his more reliable batsmen. Kelly made no
attempt to score, so I brought Tyldesley up to " silly "
point, and an over or two later he caught the New
South Wales wicket-keeper. S. E. Gregory scored
twenty-five, but he did not get them well, and half an
hour after luncheon the side were all out for 108 runs.

Rhodes had seventeen runs scored from him before
he changed ends, and thirty before he got a wicket. He
stuck up all the batsmen, with the exception of Trumper,

S. E. GREGORY.

but I have often seen him bowl a more accurate length. Arnold's was the better performance of the two. He made the ball jump up quickly from the pitch and varied his pace well. He bowled, moreover, to the end, which was by far the easier.

Though the wicket gave the bowlers some assistance, ordinary bowlers might have been scored from very freely on it by the same batsmen. Rhodes and Arnold proved their class by being able to make the utmost use of it. Still, for all that, the batting on the whole was no better than moderate, several of the men giving the bowlers assistance to get them out, and displaying no pronounced ability to cope with a wicket that was far from being one of the worst. The batsmen lacked patience. The light roller was put on between the innings in preference to the heavy one, as there was a fear that the latter might bring to the surface any wet that still remained in the ground. For the first hour or so the ball turned rather quickly at the end at which Rhodes had obtained his wickets, and Hayward and myself had to undergo some " barracking " for playing slowly. One gentleman in the pavilion was particularly loud in his remarks, but he evidently quite lost sight of the fact that every minute we stayed in the pitch was becoming drier, and that, though our tactics were probably not exhilarating to watch, we were playing the right game for our side.

Tyldesley played splendidly from the first, and Foster's graceful style was much admired. He was going very strongly when, in attempting a big drive, he was caught at slip. At the end of the day's play we had scored 172 for three wickets, Tyldesley not out seventy-two Braund not out one. There was a good attendance for a Friday, nearly 7,000 paying for admission, and the total number of spectators being estimated at between 10,000 and 11,000.

Saturday's play was chiefly remarkable for the fact that thirteen wickets fell for 261 runs on an absolutely ideal wicket for batsmen.

Both sides bowled and fielded splendidly, and in these days of high scoring it was pleasant to find the bowler more than holding his own under conditions which were certainly not in his favour. Had we made 450 runs no one would have been surprised. But one of the great charms of cricket is its deceptiveness, and, as a matter of fact, with the exception of Hirst, we had to play with our backs against the wall to get runs.

The Yorkshireman batted very sturdily, bringing off his own particular hook stroke very frequently, and when at lunch-time we had 260 on the board, with six wickets still to go, it seemed quite possible that we would exceed our totals at Adelaide and Melbourne. But a remarkable change came over the game on resuming, the last six wickets going down for fifty-four runs. Howell bowled Hirst with a beauty, which pitched about a couple of inches outside the off-stump and hit the middle; Bosanquet was finely caught at slip; Lilley played on to a good ball, and Braund was out to a great right-handed catch by Victor Trumper at cover-slip. Braund was unusually slow, being in two hours and a half for thirty-six runs while 136 were added. His innings was not exhilarating to watch, but it was invaluable, and, though he scored so slowly, it was but seldom that he did not hit the ball in the exact centre of his bat. The New South Wales men fielded splendidly, especially S. Gregory, Duff, Hopkins, and

HIRST AND P. F. WARNER.

Trumper, and Noble, after luncheon, bowled in something very like his finest form.

Trumper and Duff have so often in the past upset the calculations of opposing teams that even though we led by 211 runs on the first hands the New South Wales men were still in the game. And that these two would make a valiant effort was evidently the conviction of the crowd, for a mighty roar went up as they were seen emerging from the pavilion. I have played before some big crowds in England—at Lord's on Whit Mondays and at Leeds last August—but never before had I seen anything quite equal to that mighty throng which assembled on the Sydney cricket-ground that afternoon. Nearly 20,000 people paid at the gate, and what with members and their friends the attendance could not have been far short of 27,000 or 28,000 persons.

But away from the spectators to the actual field of play. Trumper at once made a beautiful stroke between the covers off a short ball, and was going very strongly when Braund at short-leg caught him out in dazzling fashion. Hirst sent down a fast ball just short of a good length, which Trumper turned round and hooked, not perhaps exactly in the centre of his bat, but fairly cleanly for all that. One heard the noise of the bat striking the ball—a hand shot up into the air—and Trumper was seen walking to the pavilion. There was a sort of groan from the ring, and then a tremendous cheer went up in honour of one of the finest catches I have ever seen.

C. Gregory came in first wicket down. Arnold was bowling very well indeed, and from a ball of his which got up quickly Duff gave a difficult chance to the wicket-keeper. With fifty up Bosanquet went on for Hirst, and Duff, jumping out to drive one of the slows, missed the ball, and should have been stumped by yards. Things were not going quite right for us at this point, for Rhodes missed catching and bowling Gregory from a chance which he would have accepted nine times out of ten, and a chance of running out the same batsman was also lost.

Duff was not playing up to his best form, Bosanquet frequently sticking him up, and at eighty-one he cocked a ball up in front of the wicket, and Lilley, dashing forward, caught him very cleverly. After his departure everything came off for us. C. Gregory skied one to mid-on; S. Gregory was easily caught, also at mid-on, off a full pitch; Howell fell to a well-judged catch at long-on; and Fisher was leg-before to Bosanquet. The drawing of stumps found us, therefore, in a very strong position, and on the third day we won easily by an innings and ten runs.

Bosanquet bowled his slows very well indeed—sending down that puzzling off-breaking leg break of a good length, and continually beating the batsmen. His value to the side as a bowler of infinite possibilities was never better illustrated than in this game, and his success was but the forerunner of many notable triumphs on the Sydney ground.

Hirst, Arnold, and Braund all did their share, and it was a splendid performance to get rid of New South Wales for 201, for the wicket was as perfect as it could well be. In the ranks of our antagonists were to be found seven men who afterwards played regularly for Australia, so our meeting was, in a sense, a test for a test match, and the result was correspondingly pleasing to us.

Let me sum up the games against the three principal cricketing States. At Adelaide, in the opening match of the tour, we should undoubtedly have won had the

match been played to a finish ; Victoria were no match
for us, and the powerful New South Wales Eleven also
went down in an innings.

The policy of the much-abused M.C.C. Committee in
selecting seven bowlers had so far been abundantly
justified, for not once had our bowling been collared.
There were so many different styles and types of
bowlers on the side—from the fast-swerving deliveries
of Hirst to the harmless-looking slows of Bosanquet—
while sandwiched between these two were Arnold,
Rhodes, Fielder, Relf, and Braund.   It had been a great
factor in our success, this variety in bowling, for every
change was a real change, and no makeshift.   Arnold
had been our best bowler up to date.   He was always
steady, bowled a good slow ball, a splendid fast yorker,
made a new ball swing very perceptibly, and, best of
all, get up straighter than any bowler I have seen on an
Australian wicket.   He was the mainstay of the attack.
Hirst had always bowled well—though without any
striking success ; but I found that under the hot sun
and on the hard grounds he was not able to keep his
pace for as long a time as he can in England.   Nine
or ten overs at a stretch were enough for him ; after
that he lost his pace and devil.   Rhodes had done
wonderfully well on all sorts of wickets, true and false
alike, and Relf was always trying and always useful.
If Arnold or Hirst had not been on the side Relf would
have been given more opportunities of distinguishing
himself.   For Relf likes a new ball, but so do Hirst and
Arnold ; and as they were the better bowlers, and
formed such a splendid contrast, I was forced to give
them the preference.

Fielder bowled very well indeed at the tail-end men
of the Victorian Eleven, but he has not quite the devil

of a really great fast bowler, though his usefulness to the side was undoubted. It is a pity he is not a better field.

Up to this period Braund had not done much bowling. He sent down less than a couple of dozen overs in the game against South Australia; at Melbourne he did not play at all; and at Sydney he was not wanted until the second innings. When he had been on he had showed that he had lost a little of his accuracy, though this, perhaps, was only natural considering the few opportunities he had. It was with direct intention that I gave him as little work as possible; I wanted that side of his to get quite strong, so that he might be thoroughly fit for the hard campaign we had before us.

Bosanquet had bowled fairly at Adelaide, badly at Melbourne, and exceptionally well at Sydney, and on a hard, fast wicket—the faster the better I thought then —and I am more than ever convinced now that *if he struck his length*, he was our most dangerous bowler. All round, then, our bowling had more than fulfilled my expectations, and Australian critics were unanimous in saying that we were one of the strongest bowling sides which had ever visited Australia.

Our batting had given no cause for anxiety, and Tyldesley, Hayward, Hirst, and Foster were in really fine form. Foster, indeed, was playing brilliantly and quite up to his form of the English summers of 1900 and 1901, while he and Braund made a formidable pair of slips. Against New South Wales the last five wickets did not make much of a show, but that was the one and only time that anything approaching a "heel of Achilles" was found in the team. Lilley had kept wicket very finely; Strudwick was almost equal to him in the one match he had taken part in; and the fielding was sound, keen, and full of life.

The team were fired with a splendid enthusiasm, and while realising as we did to the full that the combined Australian Eleven would be an extremely difficult side to beat, we could not but help a feeling of pride in our past work and a confidence in our future.

NEW SOUTH WALES.

First Innings.		Second Innings.	
R. A. Duff, c. Lilley, b. Arnold... ...	14	c. Lilley, b. Bosanquet.	44
V. Trumper, st. Lilley, b. Rhodes ...	46	c. Braund, b. Hirst ...	11
M. A. Noble, c. Lilley, b. Arnold ...	3	b. Hirst	16
A J. Hopkins, c. Braund, b. Rhodes..	4	st. Lilley, b. Braund ...	23
S. E. Gregory, l.b.w., b. Rhodes ...	25	c. Arnold, b. Bosanquet	8
J. J. Kelly, c. Tyldesley, b. Rhodes ...	2	l.b.w., b. Bosanquet ...	12
W. P. Howell, c. Arnold, b. Rhodes...	9	c. Relf, b. Arnold ...	8
C. Gregory, st. Lilley, b. Rhodes ...	4	c. Warner, b. Arnold...	36
R. N. Hickson, c. Rhodes, b. Arnold.	0	c. Warner, b. Braund...	30
A. Fisher, c. Foster, b. Arnold	0	l.b.w., b. Bosanquet ...	0
A. McBeth, not out	0	not out...	0
Extra	1	Extras	13
Total	108	Total	201

Bowling Analysis.

First Innings.

	O.	M.	R.	W.		O.	M.	R.	W.
Hirst	7	2	22	0	Arnold	13.2	3	30	4
Rhodes	17	2	55	6					

Second Innings.

	O.	M.	R.	W.		O.	M.	R.	W.
Arnold	19	2	62	2	Rhodes	7	2	17	0
Hirst	18	6	36	2	Braund	11.4	2	13	2
Bosanquet ...	19	1	60	4					

Hirst delivered 2 no-balls and Arnold a wide.

ENGLAND.

P. F. Warner, run out	45
Hayward, c. and b. Fisher	13
Tyldesley, b. Noble	80
R. E. Foster, c. Howell, b. McBeth	35
Braund, c. Trumper, b. McBeth	36
Hirst, b. Howell	66
B. J. T. Bosanquet, c. Howell, b. Noble	8
Lilley, b. Noble	3
Arnold, c. Duff, b. Hopkins	14
Relf, b. McBeth...	12
Rhodes, not out	0
Extras	6
Total	319

Bowling Analysis.

	O.	M.	R.	W.				O.	M.	R.	W.
McBeth	37.4	14	72	3	Fisher	...	...	11	2	35	1
Howell	26	10	48	1	Trumper	...	...	8	0	34	0
Noble	34	8	81	3	Hopkins	...	...	21	10	43	1

Noble and Trumper each delivered a no-ball.

FALL OF WICKETS.

First Innings of New South Wales.

1	2	3	4	5	6	7	8	9	10
35	55	67	68	74	86	107	108	108	108

Second Innings of New South Wales.

1	2	3	4	5	6	7	8	9	10
12	83	99	101	114	114	152	164	197	201

First Innings of England.

1	2	3	4	5	6	7	8	9	10
28	80	162	176	265	276	280	297	319	319

AT THE BLUE MOUNTAINS, N.S.W.

Horse dragging motor car up steep hill.

CRICKET GROUND, BRISBANE.

CHAPTER VI

BRISBANE

BRISBANE lies somewhat off the line of march of English Teams visiting Australia, but the M.C.C. are ever ready to encourage cricket in the most remote corners of the Empire. We made, too, a special point in accepting the offer of the Queensland Cricket Association, for the game there has not altogether received that encouragement from the more prosperous centres which one might perhaps have expected. It is a long railway journey from Sydney to the northern capital—some thirty hours in the train—but we were made very comfortable in a luxurious saloon car, and the commissariat arrangements had been well cared for by the tactful and hard-working Mr. J. A. Murdoch, but for whose powers of organisation and management we should have fared badly. Mr. Murdoch took no part with us on the actual playing-ground, but he was, in some respects, the most valuable member of the combination.

On the frontier we changed on to a narrow-gauge railway, and at every station we stopped at crowds came to stare at us through our saloon windows. The climax was reached at a station just outside Brisbane, where a brass band played patriotic airs with most unmistakable energy, and where five or six hundred people must have collected on the platform. Indeed, we might have been a collection of monkeys on the way to the Zoo.

After the usual welcome from the cricket authorities we were allowed to go to bed, and next morning our match against Queensland began on a magnificent wicket on a good ground, though the outfield in parts was rather rough. It may have been the reaction after our struggles with South Australia, Victoria, and New South Wales, or maybe we were feeling the effects of the railway; but, whatever the cause, our bowling was scarcely up to the mark, and though not a single catch was missed, there might have been more life in our fielding.

Evil prophets had predicted that Queensland would not make a hundred against our bowlers, so when the innings realised as many as 242 there was not a little rejoicing. Evans, a fine natural player, made seventy-two, and treated Rhodes with such disrespect that at one time the Yorkshireman had four men out in the country to him. Twice did Evans send the ball over the ring, and our bowling had not been treated in so cavalier a manner since we landed in Australia. His was the best innings, but Dr. MacDonald, who in recent years has rendered such good service to Leicestershire, also played admirably in his purely defensive style for fifty-nine. Arnold and Braund were our most successful bowlers, and Foster and Braund brought off two or three fine catches in the slips. We had ten minutes' batting before the close of play, and the hum of approval that went round the ground as Henry, the aboriginal bowler, shot one at Braund with the speed of a Kortright or a Jones reminded me of the enthusiasm which the black bowlers in the West Indies used to kindle in the minds of the native population. Braund liked it not at all, and practically gave away his wicket by retreating towards square leg, and tipping the second ball into point's hands, to the amusement of some of the pavilion critics. Henry has a great record in Queensland cricket, but, though very fast for half a dozen overs, he does not appear able to last long. On a fiery wicket he is bound to be very dangerous, but at present he is wanting in that finesse and subtlety which just make the difference between an ordinarily good and a really first-class bowler.

Queensland headed us by twenty-seven runs on the first innings, our batting being too much of the daring order. Knight, however, played a beautiful innings, his late cutting being wonderfully fine. He was eventually caught at the wicket on the leg-side when four runs short of fifty. Henry took two wickets for sixty runs and Byrne, a slow left-hander, five for seventy-two runs. He bowled well, but he owed more than one wicket to the somewhat over-dashing tactics which some of our batsmen indulged in.

Queensland's second attempt was but a poor imitation of their first, for against some excellent bowling by Braund, Arnold, and Fielder they were all out for ninety runs.

The wicket at the close was almost as good as when the match started, and the 119 runs set us to win were hit off for the loss of Relf, Arnold, Knight, and myself. Right up to the last ball the Queenslanders fielded keenly, and all round showed themselves an infinitely better side than we were led to expect. Their fielding in both innings was brilliant, and in Byrne (left-hand)

Griffith (medium right), and Henry the aboriginal they have three useful bowlers. In every way the match was a success, and the good show made by the home team is sure to bear fruit ; and the day should not be far distant when Queensland will take her place, together with New South Wales, Victoria, and South Australia, in the Sheffield Cup Competition.

On the second afternoon (Saturday) there was an almost record crowd for a cricket match in Queensland, something like 13,000 spectators being present. The plucky fight which the Queensland Eleven made has kindled a great enthusiasm for the game, and from every one one heard the remark, "the visit of your team has done more good for cricket here than you can possibly imagine." Future English teams should play at Brisbane, for they will assuredly enjoy themselves.

QUEENSLAND.

First Innings.		Second Innings.	
C. W. Patrick, c. Braund, b. Fielder...	0	b. Arnold	12
J. Carew, b. Bosanquet	28	run out	0
Dr. R. Macdonald, l.b.w., b. Arnold..	59	l.b.w., b. Braund ...	6
A. A. Atkins, b. Arnold	30	st. Strudwick, b. Braund	3
W. T. Evans, c. Foster, b. Rhodes ...	72	c. Arnold, b. Fielder ...	27
J. Fitzgerald, c. and b. Braund	12	b. Braund	2
E. R. Crouch, c. Bosanquet, b. Braund	0	b. Arnold	13
H. R. Griffith, l.b.w., b. Braund ...	8	c. Relf, b. Braund ...	4
N. K. Foster, c. Foster, b. Arnold ...	18	b. Arnold	20
T. J. Byrne, c. Foster, b. Fielder ...	8	c. Rhodes, b. Braund...	0
A. Henry, not out...	0	not out	0
Bye, 1 ; no-ball, 6...	7	Leg-bye, 3 ; no-ball, 1	4
Total	242	Total	91

Bowling Analysis.

First Innings.

	O.	M.	R.	W.		O.	M.	R.	W.
Fielder	14	4	30	2	Relf...	8	5	10	0
Braund	25	8	54	3	Arnold	23.1	11	38	3
Bosanquet ...	17	2	65	1	Rhodes	10	0	38	1

Fielder bowled 4 and Relf 2 no-balls.

Second Innings.

Fielder			O. 7	M. 1	R. 15	W. 1	Arnold			O. 17.4	M. 12	R. 16	W. 3
Braund	...	...	19	4	50	5	Rhodes	...	...	5	1	6	0

Fielder bowled 1 no-ball.

ENGLAND.

First Innings.		Second Innings.	
Braund, c. Foster, b. Henry	2		
P. F. Warner, c. Macdonald, b. Griffith	37	c. Fitzgerald, b. Byrne	4
Arnold, b. Henry	34	c. Atkins, b Griffith ...	8
R. E. Foster, c. and b. Fitzgerald ...	21	not out	34
Knight, c. Evans, b. Byrne	46	b. Griffith	25
B. J. T. Bosanquet, c. Crouch, b. Byrne	37	not out	20
Lilley, c. Crouch, b. Byrne	2		
Rhodes, c. Macdonald, b. Byrne ...	6		
Relf, b Byrne	0	c. Foster, b. Griffith ...	24
Fielder, not out	5		
Strudwick, c. Macdonald, b. Griffith...	17		
Byes, 4 ; leg-bye, 1 ; no-balls, 3...	8	Byes, 2 ; no-balls, 2 .	4
Total	215	Total (for 4 wkts)..	119

Bowling Analysis.
First Innings.

Henry			O. 12	M. 0	R. 60	W. 2	Griffith			O. 15	M. 1	R. 59	W. 2
Byrne	...	...	24	6	74	5	Fitzgerald	...		2	0	14	1

Second Innings.

Henry			O. 5	M. 3	R. 21	W. 0	Griffith			O. 12	M. 5	R. 34	W. 3
Byrne	...	...	16	3	60	1							

Griffith delivered 2 no-balls.

FALL OF WICKETS.
First Innings of Queensland.

1	2	3	4	5	6	7	8	9	10
0	46	70	165	178	178	188	229	241	242

Second Innings of Queensland.

1	2	3	4	5	6	7	8	9	10
7	12	16	25	29	59	63	89	90	91

First Innings of England.

1	2	3	4	5	6	7	8	9	10
6	64	99	101	166	174	191	191	194	215

Second Innings of England.

1	2	3	4
12	47	66	90

From Brisbane we journeyed to West Maitland, where we played an Eighteen, and then on to Newcastle, where Fifteen were opposed to us. Neither game was of much interest in itself, but they served their purpose in giving us some batting practice.

The Rev. P. S. Waddy, who was in the Oxford Elevens of 1896–1897, batted splendidly in both innings, and was unlucky not to get a double century. In his University days Waddy, though he often made runs, was more of a bowler than a batsman, but he seems to have lost his bowling altogether, while his batting has immensely improved. Indeed, his form was so excellent that we were surprised at his not being given a trial in the New South Wales Eleven.

There was much fine batting on our side in both games, Tyldesley (who was playing in his very best form just then) scoring two hundreds in the week, and Foster being brilliant to a degree.

Excepting Knight, who had not much luck, all the recognised batsmen came off in one match or the other, and there was some good bowling by Hirst, Arnold, and Braund.

At Maitland their wicket-keeper was very funny when Lilley and ·Bosanquet were batting. He had bet a sovereign that one of them got more runs than Tyldesley, and you could hear him at intervals muttering, " That must be sixty," or " That's about eighty." When Bosanquet was run out at ninety-nine his disgust was unspeakable. However, Lilley just beat Tyldesley's score by one, and he was happy. Their bowling and fielding got very slack towards the end of our innings, and Foster had to remonstrate. Unfortunately for him Bosanquet was unable to get a length, and at the end of the match their captain came up to him and said, " At any rate, our

LILLEY.

bowling was not much worse than Bosanquet's." To which there was no adequate reply.

At Newcastle George Hirst and Relf bowled extremely well. George went into the bar for some light refreshment; he was just on the point of drinking, when he heard a voice near him saying, " That Hirst's a ——— rotten player ! " His drink untasted, he retired to a corner, foregoing his original intention of sending the speaker through the roof, and plotted revenge. He never had a happy moment till the second innings came, and with it his justification. He was allowed to go in first, and proceeded to make fifty of the very best. The first smile for twenty-four hours then lit up his face, and he got out and went off to have the postponed and well-earned drink.

FIFTH MATCH—v. NORTHERN DISTRICT XVIII.

Played at West Maitland on December 2 and 3, and left drawn. Full score :—

NORTHERN DISTRICT XVIII.

First Innings.		Second Innings.	
T. Hogue, b. Arnold	5	l.b.w., b. Bosanquet ...	35
L. Moore, l.b.w., b. Bosanquet	31	c. Foster, b. Arnold ...	6
R. Lindsay, b. Hirst	2	not out	62
N. Ebsworth, run out	12	c. Hirst, b. Arnold ..	4
P. S. Waddy, c. Braund, b. Arnold ...	93	c. Braund, b. Lilley ...	102
C. Onus, b. Arnold	21	l.b.w., b. Bosanquet ...	0
A. E. Clements, c. Braund, b. Arnold.	8		
E. Capp, b. Arnold	0		
W. McGlinchy, c. Foster, b. Hirst ..	16	not out	12
W. Cameron, c. Foster, b. Braund ...	43	b. Hirst	6
H. Harden, l.b.w., b. Braund	0		
R. Lawrie, b. Braund	11		
M. Bourke, b. Braund	0		
D. Freeman, b. Braund	8		
J. W. Lawrie, c. Foster, b. Braund ...	9		
R. Norman, c. Tyldesley, b. Braund...	0		
J. Baker, not out	15		
C. Maguire, c. Hayward, b. Braund ...	1		
Extras	8	Extras	14
Total	283	Total (for 6 wkts)	241

Bowling Analysis.
First Innings.

	O.	M.	R.	W.		O.	M.	R.	W.
Braund	25.1	2	73	8	Bosanquet ...	8	0	55	1
Arnold	20	6	48	5	Hayward ...	3	0	21	0
Hirst	19	5	39	2	Fielder	11	0	39	0

Hirst delivered 1 no-ball, Bosanquet 1 wide, and Fielder 2 no-balls.

Second Innings.

	O.	M.	R.	W.		O.	M.	R.	W.
Hirst	7	2	19	1	Braund	6	0	41	0
Arnold	6	2	22	1	Fielder	7	2	22	0
Bosanquet ...	10.3	0	68	2	Foster	6	2	18	0
Lilley	10	0	35	1	Knight	4	0	2	0

ENGLAND.

Knight, c. Harden, b. Maguire	5
Hayward, b. J. Lawrie	59
Tyldesley, c. Ebsworth, b. Hogue	101
R. E. Foster, l.b.w., b. Ebsworth	31
Hirst, c. and b. Maguire	7
Braund, c. Hogue, b. Maguire...	10
B. J. T. Bosanquet, run out	99
Lilley, not out	102
Arnold, c. Maguire, b. J. Lawrie	25
Fielder, c. Cameron, b. J. Lawrie	5
Strudwick, l.b.w., b. Maguire...	0
Extras	9
Total	453

J. W. Lawrie, three for 108 ; Maguire, four for 64 ; Hogue, one for 40 ; Ebsworth, one for 28.

Sixth Match—v. Newcastle XV.

Played at Newcastle on December 4 and 5, and left drawn. Full score:—

ENGLAND.

First Innings.		Second Innings.	
R. E. Foster, c. Cowen, b. Dent ...	105	b. Clayton	47
Hayward, b. Fraser	87	not out	27
Tyldesley, c. Scott, b. Dent	5	c. Scott, b. Morley ...	127
Knight, c. Lott, b. Dent	5	l.b.w., b. Fraser... ...	9
Hirst, c. Dent, b. Ripon	4	c. Clements, b. Morley.	51
B. J. T. Bosanquet, c. Clements, b. Dent	1	c. Scott, b. Whiting ...	8
Rhodes, c. Clements, b. Dent	0	b. Fraser	9
Relf, c. Donald, b. Fraser	10	l.b.w., b. Hogue ...	6
Braund, not out	42	not out	64
Fielder, ht. wkt., b. Hogue	0	c. Bourke, b. Ripon ...	5
Strudwick, c. Fraser, b. Morley... ...	29		
Byes, 9 ; leg-byes, 9	18	B. 18; l.-b. 1; w. 1; n-b 8	28
Total	306	Total (for 8 wkts.).	381

FIELDER AND LILLEY COMING OUT TO FIELD.

Tyldesley and Arnold in the background.

Bowling Analysis.

First Innings.

			O.	M.	R.	W.				O.	M.	R.	W.
Dent	...	...	25	3	87	5	Morley	..	...	6	0	31	1
Fraser	...	...	14	2	49	2	Clements		...	2	0	11	0
Ripon	...	...	13	4	47	1	Clayton	...	...	3	0	20	0
Hogue	...	...	13	3	43	1							

Second Innings.

			O.	M.	R.	W.				O.	M.	R.	W.
Dent	...	...	12	1	47	0	Clements		...	10	1	76	0
Fraser	...	...	15	2	24	2	Clayton	...	...	6	0	33	1
Hogue	...	...	12	1	35	1	Whiting	...	...	7	0	43	1
Morley	...	..	9	1	36	2	Waddy	...	...	2	0	8	0
Ripon	...	...	9	0	29	1							

NEWCASTLE XV.

N. Ripon, c. Strudwick, b. Hirst	25
T. H. Hogue, c. Rhodes, b. Hirst	31
E. Clements, b. Relf...	4
W. W. McGlinchey, b. Relf	0
F. Donald, b. Hirst	0
Rev. P. S. Waddy, b. Relf	1
J. Cowen, l.b.w., b. Hirst	10
T. Dent, st. Strudwick, b. Bosanquet	26
J. Whiting, c. Strudwick, b. Relf	2
O. Scott, b. Hirst	13
M. Bourke, b. Fielder ... ..., ...	43
A. Clayton, b. Fielder	22
Morley, b. Rhodes	4
Fraser, not out	1
H. Lott, b. Fielder	12
Byes, 1 ; leg-byes, 4 ; no-balls, 4	9
Total	203

Bowling Analysis.

			O.	M.	R.	W.				O.	M.	R.	W.
Relf...	...	...	28	10	66	4	Bosanquet		...	8	0	34	1
Rhodes	...	...	11	2	26	1	Fielder	...	...	12	1	42	3
Hirst	...	...	21	7	30	5							

Umpires : A. Theevers and T. H. Raysmith.

CHAPTER VII

THE FIRST TEST MATCH

ON Friday morning, December 11, I moved in force against the Australian Eleven at Sydney, who were drawn up under the leadership of M. A. Noble. In marshalling my men for the encounter I was, I suppose, undergoing an experience which no other man has known before me; for it was my very first test match, and at the same time I was in the onerous position of Captain. I do not remember that cricket history affords any parallel, and I do not altogether envy the man who has to follow me through the same sensations! Of the team that I was privileged to lead into the field four besides myself were new to test matches, namely, Foster, Bosanquet, Arnold, and Relf, while the others were all more or less old stagers. It was Rhodes' thirteenth test match, Hirst's fourteenth, Braund's fifteenth, and Tyldesley's seventeenth, while Hayward and Lilley had each taken part in eighteen international encounters already, and turned up as fresh as paint for their nineteenth. And here perhaps I may add that Lilley's experience was of much service to me throughout the tour. He is not only a splendid cricketer, but a sound judge of the game, and his advice was frequently of the highest value and assistance.

The first duty of a Captain is to win the toss. I

THE FIRST TEST MATCH.

England taking the Field.

failed in that duty, and as the meteorological observers had predicted unsettled weather, it was commonly remarked that winning the toss meant winning the match. But it was in no spirit of dejection that we took

THE TOSS.

the field, for our triumphs over Victoria, New South Wales, and South Australia had put us in good heart, and, besides, I am said to be a cheerful optimist, and to think my geese swans.

Noble, Hill, and Johns, the selectors of the Australian Teams, had chosen a very good Eleven, and their choice had been very generally approved. There was, however, one great name missing, that of Hugh Trumble, he who during the last ten years had played so big a part on the world's cricket stage. On his return from England after the 1902 tour, Trumble had stated his decision to retire from cricket, but, as will be seen, pressure was brought to bear on him, and he subsequently appeared in the remaining tests. The interest taken in the match was intense, and there must have been 10,000 people on the ground when we took the field. The weather was ideal, and the wicket, which had a brown glazed look as if a hot iron had been passed over it, and had scorched the grass, was perfect. Fast it certainly was, very much faster, indeed, than the usual Sydney wicket. This was the sixty-seventh match between England and Australia, but I doubt very much whether any one of them has opened in so sensational a manner as this one. Trumper and Duff, as usual, were the first pair of batsmen, and Hirst began with his field placed like this.

Hayward.   Hirst.

(Umpire.)   Bosanquet.
III

                                                    Warner.
        Braund.

(Umpire.)   **III**   Arnold.
                      Lilley.
        Rhodes.

              Foster.

Relf.
                                          Tyldesley.

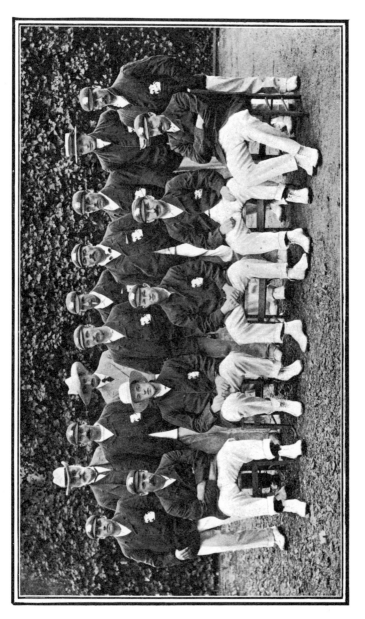

THE ENGLAND TEAM.

J. A. Murdoch.   Relf.   R. E. Foster. Knight. Arnold. Fielder.   Rhodes.   Braund.   Tyldesley.
Strudwick.   B. J. T. Bosanquet.   P. F. Warner.   Hirst.   Lilley.
           Hayward.

Almost immediately our guns found the range, for with the first ball of his opening over, Arnold got Trumper caught at extra slip by Foster, who took a remarkably fast travelling ball with his left hand. The ball was very wide of the fieldsman, who fell over in making the catch.

Trumper and Duff have often knocked the best of English bowlers off their length in the course of four or five overs, so it was a great piece of luck for us to get rid of one of the famous pair for a single. But the goddess who presides over cricket had even better fortune in store for us, for with the first ball of Arnold's next over Duff was beautifully caught at the wicket. Duff had tried a forcing stroke between point and cover, and the ball got up quickly off the pitch. So No. 2 of the famous pair had also gone! And when in Hirst's next over Lilley, standing back, caught Hill, we had good reason to be pleased with ourselves—three of the greatest batsmen in the world gone for nine runs on a perfect wicket!

But Australian cricketers were ever good fighters, and Noble and Armstrong clenched their teeth and set about to retrieve those early disasters. Runs came very slowly, but the bowling was superb, Hirst swerving in his best style, and Arnold frequently getting up quickly from the pitch. The extent of Hirst's "swerve" will be understood when I say that about three balls in every over passed well outside the legs of the batsman. Later he bowled on the wicket more, but neither batsman could get him away. At one o'clock, after fifty-five minutes' play, the score stood at twenty-four. At thirty-six Braund relieved Hirst, who had sent down eleven overs, six maidens, for eight runs and one wicket. Braund bowled one over, and then Bosanquet went on, Braund crossing to Arnold's end. At the luncheon adjournment the total was fifty-five, Noble twenty-three, Armstrong twenty-five.

During the interval the dismissal of Trumper, Duff, and Hill for nine runs was much discussed. Those who knew least about the game maintained that the wicket was fiery; but the simple explanation was that, on an exceptionally fast pitch, three great batsmen mistimed three balls and gave three chances, which were taken.

When the game was resumed there could not have been fewer than 15,000 people present. Noble and Armstrong went on batting very soundly and doggedly, but when the Victorian had put together a very well-played forty-eight Bosanquet bowled him one of those "off-breaking leg-breaks" and down went his middle stump. Bosanquet is really invaluable. He can bowl as badly as anyone in the world, but, when he gets a length, those slow "googlies," as the Australian papers call them, are apt to paralyse the greatest players. Could he be mechanically certain of his length, I venture to think that he would be the most difficult bowler in the world; for seldom indeed does one find a batsman who can detect that "off-break with the leg-break action."

Armstrong was at the wickets two hours and a half. He had made forty-eight at a time when runs were very badly wanted. His was a really good innings. Hopkins followed Armstrong, and for a time played none too well. Rhodes had gone on in place of Braund, and off him Hopkins should have been caught at cover-point when he had made seven. It was not exactly an easy catch, the ball going rather hard and somewhat low

BRAUND.

from a stroke off a full pitch, but it should certainly have been held.   Shortly afterwards Lilley might possibly have stumped Hopkins.   At tea-time Australia had got 164 for four wickets, and so, to a great extent, had recovered from their bad start.   Noble was not out eighty-one.   He had played absolutely superb cricket. On resuming Hopkins hit pretty freely, but the new ball was once again our salvation, as George Hirst going on caused Hopkins to play a ball into his wicket. Gregory was to have come in next, but a thunderstorm appeared imminent, and with the idea of getting as many runs as possible before the rain Howell was sent in, and our long fields scattered into various parts of the empire.   Howell once made ninety odd runs against A. E. Stoddart's second Team in an incredibly short space of time, and ever since then English Elevens have lived in dread of his repeating the performance.   But Howell is impatient, and loves to let drive the moment he comes in, and Relf, standing away in the Southern Hemisphere, caught him beautifully off Arnold's bowling, just as he had done in the match against New South Wales.   S. E. Gregory, whose inclusion had been somewhat criticised, came next and played very good cricket, but just upon six o'clock Bosanquet sent him a beauty which pitched on the off stump and hit the top of the middle and leg.   Stumps were then drawn, Australia having made 259 for seven wickets, Noble not out 131. He came in when his side was in a desperate position, and by superb skill and judgment put an entirely different aspect on the game.   He made one bad stroke off Bosanquet in the direction of mid-off when he had got sixty-nine, and just after he had passed his hundred he sent one uppishly through the slips.   But these were

trifling flaws in an innings which for style, defence, and
execution could not have been surpassed. He never
scored at any great pace—the bowling was too good
for that—but he never looked like getting out. It
was, indeed, a great performance. Our bowling was
splendid. Arnold seemed to me to be the most difficult
to play, and Hirst and Bosanquet in their totally
different styles also did well. Rhodes was unlucky;
for he should certainly have had Hopkins' wicket,
though the chance was not altogether an easy one.
Braund kept a fine length. Our fielding was superb, the
picking up and throwing in being of the best, and the
whole side worked like a machine.

Tyldesley in the long field cut off many fours, and
Hirst at mid-off was as good as ever; in fact, everyone
did well, and the critics were unanimous in saying that
our work was very fine.

The weather prophets were right for once, for during
the night it rained very heavily, and it was therefore
with no little anxiety that we inspected the wicket next
morning. It was very wet at one end, but the famous
Bulli soil dries rapidly; and, as there was a strong wind
and a hot sun, it was more than probable that the pitch
would pretty well have recovered by four o'clock. The
Australian innings was soon finished off for 285, Rhodes
giving strong evidence of his power to bowl on a
damaged wicket. Between the innings the light roller
was put on. We had three-quarters of an hour's batting
before lunch, and it was expected that we should have a
poor time. Hayward and myself began, and in Laver's
first over I was caught at the wicket. Tyldesley came
in after I had gone, and played perhaps the best innings
of his life. The end to which Saunders was bowling was

made for a left-hander ; but Tyldesley took him by the scruff of the neck and hit him to all corners of the field.

With the pitch as it was no one would have been surprised had we lost four wickets before lunch. In fact, Noble told me afterwards that they fully expected Saunders would have got four of us out before the interval. The Victorian is a curious bowler. On his day he is as good as anyone. On his off day—well, you may expect three bad balls an over. Tyldesley, whether he was off-driving, forcing a short ball between the covers, hooking or glancing to leg, was perfect in his timing of the ball, and in less than half an hour he had knocked off Laver and Saunders. Tom Hayward, too, played very well indeed, and we were doing infinitely better than under the circumstances we could possibly have hoped for. Hayward had got fifteen when Howell knocked down his middle stump with a very good ball which came in a trifle from the off.

Foster was to have gone in next, but as there remained only ten minutes to luncheon-time, I altered the order and sent in Arnold. At lunch we were fifty-eight for two wickets ; Tyldesley not out thirty-eight.

During the interval the wicket improved rapidly, and though up to four o'clock the ball required considerable watching, it was no longer a bowler's wicket. People had been pouring into the ground all the morning, and during the afternoon the attendance reached 36,000, over 27,000 people paying at the gate. This is not an absolute "record," for I am informed that there were 40,000 at MacLaren's first test match.

Tyldesley went on batting splendidly, but when he had scored fifty-three out of seventy-three in fifty-six minutes, Noble bowled him with one that came with the bowler's arm. Foster and Arnold played some good bowling very carefully, but after the professional had been in an hour and a half for twenty-seven runs he was beautifully caught by Laver at fine short-leg off Armstrong. It was a clean, hard stroke, straight to the fieldsman, who was standing close in. 117—4—27 At four o'clock Foster was not out thirty and Braund seven, and the total was 135 for four wickets.

The bowlers after the interval were Armstrong and Laver. The heat was oppressive, and the flies a source of worry to the batsmen and fielders. Laver was bowling very well indeed. He was keeping a capital length, and breaking back a good deal, judging by the placing of the field, for there were four men on the leg side —long-field, mid-on, short-leg in front of the umpire, and another just behind the wicket. Runs came a little more freely after a time, Braund especially playing good cricket.

The score kept on rising, and though the run-getting was never fast, scarcely an over passed without a run accruing to one or other of the batsmen. In the last twenty minutes Braund opened out, and although he made a risky hit or two several powerful and well-placed drives came from his bat. The two men were still together at six o'clock, the partnership having put on 126 runs, and the score being 243 for four wickets. Foster was batting three hours, but he was scarcely at his best. He should have been caught by Gregory at extra cover when he had got forty-nine, and there were one or two faulty hits. Every now and again he brought off a beautiful off-drive or late cut, but, taken as a whole, his display was somewhat disappointing, although invaluable to his side, and it must be

A. J. Hopkins.   W. P. Howell.

W. W. Armstrong.   R. A. Duff.

remembered that the ball always required careful watching, and that the bowling was of high quality.

Thus we ended the day in a very satisfactory position.

Monday, December 14, will long be remembered in the annals of cricket as a record-extinguishing day. The highest innings by an English side in a test match, 576 at the Oval in 1899, was beaten ; the fifth-wicket record was broken, Foster and Braund's 192 eclipsing MacLaren and Peel's 162 in March, 1895 ; and the last-wicket record for a test match also went, while Foster's marvellous 287 beat by a long way the highest individual innings in test matches.

The wicket was perfect, and Foster and Braund fairly collared the bowling. At one time their respective scores were ninety-four and ninety-three, and the race for the hundred became intensely exciting. Foster was the first to reach three figures, which he did with a magnificent late cut for four off Laver. It was about the finest stroke of the whole tour, the batsman dabbing down on an off ball with lightning-like wrists. W. G. Grace, C. Bannerman, K. S. Ranjitsinhji, H. Graham, and R. A. Duff are the only men besides Foster who have made a hundred in their first test match.

Braund got his hundred in the following over. He went from ninety-four to 102 by means of two lovely off drives, but the next ball yorked him. Braund had played a splendid innings, full of fine forcing strokes, and very sturdy in defence. He is, indeed, a great cricketer, and the bigger the match the better he plays. Always so keen—too keen, perhaps, occasionally, for he likes to bowl all day—he is a splendid man to have on one's side. With F. S. Jackson, Hirst, John Gunn (and after this tour, I think, Bosanquet), he shares the distinction of being one of the ablest all-round players in England. When Braund left the score was 309, but the game then took a turn in favour of Australia. Hirst was bowled by an exceptionally good one from Howell, Bosanquet was smartly caught at slip, and Lilley at long-off.

At this point we were but thirty-seven runs to the good, with but two wickets to fall, so it was still anybody's match. But Relf has a reputation for being a great man at a crisis, and worthily did he sustain it. For a time he acted purely on the defensive while Foster hit the Australian bowlers as I am certain they have never before been hit in all the long history of England and Australia matches. It mattered not who bowled ; it was all the same to the brilliant batsman.

Relf had gone in at 2.34, and when he was neatly caught in the slips by Armstrong off Saunders in the last over before the 4 o'clock adjournment, the score had been increased to 447—115 having been added in an hour and twenty-four minutes. Relf, at first stone-walling, later displayed capital form, driving ably and cutting very finely. The Sussex professional may have played many a greater innings numerically, but never a better one. I cannot praise him enough for his cool head at a trying time.

Foster had previously eclipsed Ranjitsinhji's 175, the record score for England against Australia. Shortly afterwards he passed Gregory's score of 201 against England at Sydney in 1894—curiously enough Gregory himself was bowling at the time—and then a few minutes later amidst cheering which W. L. Murdoch might have heard in far-away England, he beat that great batsman's

R. E. FOSTER.

211 at Kennington Oval in 1884. That innings had
stood for nearly twenty years, on what seemed an
inaccessible pinnacle, and here Foster comes along and
in his first test match beats it. In sixty-six minutes he
and Rhodes added 130 runs, and then Foster, by this
time thoroughly tired, skied one to mid-off, and his great
innings was over. He was at the wickets seven hours
and ten minutes, and hit thirty-seven fours. On the
Saturday he was in three hours for seventy-one runs;
on the Monday about four-and-a-quarter hours for 216
runs. In the last hour he scored eighty runs. He gave
a difficult one-handed chance to Gregory at forty-nine,
otherwise his cricket was practically faultless. His batting
on the Monday, was, I think, the best I have ever seen;
his off-driving and cutting have never been equalled—of
that I feel sure—while there was a Lyons-like power
about his straight driving. On the on-side, too, he was
wonderfully good, frequently forcing the ball away in a
masterly manner. His style was, as it always is, beautifully easy, and he made good use of his exceptional
quickness of foot, frequently moving a yard out of his
ground to play the ball. His cricket on the Monday
suggested that his idea was that the best method of
defence was offence. He received a magnificent reception, and the cheering could not have been more genuine
had it been at Lord's or the Oval. Malvern may well
be proud of such a cricketer.

Rhodes carried out his bat for forty. His off-driving
was beautifully timed, and more than once he hit the ball
round on the on-side. Rhodes might well go in
number five or six in any ordinary county team.

The Australians fielded splendidly, Duff in particular doing many marvellous things at mid-off

principally, but wherever he was placed drive after drive was stopped which seemed certain to reach the fence. He never flagged, and his picking up and returning were splendid. Hill, Hopkins, Trumper, Gregory, Noble, and Laver had a tremendous lot of work to do, and did it grandly ; in fact, the whole side fielded well, and never relaxed their efforts.

Howell and Noble were the most successful bowlers, and · at the time of Lilley's dismissal both had good

THE SCORE-BOARD AT SYDNEY. ENGLAND'S FIRST INNINGS.

analyses. It was Relf's defence which wore them down, and Foster's hitting which subsequently spoiled their figures. No one bowled better than Laver did on Saturday afternoon ; but Saunders, though he might have had better luck, was uncertain. For four or five overs he would bowl very well indeed, and then he would suddenly lose his length.

If there is one thing we have learnt from the long series of England and Australia matches, it is that our kinsmen are never done with until the last ball has been bowled. One can call to mind scores of matches in which the indomitable pluck and resolution of the Australians have turned many a seeming defeat into a victory. Indeed, they have inherited to the full that spirit of never giving in which we are so proud of saying is inherent in the British race.

And seldom, perhaps, was this ability to play an uphill game more strikingly demonstrated than in this first test match.

We were 292 runs ahead when an innings apiece had been played—surely a task before which even such giants as Trumper, Hill, Noble, and Duff might well quail.

But it was very evident, from the first ball of our opponents' second innings, that they meant to make us pay heavily for victory, if indeed victory was to be ours. But we too were equally determined to make the most of our initial advantage, and for a long time it was a stubborn fight, good bowling keeping the batsmen quiet even on that past-pluperfect-prestissimo wicket.

At lunch-time on the fourth day Kelly and Gregory were out and the total 108, Gregory having been caught at the wicket in the last over. I had made a good deal of use of Hirst and Arnold, both of whom were in fine form, but it was Rhodes who separated the batsmen. When the game was resumed Hill was Duff's partner, but the latter, although he made several good strokes, was not, perhaps, at his best. Our bowlers—and especially Rhodes, who kept a wonderful length—made rapid scoring difficult, and this in spite of the fact that they were not adequately supported by the fieldsmen. Indeed, our fielding—especially during the early part of this innings—was much below our previous standard. This was to some extent due to the fact that the grass had grown considerably during the progress of the match, and was rough and uneven in many places. Custom on this point seems to vary. In some games an agreement is come to between the two captains to cut the grass on each morning of the match ; on other occasions, such as this one, there is no such arrangement.

In the four subsequent test matches, Noble and I agreed that the grass should be cut on the Monday and Wednesday following the commencement of play on the previous Friday. But to return to the actual cricket. Duff was easily caught at short-leg at 191, off Rhodes, who was keeping an admirable length. Hill had made thirty-seven when Trumper came in at twenty minutes to four o'clock. The score was gradually taken to 200, when Hirst came on for the last over before the interval with the new ball. Nothing came of it, however, and at tea-time Australia had made 207 for three wickets, Hill forty-six, Trumper seven.

Trumper and Hill soon got going when play was re-started, though the left-hander's share was principally defensive play and great quickness between wickets. Trumper had started with unusual care, but after a few overs he opened out, and got runs off Relf, who had been bowling very ably and accurately ; but Rhodes still kept him quiet.

Braund was brought on to bowl, but his first over was a sensational one. The first and second balls Trumper cut magnificently for four, the third went for four byes, the fourth was hit past extra-cover to the ring, the fifth was played back to the bowler, and the concluding ball

SYDNEY CRICKET GROUND.

of the over was again forced away past mid-off. Three had been run when Hirst returned to Braund, who threw at the wicket while the fourth run was being made. He missed the stumps, and the batsmen were off again for the fifth—a dangerous one, seeing that Hill had over-run his wicket by yards. The ball was splendidly returned by Relf to Lilley, and on the unanimous appeal of those in the vicinity of the wicket, Hill was given out by Crockett. Hill had rushed past his crease, and when Crockett told him he was out, he showed by his manner that he was greatly surprised at the decision. Hill *did not say a word in protest* to Crockett, but the way in which he walked back to the pavilion could not possibly have left anyone in doubt as to what he himself thought of Crockett's ruling. Immediately after Hill had reached the pavilion, a perfect storm of groans and hisses came *from the members in the pavilion*, and this chorus of disapproval was immediately taken up by the " rinkers." A minute or two later I walked to the pavilion with the intention of asking the members to desist ; but instead of them listening to me, the " booing " became louder than ever. At this moment, Noble, who was next in, came from the pavilion, and we walked together to the pitch. We both sat down for a few minutes, waiting for the disturbance to subside. During these moments Noble and I were talking the matter over, and I told him that we should be compelled to leave the field if the demonstration against Crockett did not cease. After a while the noise abated somewhat, and Noble advised me to go on with the game. The moment we started play, the noise became, if possible, greater than ever, and shouts of " How much did you pay Crockett, Warner ? — " Have you got your coffin ready, Crockett ? —

"Which gate are you leaving by, Crockett?" rent the air.

It was a most difficult situation, but I think that, on the whole, I acted wisely in not withdrawing the team from the field. People in England, however, can have no conception of the yelling and hissing that went on that afternoon right up to the drawing of stumps ; even such hardened test-match players as Hirst and Rhodes were quite upset.

I myself was fielding deep mid-on to Braund when Hill was given out, so was not in a position to say whether the decision was correct or not; but Foster, who was standing at short-leg, and Hayward, who was at deep-point, declare that Hill was out by a foot. But this is really beside the point ; Crockett was there to decide such questions, and from his ruling there could be no appeal. There was absolutely no excuse for this demonstration, which was as disgraceful as it was un-warranted. It was started, as I have said, in the members' pavilion, from which point it was impossible to see what had occurred.

As the players returned from the field Crockett, who eventually left the ground under the care of two detectives, was " hooted " at more fiercely than ever by many of the members in the pavilion, though it is only fair to add that a large section applauded him loudly, and one member, I was informed, was so disgusted with the behaviour of his fellows, that he forthwith resigned his membership. Noble and the Australian Eleven generally were as much upset as we were, and next morning I received scores of letters condoling with us on the bad treatment we had received. The whole business was an insult to the game of cricket, and the wisest course is to forget it as quickly as one may.

Mr. F. A. Iredale, the *Daily Mail* correspondent, in a letter which he wrote to the *Daily Mail*, and which was subsequently shown to me, stated that my walking to the pavilion was the cause of the whole trouble. In answer to Mr. Iredale I would like to point out that the row had already begun before I started on my fruitless journey to the pavilion. All I intended to do was to appeal to the better feelings of the members, and if they had allowed me to do so, I feel sure I would have succeeded in persuading them to stop the demonstration against Crockett.

After tea Trumper played in the most brilliant fashion. Rhodes, with three men in the country, a long-on, a long-off, and a deep extra-cover, kept him fairly quiet, but everyone else who went on was roughly handled. The great batsman was playing in his own inimitable style, and scoring with splendid freedom and power all round the wicket. Every stroke was in evidence: the cut, the drive, the leg glance ; and that special one of Trumper's when he goes right back almost on to his wicket and forces a ball just short of a good length away past mid-on or between the off-side fielders. Rhodes continued to bowl well, but it was Bosanquet who got Noble stumped. Armstrong came in at twenty-five minutes to six, and just on time there was a very confident appeal for l.b.w. against him which was disallowed. At the close the score was 367 for five wickets ; Trumper not out 119, Armstrong not out 14. In the hour and forty minutes after tea Trumper made 112 runs, sixty-four of them in the last forty minutes.

For the first time during the tour our bowling had been severely dealt with, and what we should have done without Rhodes I do not know. He bowled magnificently all the time he was on, and every ball had to be watched. Arnold was not in his best form, frequently pitching too short, and next to Rhodes, Relf, perhaps, did best, though Bosanquet and Hirst worked hard, and the former with little luck. After the tea interval our fielding improved, but it is not easy to pick a ball up cleanly on a ground which is covered with daisies.

The magnificent fight Australia were making brought over 20,000 people to the ground on the fifth day of the match—Wednesday, December 15. Everything depended on whether the remaining batsmen would stay with Trumper. Did they do so, we might be set an almost impossible task for a fourth innings on a worn wicket. But Rhodes came to the rescue, as he has so often done before for England and Yorkshire ; and, though Trumper remained unshaken, his companions did not lend him any very great assistance.

There had been a little rain in the night, but this did not in any way affect the wicket ; in fact, it only served to bind the worn places together. Rhodes soon had Armstrong caught at slip, and after Hirst had relieved him for a few overs after the 400 had gone up, he tempted Hopkins to hit, and the ball landed in cover-point's hands.

Bosanquet had opened the bowling with Rhodes, and was in very fair form, pitching that perplexing off-break of his of a good length. With one of these he clean beat Trumper, and from another there was a loud appeal for l.b.w. against Hopkins. While Trumper and Hopkins were together the Australians had a good chance of ultimate victory, for every moment the wicket was becoming more worn, as any wicket is bound to do on which 1,300 runs have been made. After luncheon,

VICTOR TRUMPER.

however, the game took a sudden turn in our favour, Laver being easily caught at extra slip, Howell finely taken at the wicket, and Saunders run out. Trumper was, therefore, left undefeated. He gave nothing like a chance, and was Trumper at his best. Greater praise is scarcely possible. Of Rhodes' bowling during that long innings I cannot speak too highly; he was our tower of strength in the day of battle.

Those critics who prophesied that he would be harmless on the billiard-table wickets of Sydney, Melbourne, and Adelaide would assuredly have felt small had they seen his accuracy of length, his variation of pace, and his determination. He often turned the ball away a good deal, but as the one possible worn spot was not in a line with the wickets, the batsmen were able to merely look at about three

RHODES GETTING READY.

of every six balls he delivered. He did a tremendous amount of work, and bowled without a rest, except for half a dozen overs or so, from tea-time on the fourth day until the end of the Australian innings at 2.45 on the fifth day.

Our fielding during this innings was patchy—brilliant at one time, uneven at another. On the whole, though there were exceptions—such as Hirst, Tyldesley, Relf, and Rhodes—the work fell below the high standard we

K 2

had attained in previous games. Lilley, as he almost invariably did throughout the tour, kept wicket in irreproachable style.

We had 194 to get to win—no light task in the fourth innings of a match against Australian bowlers and fielders. Hayward and myself began, but at twenty-one a ball of Howell's came back quickly and, hitting me on the right thigh, rolled slowly on to the off stump. 21—1—8. Tyldesley, with Rhodes to run for him (for he had strained his leg), was splendidly caught at point at thirty-nine, but Hayward and Foster played some bowling of the highest class with much skill, and matters were going well for us when Foster was stumped. He had gone forward a long way to play the ball which beat him, and he was out by feet. 81—3—19. Another fine catch by Noble sent back Braund, and then Hirst came in. Before he had scored the Yorkshireman hit Howell hard but straight to Laver at short-leg, just behind the umpire, but fortunately for us the chance was not taken. This was a great piece of luck, for Laver is about the last man in the world one would select to hit a catch to. Had Hirst been caught, five wickets would have been down for eighty-three and the game in favour of the Australians. But cricket is full of chances, and this Hayward-Hirst partnership was destined practically to win us the match, for we were within thirteen runs of victory before Hayward was stumped on the following morning. He had played a splendid and chanceless innings, and his nerve and experience never stood him in better part than on this occasion. He was batting for four hours, and, excepting for a barely possible chance to extra cover, I could see nothing like a mistake in his beautiful ninety-one.

Hirst carried out his bat for sixty, a characteristic and fine display, but if catches were never missed, the Yorkshireman would have added another to the list of cricketers who have made two " ducks " in a test match.

And thus after six days of some of the hardest fighting the long history of test matches can show the Australians had to surrender. It was a magnificent game from start to finish, the fortunes of war inclining first to one

TOM HAYWARD, PREPARING FOR WORK.

Eleven and then to the other, and finally giving the verdict to that side which showed, on the whole, the best all-round form.

But the Australians deserved almost as much credit as we did, for I cannot recollect another instance of a side which, going in 292 in arrears, eventually sets its opponents nearly 200 runs to win. This performance of theirs will ever remain a shining example of grit and courage, and a glorious tradition for future generations.

What luck there was about the game went to Australia. They won the toss on a perfect wicket, and by magnificent bowling and fielding we got seven wickets down on the first day for 259 runs. Then the rain came, and up to lunch-time on the second day the wicket was all in favour of the bowlers, and it was then that Australia missed Hugh Trumble. After luncheon the pitch recovered rapidly, and was quite a good one for the rest of the afternoon, though never, I think, absolutely " plumb." It is not a " plumb " wicket at Sydney when Laver can pitch a ball outside the off stump and miss the leg, beating both Foster and Kelly.

Then from Monday to the end of the game the wicket was practically as good as any batsman could desire, though a worn spot or two worked up, as was only natural, on the last day.

This, I maintain, is a fair and impartial summary of that oft misleading expression " the luck of the game." But there never was a match played in which the luck of the weather and wicket did not play a part, great or small.

The *Daily News* at the time wrote that "the Australians were always overplayed"; the *Sporting Life,* " that England's bowling was a great deal the strongest." These criticisms were rather overdrawn. Our batting was more solid ; Australia's more brilliant. Our bowling was infinitely more varied, and a little better in quality. Australia's ground fielding was better than ours, but, while our catching was magnificent, Australia's was only very fair.

Practically every chance given by an Australian was accepted by us ; while Australia made two or three mistakes in the field which had far-reaching results. But these things are all in the game, and I am inclined to think that we really won the match when Arnold and Hirst, ably seconded by Foster and Lilley, got rid of Trumper, Duff, and Hill for nine runs.

AUSTRALIA.

First Innings.		Second Innings.	
R. A. Duff, c. Lilley, b. Arnold... ...	3	c. Relf, b. Rhodes ...	84
V. Trumper, c. Foster, b. Arnold ...	1	not out	185
C. Hill, c. Lilley, b. Hirst	5	run out	51
M. A. Noble (capt.), c. Foster, b. Arnold	133	st. Lilley, b. Bosanquet	22
W. W. Armstrong, b. Bosanquet ...	48	c. Bosanquet, b. Rhodes	27
A. J. Hopkins, b. Hirst	39	c. Arnold, b. Rhodes ...	20
W. P. Howell, c. Relf, b. Arnold ...	5	c. Lilley, b. Arnold ...	4
S. E. Gregory, b. Bosanquet	23	c. Lilley, b. Rhodes ...	43
F. Laver, l.b.w., b. Rhodes	4	c. Relf, b. Rhodes ...	6
J. J. Kelly, c. Braund, b. Rhodes ...	10	b. Arnold	13
J. V. Saunders, not out	11	run out	2
No-balls	3	B. 10, l.-b. 15, w. 2, n.-b. 1	28
Total	285	Total	485

Bowling Analysis.

First Innings.

	O.	M.	R.	W.		O.	M.	R.	W.
Hirst	24	8	47	2	Braund	26	0	39	0
Arnold	32	7	76	4	Bosanquet ...	13	0	52	2
Rhodes	17.2	8	41	2	Relf...	6	0	27	0

Hirst delivered 2 no-balls and Relf 1 no-ball.

Second Innings.

	O.	M.	R.	W.		O.	M.	R.	W.
Arnold	28	3	93	2	Braund	12	2	56	0
Hirst	29	1	79	0	Rhodes	40.2	10	94	5
Bosanquet ...	24	1	100	1	Relf	13	5	35	0

Hirst and Bosanquet each bowled 1 wide and Arnold 1 no-ball.

ENGLAND.

First Innings.		Second Innings.	
P. F. Warner, c. Kelly, b. Laver	0	b. Howell	8
Hayward, b. Howell	15	st. Kelly, b. Saunders	91
Tyldesley, b. Noble	53	c. Noble, b. Saunders	9
Arnold, c. Laver, b. Armstrong	27		
R. E. Foster, c. Noble, b. Saunders	287	st. Kelly, b. Armstrong	19
Braund, b. Howell	102	c. Noble, b. Howell	0
Hirst, b. Howell	0	not out	60
B. J. T. Bosanquet, c. Howell, b. Noble	2	not out	1
Lilley, c. Hill, b. Noble	4		
Relf, c. Armstrong, b. Saunders	31		
Rhodes, not out	40		
B., 6 ; l.-b., 7 ; w., 1 ; n.-b., 2...	16	Byes, 4 ; wides, 2...	6
Total	577	Total (5 wkts.).	194

Bowling Analysis.

First Innings.

	O.	M.	R.	W.		O.	M.	R.	W.
Saunders	36.2	8	126	2	Armstrong	23	3	47	1
Laver	37	12	116	1	Hopkins	11	1	40	0
Howell	31	7	113	3	Trumper	7	1	12	0
Noble	34	8	99	3	Gregory	2	0	8	0

Noble delivered 2 no-balls and 1 wide.

Second Innings.

	O.	M.	R.	W.		O.	M.	R.	W.
Howell	31	18	35	2	Noble	31	18	37	0
Saunders	18	3	51	2	Laver	16	4	37	0
Armstrong	18	6	28	1					

Saunders bowled 2 wides.

Umpires, Crockett and Jones.

FALL OF WICKETS.

First Innings of Australia.

1	2	3	4	5	6	7	8	9	10
2	9	12	118	200	207	259	263	271	285

Second Innings of Australia.

1	2	3	4	5	6	7	8	9	10
36	108	191	253	334	393	441	468	473	485

First Innings of England.

1	2	3	4	5	6	7	8	9	10
0	49	73	117	309	311	318	332	447	577

Second Innings of England.

1	2	3	4	5
21	39	81	82	181

The gate receipts (including stand) for the match beat all records, amounting to £4,250. Of this, £1,521 14s. 3d. went to the M.C.C., a similar amount to the N.S.W. Association, and £1,230 11s. 6d. to the trustees of the ground.

There was little interest in the next game against eighteen Melbourne Colts, the reaction after the long-drawn-out excitement of the test match being great. The Juniors showed poor form, though Sharpe, a left-hander with a nice action, bowled with promise, and Delves and Grace batted well. The wicket was perfect and so was the weather, and on the first day about 4,000 spectators were present. Full score :

ENGLAND.

Hayward, c. Delves, b. Smith...	37
P. F. Warner, b. Sharpe	76
Knight, b. O'Loughlin	50
Relf, c. Smith, b. Lewis	30
Braund, c. Lanigan, b. Dwyer...	33
Hirst, b. O'Loughlin...	87
B. J. T. Bosanquet, c. Cogle, b. Dwyer...	10
Lilley, b. Dwyer	10
Rhodes, not out	42
Fielder, b. O'Loughlin	9
Strudwick, b. Lanigan	16
Byes, 11 ; leg-byes, 2 ; wides, 2 ; no-ball, 1... ...	16

Total 416

Bowling Analysis.

	O.	M.	R.	W.		O.	M.	R.	W.
O'Loughlin ..	26	1	85	3	Howe	4	0	16	0
Sharpe	25	3	59	1	Lewis	7	0	18	1
Smith	14	1	49	1	Cogle	3	0	8	0
Horgan	6	0	16	0	Williams... ...	4	0	19	0
Lanigan	7	0	30	1	McSperrin ...	6	1	23	0
Dwyer	19	0	77	3					

Smith bowled 1 no-ball and Lewis 2 wides.

THE JUNIORS.

First Innings.		Second Innings.	
F. Delves, c. Relf, b. Fielder	3	run out...	52
A. V. Moon, c. and b. Relf...	2	c. Hirst, b. Braund ...	13
J. Howe, run out	11	b. Relf...	0
C. Kiernan, st. Strudwick, b. Rhodes .	14	c. Braund, b. Bosanquet	16
L. Cogle, b. Braund	1	c. Whitfeld (sub.), b. Braund	8
M. Grace, c. Bosanquet, b. Fielder ...	10	st. Strudwick, b. Braund	54
J. Hexter, run out	1	b. Rhodes	0
D. Lanigan, st. Strudwick, b. Braund.	0	b. Braund	2
J. Cattanach, c. Relf, b. Fielder... ...	6	b. Relf...	3
T. Lewis, c. Bosanquet, b. Fielder ...	8	c. Hirst, b. Braund ...	1
W. McSperrin, st. Strudwick, b. Bosanquet	24	c. and b. Bosanquet ...	9
J. Horgan, b. Bosanquet	3	c. Bosanquet, b. Braund	12
M. Dwyer, run out	18	b. Relf...	9
L. Smith, b. Bosanquet	1	c. Whitfeld (sub.), b. Braund	0
P. O'Loughlin, c. and b. Bosanquet ..	4	not out	6
J. Williams, not out	8	b. Rhodes	1
A. Sharpe, c. Fielder, b. Bosanquet ...	1	c. Strudwick, b. Relf...	0
F. Manallack, b. Bosanquet	0	b. Braund	0
Extras	9	Extras	7
Total	124	Total	193

Bowling Analysis.

First Innings.

	O.	M.	R.	W.		O.	M.	R.	W.
Relf...	15	7	17	1	Rhodes	5	1	8	1
Fielder	19	7	37	4	Bosanquet ...	14.5	4	27	6
Braund	14	5	26	2					

Fielder bowled 3 no-balls and Relf 2.

Second Innings.

	O.	M.	R.	W.		O.	M.	R.	W.
Relf...	24	8	40	4	Rhodes	10	7	14	2
Bosanquet ...	11	2	53	2	Braund	19.5	4	48	8
Fielder	12	2	26	0	Hirst	1	0	5	0

Bendigo is just a hundred miles north of Melbourne, but the Victorian trains are in no sense of the word "rapides," and the journey took us four hours and a half. Bosanquet, Lilley, Tyldesley, and Arnold stayed behind in Melbourne, the Eleven being made up by the inclusion of G. S. Whitfeld, an old Etonian, who had just come out from England.

The weather was intensely hot on Boxing Day, and the pitch scarcely a good one. Moreover, the wickets were pitched at right angles.

Fielder was in great form. With a slight breeze behind him he bowled at a great pace, and as the ball frequently got up quickly and occasionally shot he was not easy to play.

After the luncheon interval the wicket seemed to play truer, and, when our turn came to go in, seemed all right, though very likely a fast bowler like Fielder, had there been one in the Bendigo Team, would have proved awkward.

Hayward once more showed fine form, and Knight got seventy-eight; but he was missed at the wicket when he had made a single, and twice at least in the last ten runs of his innings, when the wicket was sticky. He made several fine cuts in the middle portion of his display.

We should, in all likelihood, have won in an innings, but heavy rain fell at about a quarter to four on the second afternoon, and the ground, and town too, was soon flooded. Rhodes bowled finely on the false turf, and astonished our opponents by the amount of work he got on the ball.

It is very much of a question whether these matches against odds do any good, for the test matches and the State games give quite enough hard work, and the constant travelling about in trains, especially in hot weather, is not conducive to that absolute physical fitness which the highest class of cricket demands. Full score :

BENDIGO AND DISTRICT XVIII.

First Innings.		Second Innings.	
E. J. Keogh, c. Braund, b. Fielder ...	13	c. Foster, b. Braund ...	12
G. H. Freeman, b. Hirst	1	c. Relf, b. Rhodes ...	3
T. E. Green, b. Rhodes	1	c. and b. Rhodes ...	25
G. De Ravin, b. Rhodes	10	c. Knight, b. Rhodes...	1
T. Hall, b. Fielder	0		
Wyn. Murray, b. Fielder	16	b. Braund	5
H. Seelenmeyer, c. Braund, b. Fielder	14	c. Strudwick, b. Rhodes	5
H. Woolley, b. Fielder	0	not out	4
J. Harry, c. Strudwick, b. Fielder ...	14	b. Braund	0
H. Kennedy, b. Relf	0		
H. Hall, b. Fielder	0		
T. Garlick, c. Rhodes, b. Fielder ...	1		
H. C. Boydell, not out...	8	not out	0
J. Sarvaas, run out	0		
T. Manallack, b. Fielder	4		
H. Moore, b. Relf	3		
F. Jinks, c. Strudwick, b. Fielder ...	0		
C. F. Gibson, b. Fielder	0		
Byes, 5 ; no-balls, 4	9	Extras	9
Total	94	Total (for 7 wkts.).	64

Bowling Analysis.

First Innings.

	O.	M.	R.	W.			O.	M.	R.	W.
Hirst	8	4	7	1	Fielder		15.4	5	32	11
Rhodes	12	0	29	2	Relf...		11	5	17	2

Fielder and Relf each delivered 2 no-balls.

Second Innings.

	O.	M.	R.	W.			O.	M.	R.	W.
Rhodes	14	2	29	4	Braund		14.4	6	26	3

ENGLAND.

P. F. Warner, c. Moore, b. T. Hall	20
Hayward, c. Garlick, b. H. Hall	115
Knight, c. Kennedy, b. De Ravin	78
R. E. Foster, b. De Ravin	0
Rhodes, not out	42
Whitfield, c. H. Hall, b. Gibson	12
Extras	6
Total (for 5 wickets)	273

Innings declared closed.

Braund, Hirst, Relf, Strudwick, and Fielder did not bat.

CHAPTER VIII

THE SECOND TEST MATCH

THE second of the five great contests between England and Australia created a vast amount of interest, not only in Melbourne itself, but all over Australia. Supporters of the Colonials argued that history would repeat itself, and that, although we had won the first test match, we were destined to lose the remaining four games of the rubber. On the other hand, elated by our initial success, we maintained that we did not intend that history should repeat itself; and so the chances of the two sides were keenly discussed, in club smoking-rooms, in trains, in hotels, and, indeed, wherever men foregathered, and when the day of battle arrived an immense crowd collected round the Melbourne Cricket Ground. The official estimate was that nearly 21,000 people paid gate, and, with members and their friends, there must have been quite 32,000 spectators. Two changes had to be made in the side which played at Sydney, Bosanquet and Arnold—the former suffering from a displaced bone in his right hand and the latter from a strained knee—being replaced by Knight and Fielder, so, although our bowling strength was considerably reduced, the batting was not thereby materially weakened.

THE SECOND TEST MATCH.

P. F. Warner and Hayward going to bat.

I began the New Year well by winning the toss, always of importance in Australia, but doubly so at Melbourne, where, from the experience of this tour, rain on Saturday or Sunday is always a certainty.

The weather on Friday was glorious, the heat being tempered by a cool south-west breeze, and the wicket of that pace where one could play back or forward at will. There seems to be a prevalent idea in England that the Melbourne wicket is not unlike Lord's, that is to say, fast, with plenty of life in it, and a tendency to become fiery. When I was in Melbourne with Lord Hawke's Team, in March of 1903, the wicket there was like lightning, even faster, if anything, than Lord's, but from what I saw on this tour I cannot imagine a wicket less like Lord's than the Melbourne one. No doubt the exceptionally wet summer had much to do with this alteration in pace.

People were pouring through the turnstiles when Hayward and I went out to bat. Trumble and Noble began, and from the start we set ourselves to wear down the bowlers. The first hour's play produced only thirty-eight runs, Hayward making but seven of these ; and at lunch-time, after an hour and twenty-five minutes' play, the total was fifty-five ; Hayward twenty, myself thirty-five.

After luncheon the rate of scoring increased, and we were both going strongly when Gregory, whose fielding had been magnificent, caught my partner very cleverly at extra-cover. Hayward was batting for two hours and a half. Before lunch he was by no means at his best, but his last thirty or forty runs were splendidly got. He should have been stumped off Trumble when

L

seven, but Kelly thought the ball was going to hit the wicket. This partnership of 122 runs—curiously enough exactly the same figure as we had put up at Adelaide in the opening match of the tour—was, if I may say so, invaluable.

It took us a long time to put the runs together, and though a great number of spectators passed adverse comment on what they termed " very slow play," it seems to me that, looking at it from the true cricket standpoint, this slow play was, after all, the highest possible tribute to the bowling of the Australians. When you have very accurate bowling, splendidly supported by a well-placed field, run-getting is bound to be slow. Ten minutes after Hayward had gone I tried to drive Trumble wide of mid-on, but the bat slipped round in my hands, and the ball went soaring over the bowler's head, where Duff, running from mid-off, brought off a good catch. 132—2—68. The flies were a dreadful worry, and during my innings I kept mopping my face with a sponge saturated with eucalyptus oil.

Tyldesley and Foster were together at the tea interval, with two wickets down for 141, and were still there at the drawing of stumps, the Lancastrian forty-six and Foster forty-nine. Two hundred and twenty-one runs in just under five hours is not, to say the least of it, an excessive rate of scoring ; but the Australian bowlers were wonderfully accurate in their length, and though Trumble did miss Foster at slip from an easy chance when thirty-nine, the fielding could scarcely have been finer. S. E. Gregory, in particular, at extra-cover, was superb, and must have saved between thirty and forty runs, and very interesting was it to notice how he

THE SECOND TEST MATCH AT MELBOURNE.

P. F. Warner and Hayward at the wickets. Hayward cuts Howell for four.

anticipated the batsmen's strokes. The Australians were severely handicapped by the inability of Noble to bowl more than half a dozen overs owing to a strained arm.

We should, I think, have made something between 250 and 260 runs. Neither Hayward nor myself are, as a rule, quick scorers, but one would have expected brilliant batsmen like Foster and Tyldesley to score more than eighty runs in an hour and three-quarters. That they did not do so was another proof of the excellence of the Australians' out-cricket. As I have said, many critics blamed us for not forcing the game more ; but if one studies closely the history of English cricket in Australia it will be found that much of our non-success in recent tours has been due to the inability of our men to adapt themselves to the conditions of four-, five-, and even six-day cricket. It is no earthly use risking one's wicket in the desire to make runs fast when one has an un-limited amount of time to finish a game in. Wear down the bowling was our fixed line of policy. Let the later batsmen go for the bowling if they like, but take your time and no risks, is, I am convinced, the right game for the opening batsmen under Australian conditions.

Only once before in Australia has England managed to keep possession of the wickets throughout the day with the loss of only two men. This was at Adelaide on December 13, 1884, when England scored 232 for the loss of Shrewsbury and Ulyett, both, alas ! now dead.

With 221 runs on the board, and only two men out, we started the second day in a very strong position, and the news that Foster was suffering from a severe chill, which subsequently developed into tonsilitis, came as a great blow. He very pluckily went down to the ground, but soon had to retire to bed, where he remained for several days.

Bar the easy chance to Trumble overnight, Foster had played so well that it was quite likely that he would have got another three-figure score, and his inability to continue his innings was indeed a cruel disappointment to all of us. To make matters worse, the rain came down in torrents, and no cricket took place until 2.15. From then till tea-time the game was not interrupted, but further heavy showers rendered play after four o'clock impossible.

In the hour and three-quarters' batting we did, under the circumstances, quite well; for though the ball came along easily for the first half-hour, the pitch soon dried, and Trumble and Howell were able to make the ball jump about very awkwardly. It was our first experience of a sticky Melbourne wicket. In England when a wicket is sticky the ball turns quickly enough in all conscience, but it does not get up straight in your face as is its habit under similar conditions at Melbourne. There is one Bulli soil wicket on the Melbourne ground, but it is not often used, and this match was played on a wicket made of Merri Creek soil. Trumble is a past master on a wicket like this one. He bowled round the wicket—pitched a fine length on or just outside the off stump, and got up perfectly straight. He had eight of his men on the on-side. In England we frequently find men, and the best batsmen too, bowled out neck and crop on a sticky wicket, but on a similar wicket at Melbourne the ball gets up so straight that it is but

THE SECOND TEST MATCH.
Hayward playing back to Noble.

seldom that the wicket is hit. Only three of the thirty-eight wickets which fell in the match were bowled—all of them on our side. In neither innings of the Australians was the wicket hit.

Tyldesley had not, perhaps, been in his best form overnight, but now he played superbly, getting the breaking ball away to the on and on the leg side in masterly fashion, and every now and then whipping round and flicking one off his head. It was a great innings by a great batsman under adverse conditions.

Braund batted in most attractive style. Two or three of his strokes in front of cover-point were charmingly made, for with hardly an effort the ball flew to the ring. Mr. F. A. Iredale, in cabling to the *Daily Mail*, stated that Braund was missed three times! As a matter of fact his only chance was a barely possible one from a very hard drive to Trumble's right hand. Now Mr. Iredale was, and I believe still is, a very fine batsman, one who has made his century in a test match; but, to judge him by the cables he sent home, he really does not know what is a catch and what is not. Indeed, he reminds me of that type of reporter who, together with the more ignorant section of a crowd, always imagines a "bump" ball is a catch. Trumble was especially reserved for Mr. Iredale's censure, for he credited him during this match with having missed eight catches! Poor Hughie—that was drawing the long bow with a vengeance.

Braund was out just as the wicket was beginning to be nasty, and Knight, Hirst, and Rhodes fell in quick succession. Hirst was magnificently caught at short leg, Noble springing sideways and taking a hard hit low down with the left hand. This brilliant catch made up, from an Australian point of view, for an easy chance which Tyldesley had given him off Trumble when standing in the same position a few minutes earlier. At four o'clock Tyldesley was not out ninety-seven, and the total 306 for six wickets.

The torrents of rain which fell shortly after the players reached the pavilion prevented any possibility of further play ; but the unthinking portion of the crowd clamoured incessantly for the game to proceed, and two men jumped the fence and proceeded theatrically to judge for themselves of the state of the wicket. The police—forewarned by a similar scene at a recent inter-State match —at once took the matter in hand, and the intruders were bundled over the fence again. As the crowd still noisily protested, numbers of police were strategically placed in the playing area in case of a rush. The rain stopped about five o'clock, and shortly afterwards the umpires went out and returned to the pavilion, the pitch being found unfit for play. Again at half-past five o'clock they went out and drew the stumps.

There was much rain on the Sunday, and the game could not be continued until 1.20 on Monday afternoon, though why the umpires decided that play could be started ten minutes before luncheon was a little puzzling. The wicket was very difficult, and Tyldesley was at once caught at slip. His was a grand innings, and he was unlucky to just miss making a hundred. Lilley was caught at slip and Fielder clean bowled, and with Foster absent the innings closed for 315. The wicket

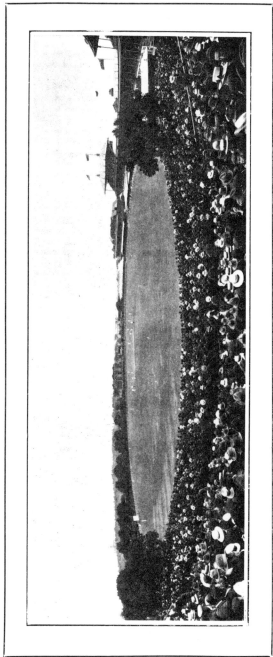

THE SECOND TEST MATCH.

Melbourne Cricket Ground.

was a real "beast" when the Australians went in, and we ought certainly to have got them out for less than 122 and thus made them follow-on. Had we done so, the match would in all probability have been over that evening. But the follow-on was saved by a mighty effort on the part of the mighty Trumper, who went in first and was last out, caught at long-off. It was a grand achievement on a bowler's wicket; but he was very lucky, for he was missed four times.

The first chance was to Lilley. Trumper popped the ball up in front of the wicket, and Lilley, darting forward, got it into both hands, but unaccountably dropped it. Trumper had then made but three. His next escape was at the hands of Hayward at long-on when he had got over fifty, and the third was to myself at point when he had got sixty-four. All these chances were off Rhodes' bowling, whilst the fourth was to Strudwick at short-leg behind the wicket off Braund. Had either of the first three catches which the great batsman gave been accepted, we would almost certainly have made our opponents follow-on, and had Lilley's catch come off I very much doubt whether the whole side would have made seventy runs. In spite of his luck Trumper played magnificently, jumping out to hit frequently, and as frequently jumping out and then, finding the ball too short to drive, getting quickly back and cutting it.

Rhodes bowled grandly, but was very badly supported by the field. It was the first really sticky wicket upon which Rhodes had had a chance to perform in Australia, and he showed himself to be a worthy successor of those other famous left-handed Yorkshiremen Emmett, Peate, and Peel.

Of the fifty-six runs hit from him Trumper must have made at least thirty-five.   Strudwick, as substitute for Foster, fielded very smartly, catching Noble and Trumble at "silly point"—a useful place on an

THE SECOND TEST MATCH.
English Team taking the field.

Australian sticky wicket to the Rhodesian type of bowler—and Hopkins at short leg.   It would have been better, perhaps, had Rhodes and Hirst changed ends. This was my own view after a few overs, but Rhodes *was particularly anxious* to keep on at the end at which

he began, and as he was our mainstay on the conditions
which prevailed I let him stay there. Whether I was
wise or not in so doing I am not sure. It is an open
question ; but on the whole it is best, I think, to leave
the choice on such an occasion to the bowler who is
most likely to get the other side out.

With the pitch as it was, it was only to be expected
that we should have a bad time when we went in again,
and goodness knows what might have happened had not
Tyldesley played another splendid innings. His forty-
eight (not out) was as fine a piece of batting on a bad
wicket as I have ever seen. The wicket was even worse
than when the Australians were in, for the sun had got
to work on it. Therefore Tyldesley's innings was an
even greater one than Trumper's, and, besides, except
for a possible chance to Trumble at slip off Saunders,
he did not give a chance. He hit Trumble for a fiver,
and roused the thousands to enthusiasm by smiting
Saunders off three successive balls for four, four, and five,
the latter being a grand hit right into the ladies' reserve,
the ball landing over the sight-board placed across the
path leading from the north gate of the pavilion fence.
One may safely say that Tyldesley is without a
superior on a bowler's wicket. At the drawing of
stumps Hayward, Braund, Knight, Hirst, and Rhodes
were out for seventy-four runs, Tyldesley not out
forty-eight.

The heavy rain of Monday night being followed by
light showers on Tuesday morning, play was not resumed
on the fourth day until 3.30. The previous night's
downpour made ultimate victory a certainty for us, for
the wicket was bound to be as bad as it could possibly

be. Our only fear was that the ground would be so wet that play would be impossible on Tuesday, and that if the rain kept off the wicket might roll out true when the Australians went in again on the Wednesday, for wickets in Australia recover twice as quickly as they do in England. It was obviously our best policy to get out as quickly as possible, and in less than half an hour the innings was over for an additional twenty-nine runs. Tyldesley was ninth out, and a better innings has surely never been played on a bad wicket than his sixty-two.

Trumble bowled very finely—for the most part round the wicket—keeping an accurate length and making the ball turn quickly; but Saunders was erratic. Every now and then he would send down a rattling good over, and then would come three or four long hops or half volleys in succession. He is certainly not the bowler he was.

The fielding all round, but especially Trumper's and Gregory's, was superb.

By ten minutes past four we were in the field, and an hour and three-quarters later the game was all over. Rhodes bowled splendidly, as did Hirst, but our catching was wretched. Never have I seen a first class side catch so badly. Braund and Rhodes missed the easiest catches imaginable at short-slip and mid-off. Trumper played with all his usual dash and skill, but he was twice let off—by Braund at slip off Hirst, when he had made nineteen, and by myself at cover-point when thirty-three. Then Hill was missed at mid-off. The batsman tried to hook the ball, which went softly to Rhodes, who, to the dismay of everybody, dropped it.

THE AUSTRALIAN TEAM.

A Gehrs.   W. W. Armstrong.   W. P. Howell.   H. Trumble.   A. J. Hopkins.   C. McLeod.
J. J. Kelly.   C. Hill.   M. A. Noble (Capt.).   R. A. Duff.   S. E. Gregory.   V. Trumper.

M

Hill and Trumper were hitting at everything, and both eventually fell to Rhodes, who got them caught in the country by Relf, who is a very safe catch anywhere. The bowlers had by this time changed ends, and the moment Trumper was dismissed, it was only a question of time.

In the match Rhodes took fifteen wickets for 124 runs and had half a dozen chances missed off him. It was—even under the conditions—a great performance, and worthy of England's champion bowler. What came over our fielding—or rather catching—in this game no one can tell. When men like Rhodes and Braund, who are admittedly among the great fielders of the world, take to dropping the easiest chances, it is useless to try to make excuses. They were just the accidents of the game which occasionally do occur; but some excuse may be found in the light, for the high stands and number of trees handicap the field materially.

Lilley, although through lack of opportunity he only disposed of one batsman in each innings, can seldom have kept wicket better. On such a pitch a record of no byes is something he may well be proud of. I am the first to admit that, as the weather turned out, tossing for choice of innings meant tossing for the match. The weather smiled on the side which batted first; wept on their opponents. But it is all in the game, and it is as well to regard things of this sort with the same degree of philosophy as the Australians did. As Clem Hill said, " Well, you had all the luck this time, perhaps we shall have it next ! "

Still, one must not forget that we, too, had some ill-fortune to contend against, as Foster had to retire after the first day's play, and, furthermore, we were weakened by the absence of Bosanquet and Arnold, two of our very best bowlers.

ENGLAND.

First Innings.		Second Innings.	
P. F. Warner, c. Duff, b. Trumble ...	68	c. Trumper, b. Saunders	3
Hayward, c. Gregory, b. Hopkins ...	58	c. Trumper, b. Trumble	0
Tyldesley, c. Trumble, b. Howell ...	97	c. Trumble, b. Howell.	62
R. E. Foster (retired ill)	49	absent	0
Braund, c. Howell, b. Trumble	20	b. Saunders	3
Knight, b. Howell	2	l. b. w., b. Trumble ...	0
Hirst, c. Noble, b. Howell	7	c. Gregory, b. Howell .	4
Rhodes, l.b.w., b. Trumble	2	l.b.w., b. Trumble ...	9
Lilley, c. Howell, b. Trumble	4	st. Kelly, b. Trumble ..	0
Relf, not out	3	not out	10
Fielder, b. Howell	1	c. Hill, b. Trumble ...	4
Extras	4	Extras	8
Total	315	Total	103

Bowling Analysis.

First Innings.

	O.	M.	R.	W.			O.	M.	R.	W
Trumble ...	50	10	107	4	Hopkins	20	2	50	1
Noble	6	3	4	0	Armstrong ...	25	6	43	0
Saunders ...	16	3	60	0	Trumper	1	0	4	0
Howell	34.5	14	43	4					

Hopkins bowled 1 wide.

Second Innings.

	O.	M.	R.	W.			O.	M.	R.	W
Trumble	10.5	2	34	5	Howell	8	3	25	2
Saunders... ...	8	0	33	2	Hopkins	2	1	3	0

AUSTRALIA.

First Innings.		Second Innings.	
R. A. Duff, st. Lilley, b. Rhodes ...	10	c. Braund, b. Rhodes...	8
V. Trumper, c. Tyldesley, b. Rhodes...	74	c. Relf, b. Rhodes ...	35
C. Hill, c. Rhodes, b. Hirst	5	c. Relf, b. Rhodes ...	20
M. A. Noble, c. sub., b. Rhodes ...	0	not out	31
S. E. Gregory, c. Hirst, b. Rhodes ...	1	c. Rhodes, b. Hirst ...	0
A. J. Hopkins, c. sub., b. Relf	18	c. and b. Rhodes ...	7
H. Trumble, c. sub., b. Rhodes.. ...	2	c. Braund, b. Rhodes..	0
W.W. Armstrong, c. Braund, b. Rhodes	1	c. Hayward, b. Rhodes	0
J. J. Kelly, run out	8	c. Lilley, b. Rhodes ...	7
W. P. Howell, c. Fielder, b. Rhodes..	0	c. Hirst, b. Rhodes ...	3
J. V. Saunders, not out	2	c. Fielder, b. Hirst ...	0
Leg-bye	1	Extras	0
Total	122	Total	111

Bowling Analysis.

First Innings.

	O.	M.	R.	W.				O.	M.	R.	W.
Rhodes	15.2	0	56	7	Relf...	...	...	2	0	12	1
Hirst	8	1	33	1	Braund	...	...	5	0	20	0

Second Innings.

	O.	M.	R.	W.				O.	M.	R.	W.
Rhodes	15	0	68	8	Relf...	...	...	1	0	5	0
Hirst	13.4	4	38	2							

FALL OF WICKETS.

First Innings of England.

1	2	3	4	5	6	7	8	9
122	132	277	279	297	306	306	314	315

Second Innings of England.

1	2	3	4	5	6	7	8	9
5	7	27	40	74	74	74	90	103

First Innings of Australia.

1	2	3	4	5	6	7	8	9	10
14	23	23	33	67	73	79	105	116	122

Second Innings of Australia.

1	2	3	4	5	6	7	8	9	10
14	59	73	77	86	90	90	102	105	111

Umpires : Crockett and Argall.

Who has not heard of Ballarat, the Eldorado of sixty years ago, whither adventurers from all parts of the world flocked ? Here we tarried for three or four days on the way to Adelaide for the third test match, and the local Eighteen were rather better than the usual odds team, though, had we played to a finish, we should have won comfortably. Knight is far from a good batsman on a soft wicket ; but with the turf hard and fast he is a very difficult man to shift, and the most noteworthy incident about this match was his admirable innings of 109. He gave but one difficult chance, and his cutting, and that characteristic stroke of his between point and cover, were well executed. Strudwick is fast improving as a batsman, and in his forty-two made several capital strokes on the leg side.

Stevens and Hennah, right hand, and Hele, medium left, bowled well, and the fielding in our first innings was smart and clean, while Baker played a first class innings. Of course, all the critics at once said that he ought to play in the next test match, but that is always the way with the local partisan.

Our casualty list was still a long one, and neither Tyldesley, Arnold, Bosanquet, nor Foster was able to play. Eton and Harrow, however, in the shape of G. S. Whitfeld and G. Drummond, came to our rescue, and the former made a great catch at point, which enabled me to obtain my first wicket in Australia. It was a slow long-hop that did it—a ball I not infrequently bowl— and the striker put some weight into the stroke.

The gate on both days was very poor indeed, and the small boys showed a strong inclination to make noisy and frequently insulting remarks.   These youths should be put down with a rod of good birch, for, if they are not suppressed now, in eight or ten years' time they will grow up into the type of man who " barracked " Crockett so disgracefully at Sydney.   But, as they are apparently encouraged in their behaviour by many of their elders, it is, I suppose, hopeless to expect any improvement. Most of their comments are, I admit, quite good-natured ; but it is, to say the least of it, unseemly that the players should have to stand up before a running fire of noisy impertinence.

These games against odds are rather a weariness of the flesh, and I doubt very much whether they do any real good locally.   In future years it would be a good plan to play nothing but eleven aside matches in Australia, viz., five test games, a couple of games against each of the three principal States, and a visit to Brisbane and Western Australia where the tour might open. That would make thirteen or fourteen matches in Australia. Then a couple of games might be played in Tasmania, and four or five in New Zealand, where cricket is fast going ahead.   The return to England might be made *via* Honolulu, San Francisco, and across the American Continent, and thus save the monotony and heat of a second journey through the Canal.   Financially, too, the programme I have sketched would be far more profitable than the present arrangement.

There are doubtless objections to so radical a departure from precedent, but the suggestion is, I think worthy of consideration.

ENGLAND.

First Innings.		Second Innings.	
Hayward, b. Stevens	12	l.b.w., b. Stevens ...	0
Braund, b. Mitchell	37	c. Champion, b. Bailey	37
Knight, c. and b. Hennah	109	c. Hore, b. Cockburn	47
Lilley, b. T. Baker	59	b. Mitchell	12
G. S. Whitfeld, b. T. Baker	3	c. and b. Stevens... ...	0
G. Drummond, b. T. Baker	0	c. Bailey, b. Hennah ...	8
Hirst, c. Bray, b. Hele...	22	c. Champion, b. Stevens	20
Relf, c. and b. Hele	10	b. Stevens	8
Rhodes, not out	43	b. Stevens	36
P. F. Warner, b. Hennah	2	b. Hele...	8
Strudwick, b. Hennah	2	b. Stevens	42
Fielder, b. Hennah	4	not out	2
Extras	23	Extras	6
Total	326	Total	226

Bowling Analysis.
First Innings.

	O.	M.	R.	W.			O.	M.	R.	W.
Stevens	16	1	65	1	Hele	... ...	15	8	18	3
Cockburn	11	3	45	0	Bray	... ...	2	1	8	0
Mitchell . . .	15	0	48	1	Bailey	... ...	8	0	31	0
Morgan	6	4	6	0	Baker	.. ...	14	3	34	2
Hennah	17	5	46	4						

Hennah bowled 1 wide and 1 no-ball.

Second Innings.

	O.	M.	R.	W.			O.	M.	R.	W.
Stevens	18	3	55	6	Baker, T.	...	13	3	37	0
Mitchell	6	0	38	1	Cockburn	...	3	1	5	1
Hele	7	1	38	1	Bailey	.. ...	3	0	17	1
Hennah	5	0	30	1						

BALLARAT.

Baker, c. and b. Braund	61
Watson, b. Fielder	18
Mailer, c. Hirst, b. Braund	15
Hore, b. Braund...	19
Bray, run out	7
Champion (Capt.), c. Fielder, b. Braund	1
Hodge, l.b.w., b. Braund	7
Kennedy, b. Rhodes	0
Hennah, st. Strudwick, b. Braund	9
Bailey, run out	4
Stevens, c. Drummond, b. Braund	0
Trethowan, b. Braund	2
Mitchell, st. Strudwick, b. Braund	9
Hele, b. Braund	4
Dillon, c. Whitfeld, b. Warner	17
Baker, b. Relf	10
Cockburn, not out	9
Extras	5
Total	197

Bowling Analysis.

First Innings.

	O.	M	R.	W.		O.	M.	R.	W.
Braund	27	5	87	10	Relf...	11	3	34	1
Hirst	10	1	21	0	Fielder	10	4	27	1
Rhodes	11	3	19	1	Warner	3	1	4	1

CRICKET IN THE BUSH.

THE TOSS FOR THE THIRD TEST MATCH.

CHAPTER IX

THE THIRD TEST MATCH

THE Adelaide Oval has always had the reputation
of being an ill-omened ground for English Teams,
and certain it is that since 1891 we have failed to win
a test match there. Great preparations had been going
on at the Oval for weeks past. More care than usual
had, if possible, been bestowed on the wicket, and the
outfield had been rolled and mown and watered, with
the result that a good deal of the unevenness and
roughness which usually characterise the ground had
disappeared. As in the match against South Australia,
the ground was roped off at each end, leaving a
maximum distance of 110 yards from the striker's wicket
to the boundary. The Australian Eleven differed in only

THE FIRST RUN OF THE THIRD TEST MATCH.

Duff hooks Fielder for four.

one instance from the side which had played at Melbourne, McLeod taking the place of Saunders. From the M.C.C. Eleven Relf, Knight, and Strudwick stood down, Fielder being given the preference over Relf, as it was thought that his bowling might be useful on the extra fast Adelaide wicket.

In the last few games Fielder had been doing wonderfully well, combining pace with accuracy, and sending down an occasional ball which went away with his arm. There was no bowler of his pace at the time in Australia—Cotter had not then appeared—and I thought that he might possibly "snick out" one or two of the great Australian cracks.

The weather in Adelaide on the Friday was ideal, and all Adelaide was talking of the third test match or down at the ground looking at it during the day, while hundreds of telegrams concerning it were flying across land and sea. Long before twelve o'clock the white fence round the ground was ringed with spectators, while the seats in the stands and pavilion were gradually filling up.

The Australian papers are very funny over the tossing, as, from their accounts, one would imagine that I had won every toss in Australia. Even so well known a writer as " Felix," commenting on the third test match, said that it was quite time my phenomenal luck with the coin gave out and Australia won the toss. As a matter of fact, up to this match we had won five and lost five, and counting this match, they had won the toss in two out of the three test matches already played. Such are the disadvantages of a reputation! This is a small matter, but it is illustrative of the tone adopted by some of the best papers. They are too anxious, really, to make out that any luck there may be always goes our way. Of course, all the luck was with us at Melbourne; but when you read that the luck was with us in the first test because "the rain on Friday night made the wicket difficult for the last three Australian batsmen" (who, as a matter of fact, made more runs than they have in any innings since), it borders on the ridiculous, when you consider that some of our best batsmen had an hour's batting on the same wicket before it became easy!

A MIGHTY PAIR.
R. A. Duff and V. Trumper.

Accompanied by half a dozen camera - fiends, Noble and I tossed for choice of innings in front of the members' reserve. Fortune favoured the Australian Skipper, and it was just mid-day when we took the field, Trumper and Duff opening to Fielder and Arnold. The Kent man did not bowl well, and Duff repeatedly hooked him round to leg, though a man was placed there to stop the boundary. Duff got most of the bowling, and, as he took every opportunity of scoring, runs came at a

THE THIRD TEST MATCH.

Hill hits Braund for four.

tremendous pace. The wicket was absolutely perfection
—of the sort on which a three-day match in England
between two strong Elevens would have no earthly chance
of being finished—and, though our bowling was good
and the fielding excellent, the total was increased every
over.

With the total at forty-four, Duff having made twenty-
eight and Trumper fifteen, Rhodes replaced Fielder, for
whom the batsmen, especially Duff, had shown great
partiality. One of Duff's strokes off the fast bowler was
a beautiful square cut. Duff continued to bat brilliantly,
and the hundred went up after an hour and ten minutes'
cricket, of which he claimed sixty-seven.

The six regular bowlers had a try, and it was left to
Hirst to bring about a separation with the very last
delivery before lunch. The ball made haste off the
pitch, kept a little low, and clean beat Duff, who had
batted beautifully all round the wicket. He might,
perhaps, have been caught at deep square-leg by Fielder
when he had made thirty-two, and Lilley should have
stumped him by yards off Bosanquet when he was sixty-
four.

When play was resumed after luncheon, Trumper, not
out forty - seven, was joined by Hill, Hirst and
Braund bowling. The two Australian champions were
in great form, and runs came off every over. Indeed, it
was not until half an hour after lunch that the first
maiden over of the day was bowled, the distinction
falling to Hirst, who bowled it to Hill.

The second hundred was reached in two hours and a
quarter, and at 219 Bosanquet relieved Hirst, who had
been on for over three-quarters of an hour and had kept
a fine length. Bowlers and fielders worked their hardest,

N

but Trumper and Hill were now so thoroughly set that a total of five or six hundred seemed possible. Just before the tea interval Hirst went on again, and his fourth ball, which was rather wide, Trumper dragged into his wicket. He played a grand innings, never attempting strokes which might be risky, but waiting for the loose ones, which he punished. He did not make a bad stroke, hit twelve fours, and was batting three hours nine minutes. He received a great ovation. The second wicket fell for 272 ; Hill seventy-two not out. It was a coincidence that the only two wickets so far obtained should have each been got by Hirst immediately prior to an adjournment. This innings of 113 is the fourth hundred Trumper has made against England.

During the last stage of the day's cricket matters veered round in our favour. Hill cut at a wide ball and was well caught by Lilley, Gregory tried to place Arnold to leg and was caught at mid-on, Hopkins played on, and Armstrong was palpably l.b.w. Noble batted slowly but with great determination and skill, and he had some very good bowling to play from Arnold and Bosanquet. The latter, indeed, has never bowled his slows better, for he had his length under something like control, and was repeatedly sticking up the batsmen with that off-breaking leg-break of his. From the last ball of the day Trumble should have been caught at short-leg behind the umpire by Bosanquet off Braund's bowling, but the fieldsman was slow in coming to the ball, which was cocked up gently.

At the close of play we had six wickets down for 355—a by no means unsatisfactory position for us, seeing that at one time 280 runs were on the board with two wickets down.

THE THIRD TEST MATCH.

P. F. Warner, c. McLeod, b. Trumble, 48.

We fielded extremely well throughout the afternoon, Arnold at point, Bosanquet, more particularly to his own bowling, Hirst, Rhodes, and Tyldesley being most conspicuous. In the beginning, owing to the long stands made by Duff, Trumper, and Hill, the outlook was not pleasant, but we stuck to our work well, and were cheered up by the later events of the afternoon. Even in face of the huge total being put up by Hill, Trumper, and Duff, the bowlers never lost heart, and attacked manfully all through. Bosanquet, on the whole, did the best work with the ball. He was unlucky in having Duff missed off him, and there was not a man on the side who played him with full confidence. Braund did not give much trouble, but Arnold, Rhodes, and Hirst all did admirably, and it was only the magnificent batting of Australia's champion batsmen that made them at time look cheap.

After Hill left the bowlers held the upper hand. This shows what a splendid quartette of batsmen Australia has to start with. They made the bowling seem easy because of their superb judgment and skill.

I have been blamed for playing Fielder, and especially for putting him on first. It may interest these critics to know that I acted on the advice of the most experienced members of my team in playing him, and as for beginning the bowling with him, it was Hirst, who suggested this course, when I was discussing the plan of campaign with him before the match started ; and he would be a rash man who lightly dismissed the advice of such a seasoned and experienced cricketer.

On Saturday morning Arnold and Bosanquet bowled as well, if not better than, they had done during the last hour of Friday afternoon, and the innings was soon over for 388—exactly the same total as MacLaren's Eleven made in the corresponding match two years ago. Of Arnold's and Bosanquet's good work I have already spoken, but everyone who went on—with the exception of Fielder, who was, I think, rather nervous—did well. Hirst, indeed, bowled better and faster than he has done all the tour. He rendered fine service in dismissing both Trumper and Duff, but Arnold and Bosanquet bowled so well after the fall of the third wicket that, except for three or four overs after tea, I did not make any use of him. Without being exactly brilliant the fielding was safe, though many brilliant things were done. Tyldesley, Hirst, Rhodes, and Bosanquet saved heaps of runs. Lilley has been in better form. He stumped Noble splendidly, but he was in and out. The Australian leader played a sound innings and one very characteristic of him.

Our innings was a failure. Excuse and explain as one may, it was not at all the exhibition of batting expected. Tom Hayward, when looking very solid— and this is a ground upon which he has made many good scores—was unlucky in pulling an off ball from Howell into his stumps. Tyldesley, as usual, was first wicket, and was dismissed by one of the most wonderful catches at the wicket I have ever seen. He glanced Hopkins to leg, but Kelly anticipated the stroke, and, dashing across, secured the ball quite four feet wide of the wicket. It was a catch such as Halliwell, the South African, whom I consider the best wicket-keeper of the present time, occasionally brings off. Foster and myself played very steadily for a while, but runs were just beginning to come fast when I was splendidly caught at mid-on by McLeod, who took a hard drive with his

THE THIRD TEST MATCH.

Hirst's fatal stroke.

right hand. It was the sort of catch that comes off once in twenty times. Foster was in over an hour for twenty-one, and was then caught at second slip. He batted fairly, but his recent illness had left him rather weak, and he was further handicapped by a bruised thumb.

The rest of our innings needs little comment. Hirst played in his best style, but Braund, Bosanquet, and Rhodes literally threw their wickets away. Braund and Bosanquet skied the ball to mid-off and Rhodes was caught at cover—all three were wretched hits. Hirst was finely caught at long-off at five minutes to six, and the day's play ended with our total 199 for eight. This was a poor performance on such a perfect wicket. Hayward, Tyldesley, and myself were somewhat unlucky in the way we were dismissed, but, as a whole, there was no excuse for our poor show.

The wicket was a fast one, but not quite so fast as the pitch we played on at Sydney in the first test match. Our batsmen got on all right so long as they acted strictly on the defensive, but the moment they tried to force runs they were in trouble. Braund, Bosanquet, and Rhodes were all out in this way from strokes that, owing to mis-timing, looked very weak.

All the bowlers were accurate, but Hopkins mixed them most judiciously.

The fielding all round was brilliant, particularly that of Duff and Gregory. Kelly was in fine form with the gloves.

Taking the tail end of the Australians and the flower of the Englishmen, only 232 runs were made on Saturday for twelve wickets, as against 355 made on the previous day for six wickets, a sufficient indication of the difference in the description of the play from a spectator's standpoint.

There was a crowd of 18,000—a very big gate for Adelaide—and amongst the alumni were the Governor General (Lord Tennyson), Lord Northcote, who four days later succeeded him, Sir George Le Hunte, the

FIELDER BOWLING.

Governor of South Australia, Admiral Fanshawe, and our keenest supporter and Chaplain of the Forces Bishop Welldon, whose enthusiasm was so intense that when Braund started for a short run he was heard to *murmur*, "My dear Braund, do be careful."

The weather was variable and threatening on the third day, and at one time rain looked a certainty. Again, at about midday, one of those dust-storms which so often seriously mar the success of cricket on the Adelaide Oval started, but ended with little more than a threat, and, all things considered, the day was fairly pleasant. Lilley batted so well, and Arnold was so safe in defence, that we were rapidly making up our lost ground when a misunderstanding ended in a run out. Our wicket-keeper had played such a free, confident game that one looked for a big score from him. Fielder was bowled off his pads, and Arnold was therefore left not out. He had played a sound defensive innings.

THE THIRD TEST MATCH AT ADELAIDE.

A Corner of the Grand Stand.

Trumble's was the best analysis. He got on a good deal of spin, and said afterwards that he felt more like bowling than he had done at any time since he resumed cricket in December.

Hopkins seemed to me to be the most difficult. He made the ball swerve in the air, and often deceived the batsmen in the pace. He kept the ball well up. The fielding could not have been better, Duff and McLeod being very much in evidence.

The Australians did not start their second innings too well, Trumper, Duff, and Hill being out for 101 runs. Trumper played exquisite cricket for an hour and a quarter. He looked good for another hundred when Rhodes got him l.b.w. with his first ball.

Neither Duff nor Hill were ever masters of the situation. Hill was out to a fine ball which came with Fielder's arm, and made great pace off the pitch. Noble was still there, fighting gamely in that quiet and perhaps uninteresting but, oh! so determined style of his; but, judged by recent cricket, Gregory, Armstrong, Hopkins, and Co. might with any luck have been disposed of fairly cheaply. But it has often been said that a good old cricketer is better than a good new one, and Gregory fully lived up to that saying. At first he might have been out any ball, for he could not time Fielder, who looked certain to secure him. However, after a quarter of an hour or so, he got the pace of the wicket, and from then until the last over of the day he batted superbly. He was the Gregory of eight or ten years back. Every bowler brought against him was punished unmercifully, but in the last over of the day he mis-hit Braund and Rhodes caught him easily at backward point. After his shaky start nothing could have been finer than the way in which he timed the ball. He was in two hours and hit seventeen fours. He gave no chance. A couple of balls off Fielder went dangerously near the slips ; indeed, after a mighty jump, Foster just touched one with his finger-tip, but no actual possible chance can be set down against him. Our fielding all day was splendid, and there was never the slightest inclination to give in, even when Gregory was making hay of the bowling.

Noble at the close of play was not out fifty-two and the total 263 for four wickets. The Australian Captain had not played so well as usual, and ought to have been out twice, for he was missed being stumped off Bosanquet and gave a chance to Hirst at mid-off from Arnold. Not exactly an easy catch, but one which I have often seen the Yorkshireman take.

The fourth morning of the match saw us apparently fairly cornered, but the day's cricket brought us nothing but honour, for we secured the six remaining Australian wickets for eighty-eight runs, and then scored 150 for two wickets. It was a recovery which we can all look back on with a certain amount of pride. Bosanquet has been aptly described as the " worst best bowler " in the world. On the previous afternoon he had sent down nothing but the slowest full pitches and long hops—stuff that would have disgraced " Two Belows " at Rugby. On this day he was a different bowler altogether, and in seven overs obtained four wickets for twenty-three runs. He got his length at once, and that perplexing off-breaking leg-breaker never stuck up batsmen more. Could Bosanquet be mechanically certain of his length he would be the best bowler in the world. When he does get a length, not even Trumper, Duff, Noble, and Hill care for him in the least. Bosanquet is, in a sense,

THE ADELAIDE OVAL DURING THE THIRD TEST MATCH.

one of the pioneers of cricket, for he has cultivated a method of bowling which is extraordinarily full of possibilities. Braund got Noble caught at mid-off, but, though he kept the batsmen quiet, he was not at this period of the tour bowling at his best.

Fielder was again very useful, keeping a good length with plenty of pace. He is a decidedly promising fast bowler, and may do great things in the future, for he is young and keen and so strong. Our fielding was quite A1—altogether our out cricket was of a high standard of efficiency.

When Hayward and myself went in we were faced with the almost superhuman task of making 495 runs—but when after two hours and three-quarters' batting we were still undefeated, visions of a glorious victory flashed through my mind. But cricket is full of changes and chances, and at ten minutes before time a good ball from Hopkins got Hayward l.b.w. He had played superbly—and there is no better man for a test match—so sound and watchful, and so strong when he does make up his mind to have a go. I know, for I was near.

It was a great start, and had we two remained together until six o'clock, our chances of ultimate victory would not have been altogether hopeless. This was the third time that Hayward and I had put up over a hundred for the first wicket. Against South Australia we scored 122, then in the Melbourne test a similar figure, and now 148.

There were many anxious Australians on Tuesday night. They were afraid of Tyldesley. As one man said, "You never know when he is going to make a hundred, and a century from him would make a hole in the 345 England still needs."

O

But Adelaide is not Tyldesley's lucky ground. When he made a couple of lovely off-drives off Hopkins, many an Australian supporter felt uneasy, but in the next over he was out in a sensational manner. He let go at a loose long hop from Hopkins. It went straight, breast high, to Noble, who was standing ten or twelve

THE THIRD TEST MATCH.

Englishmen leaving the field.

yards away, just in front of square-leg. It was hard but not too warm. I dare say a fieldsman like Noble would in such circumstances make the catch clean four times out of five. This time was the fifth. The ball struck Noble on the chest. He clutched at it, and smothered it ; got it in his right hand, and juggled with it from hand to hand. Then the ball was seen to fall, and a sharp

THE THIRD TEST MATCH.

Hayward just out : l.o.w.. b. Hopkins, 67.

"Oh!" came from a hundred voices. But the fieldsman made a desperate dive at it with his left hand, clutched it a few inches from the ground and rolled over. Tyldesley had watched it all, and as Noble rolled over he walked away, shaking his head, in a way which said, "Well, I'm——unlucky." The crowd, worked up to a high pitch of excitement in that second or two, gave a yell of delight when they saw the batsman leave his crease. Until then few could tell whether Noble had clinched the catch. It was the most exciting and longest bit of juggling with a ball I ever saw a fieldsman do.

Subsequently no real stand was made, though Foster and Braund were both missed—Foster by McLeod at mid-on off a swerving full pitch from Hopkins, and Braund at cover by Trumper off McLeod, a very easy chance. Victor looked so woe-begone when it escaped him that he buried his face in the grass. In the end both played on. Hirst played splendidly for forty-four, and looked thoroughly well set when Trumble bowled him with one that came back. Hirst batted with splendid consistency throughout the tour. He did not get many runs on the sticky wicket at Melbourne, but there was that sixty not out of his at Sydney in the first test, his ninety odd at Melbourne against Victoria, sixty against New South Wales, and now fifty-eight and forty-four. So plucky, so full of resource, and always so cheerful; he is a fortunate captain who has him on his side.

The wicket was almost as good at the finish as at the commencement of the game. On the last morning one end was, I thought, a shade faster than the other, and the surface, possibly, was a wee bit rough; but I do not suppose there has ever been a wicket which lasted better than this one.

Bad batting lost us the game, for our bowling and fielding were excellent. If one looks at the score-sheet one can see how badly our batsmen failed. In the two innings we made 510 runs from the bat, and of this Hirst, Hayward, and myself scored 316. Had we batted at all up to our bowling and fielding form we might well have made a close fight. The Australians' totals of 388 and 351 must seem big enough in England, but on the perfect Adelaide wicket they are nothing like so formidable as they look. Indeed, I think we did well to dismiss them as cheaply as we did. Once more was the overpowering personality and skill of their four great batsmen very much in evidence. The present Australian Eleven has been called, and with some truth, a four-man team so far as batting is concerned, but on this occasion one, who by many critics had been long regarded as a "has been," came out in his most brilliant form.

And so for the first time since I landed in Australia I was compelled to haul down my flag. Never, perhaps, was a match fought out under more even conditions; for the wicket, as I have already said, remained practically perfect to the end, and not one drop of rain fell during the five days over which the battle waged. It was a thoroughly well-deserved victory. We had to surrender, but we marched out with all the honours of war, and there was nothing that savoured of disgrace about our downfall.

I slept in a room numbered thirteen! Perhaps this may have had something to do with the result!

FINISH OF THE THIRD TEST MATCH.

Rhodes, run out, 8.

AUSTRALIA.

First Innings.		Second Innings.	
R. A. Duff, b. Hirst	79	c. Braund, b. Hirst ...	14
V. Trumper, b. Hirst	113	l.b.w., b. Rhodes ...	59
C. Hill, c. Lilley, b. Arnold	88	b. Fielder	16
S. E. Gregory, c. Tyldesley, b. Arnold.	8	c. Rhodes, b. Braund...	112
M. A. Noble, st. Lilley, b. Arnold ...	59	c. Bosanquet, b. Braund	65
A. J. Hopkins, b. Bosanquet	0	run out...	7
W. W. Armstrong, l.b.w., b. Rhodes..	10	c. Hirst, b. Bosanquet..	39
H. Trumble, b. Bosanquet	4	c. and b. Bosanquet ...	9
C. E. McLeod, run out	8	b. Bosanquet	2
J. J. Kelly, l.b.w., b. Bosanquet ...	1	st. Lilley, b. Bosanquet	13
W. P. Howell, not out...	3	not out	1
Byes, 7 ; leg-byes, 5 ; wides, 3 ...	15	B. 8 ; l-b. 2 ; w. 3 ; n-b. 1	14
Total	388	Total	351

Bowling Analysis.

First Innings.

	O.	M.	R.	W.			O.	M.	R.	W.
Fielder	7	0	33	0	Bosanquet ...		30.1	4	95	3
Arnold	27	4	93	3	Braund		13	1	49	0
Rhodes	14	3	45	1	Hirst		14	1	58	2

Fielder, Rhodes, and Hirst each bowled 1 wide.

Second Innings.

	O.	M.	R.	W.			O.	M.	R.	W.
Arnold	19	3	74	0	Fielder		24	11	51	1
Hirst	13	1	36	1	Rhodes		21	4	46	1
Bosanquet ..	16	0	73	4	Braund		21	6	57	2

ENGLAND.

First Innings.		Second Innings.	
P. F. Warner, c. McLeod, b. Trumble	48	c. and b. Trumble ...	79
Hayward, b. Howell	20	l.b.w., b. Hopkins ...	67
Tyldesley, c. Kelly, b. Hopkins... ...	0	c. Noble, b. Hopkins...	10
R. E. Foster, c. Howell, b. Noble ...	21	b. McLeod	16
Braund, c. Duff, b. Hopkins	13	b. Howell	25
Hirst, c. Trumper, b. Trumble	58	b. Trumble	44
B. J. T. Bosanquet, c. Duff, b. Hopkins	10	c. Trumper, b. Hopkins	10
Rhodes, c. Armstrong, b. McLeod ...	9	run out...	8
Arnold, not out	23	b. Hopkins	1
Lilley, run out	28	c. and b. Howell... ...	0
Fielder, b. Trumble	6	not out	14
Byes, 4 ; leg-bye, 1 ; wides, 4 ..	9	Leg-byes, 2 ; wides, 2	4
Total	245	Total	278

Bowling Analysis.

First Innings.

	O.	M.	R.	W.		O.	M.	R.	W.
McLeod	24	6	56	1	Hopkins	24	5	68	3
Trumble	28	10	49	3	Armstrong ...	11	3	25	0
Howell	13	4	28	1	Noble	3	0	10	1

Trumble bowled 2 wides, and Hopkins and Noble 1 each.

Second Innings.

	O.	M.	R.	W.		O.	M.	R.	W.
Howell	20	5	52	2	Hopkins	28.1	9	81	4
McLeod	25	4	46	1	Armstrong ...	7	2	15	0
Trumble	33	8	73	2	Trumper	4	0	7	0

Hopkins and Trumper each bowled 1 wide.

FALL OF WICKETS.

First Innings of Australia.

1	2	3	4	5	6	7	8	9	10
129	272	286	308	310	343	360	384	384	388

Second Innings of Australia.

1	2	3	4	5	6	7	8	9	10
48	81	101	263	289	320	324	326	350	351

First Innings of England.

1	2	3	4	5	6	7	8	9	10
47	48	88	99	116	146	173	199	234	245

Second Innings of England.

1	2	3	4	5	6	7	8	9	10
148	150	160	160	195	231	231	256	256	278

Umpires : Messrs. P. Argall and R. Crockett.

CHAPTER X

TASMANIA

FOLLOWING on the test match at Adelaide, we once more made our way to Melbourne, embarking there on the *Burrumbeet* for Launceston on Saturday afternoon, January 23. Now the *Burrumbeet* is not a good boat; she is small, rolls alarmingly, and has a peculiar awesome smell about her, and as the sea was rough we had a poor time. The test match finished just too late to enable us to catch the boat we had intended, so we had of necessity only booked our passages at the last minute. Our cabins, therefore, were not the pick of the bunch; they were, indeed, just over the screw, *and the previous crossing must have been a bad one.* Six of the professionals found themselves in a kind of geometrical figure containing six bunks, four of which were promptly seized on by Knight and other sailors of the same poor quality. When the other two occupants arrived the groaning and moaning and other sounds too awful to mention affected them so much that they beat a hasty retreat and spent the night on deck. In future the one word *Burrumbeet* will make George Hirst pale with a deathly fear.

Arriving at Launceston, we were hurried into the train, and after a wearisome journey reached Hobart, where we were to play the first of two matches against Tasmania.

After all this travelling, it was very annoying to find our hotel so overcrowded that we had to sleep two in a room, and our tempers were not improved by the exceedingly badly-mannered female who ran the show. It was race week, and rooms in the town were at a premium ; but, as our coming had been known for at least a fortnight before, one might reasonably have expected better accommodation. The Tasmanians had selected a very good side to oppose us—not quite their best, for J. H. Savigny, who was subsequently to do so well against us at Launceston, was unable to play, but C. J. Eady and K. E. Burn were in the team, as well as E. A. Windsor.

Nine years had elapsed since an English Eleven had visited the island, and our coming had been eagerly anticipated for weeks past, so that it was not surprising to find a fairly large crowd on the ground when play commenced. We won the toss, but the *Burrumbeet*, of evil memory, had taken all the sting out of us, and we could make no more than 185 on a perfect wicket. Eady, Windsor, and Smith got us out. Eady bowls almost as fast to-day as he did when he was in England eight years ago, and would have taken more than three wickets, had not a catch or two been dropped of him. There are many people in Australia who think he ought to be played in the test matches, but, as was shown subsequently in our second innings, he is not able to keep up his pace for long. Windsor is a bowler of quite a different type—right hand slow, with a break both ways—a really good bowler this—always varying his pace and full of tricks. Had he lived on the mainland he would, I venture to think, have been in a representative Australian Eleven ere this. Only the other day Joe Darling told me that he was very keen on bringing Windsor over with his 1899 Eleven. Smith is quite a boy, but he can turn the ball back, and when he learns to bowl not quite so short will be a good man, for he has a deceptive flight in the air. Tasmania just headed our first innings. There was nothing remarkable about their batting, Douglas, Hawson, Dodds, and K. E. Burn, their Captain—like Eady, one time a member of an Australian Eleven—doing best. Fielder was suffering from "Burrumbeetis," and collapsed after two overs, while Relf, owing to a bruised heel, was able to send down but half a dozen overs. Hayward, Hirst, and Braund were not playing, so Arnold and Rhodes, with an occasional change to Bosanquet, who bowled abominably, had to do nearly all the work. There had been a good deal of rain after the close of play on the first night, but the wicket recovered splendidly, and was almost perfect next morning. That it was not *quite* right was evident by the way in which Rhodes and Arnold turned the ball during the first hour. The Yorkshireman especially bowled splendidly, time after time beating the bat and then missing the wicket. His analysis gives a poor idea of how he bowled.

Our second innings was very different from our first, for we got fairly going and knocked up 350 for four wickets. Tyldesley played a superb innings of eighty-seven, but the great thing was Bosanquet's 124 not out.

Bosanquet had not done so well as I had hoped with the bat, and the fast wickets at Sydney, Melbourne, and Adelaide did not up to this time seem to suit his methods. He does not like the ball which goes with the bowler's arm, and men like Noble and Hopkins know this, and usually secure his wicket before he has got

THE RACES AT HOBART.

going. On this occasion, however, he returned to his finest form. There was no Noble or Hopkins against him, and the sting had been to a large extent knocked out of the bowling by the time he went in. He was missed at mid-on from a skier when he had made nineteen, but this was the only fault in a really magnificent display of hitting. He hit four fives and eighteen fours, and made two of the biggest straight drives I have ever seen. The first went straight over the bowler's head and cleared the pavilion; the second went slightly to the right of the first and pitched at the entrance-gate. Then he hooked Eady wonderfully well. Altogether it was a most exhilarating and delightful piece of strong, forcing, determined cricket.

With an hour left for play I declared, and the match fizzled out. Hobart is a charming place, and one of its prettiest spots is the cricket-ground, which for beauty will bear comparison with any other in the world.

Albert Knight was very funny during the match; he would tell you after one ball that he was still so bad that he could not bat, and did not want to run at all; the next ball would go to point, and off he would go down the wicket. Ask him again how he felt, and you would think he was in the last stage of collapse, till he would nearly run you off your legs in trying to get four for a possible three. At the end of the match he was so far recovered as to be able to bowl (with nine men on the on-side). We finished up our visit to Hobart by a day at the races, which the whole team enjoyed immensely, without adding greatly to their exchequer.

ENGLAND.

First Innings.

P. F. Warner, c. Cuff, b. Smith	26
R. E. Foster, c. Cuff, b. Smith	43
Tyldesley, b. Eady	4
Arnold, c. Cuff, b. Smith	4
Knight, c. Smith, b. Windsor	19
B. J. T. Bosanquet, b. Eady	35
Lilley, c. Cuff, b. Windsor	11
Relf, run out	24
Fielder, c. Eady, b. Windsor	1
Rhodes, not out	6
Strudwick, b. Eady	1
Extras	11
Total	185

Second Innings: Warner, c. Paton, b. Smith, 64; Foster, b. Windsor, 23; Tyldesley, st. Dodds, b. Windsor, 85; Arnold, b. Windsor, 8; Knight, not out, 45; Bosanquet, not out, 124; extras, 5. Total (for 4 wickets), 354.

Innings declared closed.

Bowling Analysis.

First Innings.

	O.	M.	R.	W		O.	M.	R.	W
Paton	5	1	24	0	Smith	12	0	42	3
Eady	22.2	5	40	3	Windsor	16	3	68	3

Eady delivered 1 no-ball.

Second Innings.

	O.	M.	R.	W		O.	M	R.	W.
Paton	4	9	25	0	Smith	20	0	97	1
Eady	19	4	80	0	Hall	3	0	38	0
Windsor	24	2	96	3	Bailey	3	1	13	0

TASMANIA.

First Innings.

R. Hawson, c. Arnold, b. Bosanquet	29
L. A. Cuff, c. Tyldesley, b. Relf	9
O. Douglas, c. Foster, b. Arnold	38
N. Dodds, c. Rhodes, b. Arnold	24
E. A. Windsor, c. Arnold, b. Rhodes	2
C. J. Eady, b. Rhodes	16
K. Burn, not out...	28
Hale, b. Arnold	9
D. R. Smith, c. Relf, b. Arnold	13
D. Paton, run out	18
K. Bailey, b. Fielder	3
Extras	2
Total	191

Second Innings : Burn, c. Strudwick, b. Foster, 24 ; Hawson, not out, 37 ; Dodds, not out, 2 ; extras, o. Total (for 1 wicket), 63.

Bowling Analysis.

First Innings.

	O.	M.	R.	W.		O.	M.	R.	W.
Arnold	34	15	44	4	Bosanquet ...	11	2	55	1
Fielder	4.1	0	18	1	Rhodes	31	13	52	2
Relf	8	2	20	1					

Second Innings.

	O.	M.	R.	W.		O.	M.	R.	W.
Foster	7	2	34	1	Lilley	2	0	4	0
Warner	6	2	16	0	Knight	2	0	9	0

The return game at Launceston—limited, like the first, to two days—was likewise drawn with scores of 141 and 259 for three wickets to Tasmania and 354 to us. Hayward played a superb innings of 134, but the most noteworthy batting was by Savigny, whose 164 not out was, except for a comparatively easy chance to Lilley at mid-off, quite faultless. He had strokes all round the wicket—being especially strong in the off drive, and he watched the ball closely. Hirst, who had a good bowl at him, told me he was a really high-class batsman. Our long lead on the first innings gave

P

hopes of a victory, but Savigny and Douglas quite upset
all our calculations by putting on 202 for the first wicket
—a feat which not even that famous pair Trumper and
Duff approached.   Douglas, a left-handed batsman, with
all the virtues of a Scotton or a Barlow, was batting over
four hours.   His defence was magnificent, but he entirely
ignored the slow long hop.   His patience was invaluable,

THE CRICKET GROUND AT LAUNCESTON.

but it was, to say the least of it, monotonous. Hirst and
Fielder did most of our bowling, but with much hard
cricket before us I did not think it wise to risk over-
working either Arnold or Rhodes.   Consequently we all
had a bowl, and Tom Hayward showed that he can still
send down a difficult ball, and Knight, just to be in the
fashion, bowled leg-breaks by no means badly.

The Launceston ground is small, but the wicket excellent
and the surroundings perfect.   It was like a bit of Kent,

and everything smelt of England. Finer weather could not have been wished for, and as Friday, January 29th, was a holiday, there was an attendance of over 3,000— not a bad proportion out of a population of 20,000.

Tasmania can boast of many good cricketers, and the form shown in the two matches we played was a great deal better than we had been led to expect. Cricketers like Windsor, Savigny, Dodds, Hawson, and Douglas would strengthen almost any Eleven. Most enjoyable in every way was our stay in the lovely island, and future Teams to Australia should take care to include Tasmania in their programme.

TASMANIA.

First Innings.

J. H. Savigny, c. Hirst, b. Fielder	0
R. Hawson, b. Hirst	0
O. Douglas, b. Fielder	1
L. A. Cuff, b. Hirst	6
N. Dodds, c. Strudwick, b. Fielder...	48
E. James, b. Hirst	4
E. A. Windsor, c. Strudwick, b. Hirst	33
N. R. Westbrook, st. Strudwick, b. Arnold	26
D. R. Smith, b. Hirst	5
A. G. Addison, b. Arnold...	0
E. W. Harrison, not out	7
Byes, 4 ; leg-byes, 6 ; no-ball, 1	11
Total	141

Second Innings : Savigny, not out, 164 ; Douglas, c. Rhodes, b. Hirst, 59 ; Cuff, b. Knight, 15 ; Dodds, st. Strudwick, b. Knight, 2 ; Hawson, not out, 1 ; extras, 18. Total (for 3 wickets), 259.

Bowling Analysis.

First Innings.

	O.	M.	R.	W.		O.	M.	R.	W
Hirst	16	7	37	5	Rhodes	9	2	33	0
Fielder	12	3	44	3	Arnold	11	4	16	2

Hirst delivered 1 no-ball.

Second Innings.

		O.	M.	R.	W.			O.	M.	R.	W.
Hirst		19	8	32	1	Rhodes		11	4	21	0
Strudwick ...		5	2	6	0	Warner		4	0	12	0
Fielder		16	6	29	0	Knight		12	2	34	2
Tyldesley ...		8	1	28	0	Hayward ...		10	4	17	0
Arnold		8	3	22	0	Lilley		5	1	19	0
Drummond ...		5	0	21	0						

ENGLAND.

P. F. Warner, b. Windsor...	4
Hayward, c. Douglas, b. Smith	134
Tyldesley, b. Smith	1
Knight, b. Addison	30
Hirst, c. Cuff, b. Windsor...	51
Arnold, l.b.w., b. Smith	5
Rhodes, run out	39
G. Drummond, b. Smith	1
Lilley, not out	37
Fielder, b. Windsor	23
Strudwick, b. Windsor	21
Byes, 4 ; leg-byes, 3	7
Total	353

Bowling Analysis.

		O.	M.	R.	W.			O.	M.	R.	W.
Smith		28	5	111	4	James		7	0	36	0
Windsor		30	4	106	4	Savigny		2	0	29	0
Addison		10	0	64	1						

CHAPTER XI

THE SECOND MATCH *v.* VICTORIA

THE return voyage from Launceston to Melbourne was a very different affair to that first crossing. The sea was in a far quieter frame of mind, and the *Pateena* was greatly superior to the *Burrumbeet*. It was on Wednesday morning, February 3, that we arrived back again at Menzies' Hotel, and on Friday commenced the return game with Victoria.

The committee of the Melbourne Cricket Club selected this match as an opportunity to try three or four new men, and as a consequence the Victorian side had a somewhat unfamiliar look about it.

The encouragement of new blood is doubtless a very praiseworthy object, but the Melbourne Club would have been paying us something more of a compliment had they not hit on this game to experiment with the young generation. Harry Trott captained the Victorians, and, winning the toss, his side kept us in the field all day.

Neither Fielder nor Relf were able to play on account of minor injuries, Arnold had a troublesome knee, and Hirst was not quite fit. Consequently, the bulk of the work fell on Bosanquet, Braund, and Rhodes.

It was hot with a burning wind, and during the day

we succeeded in dismissing but four of the Victorians for 269 runs. McAlister played a splendid innings of

IN THE FIELD.

133 not out. He gave nothing like a chance, and always seemed to get the ball in the centre of the bat. His cricket was of the quiet rather than the forcible order; but there was a deal of certainty about every stroke, and, though he hit but six fours, his batting was always attractive. For two or three years past McAlister has been the best batsman in the Victorian Eleven, and I am rather surprised that he has not yet appeared in this country, especially as he is a fine field at slip and in the country.

In this long innings of his he gave nothing like a chance; indeed, the only blemish in his display was that he once edged a ball from Rhodes between the wicket-keeper and slip.   McLeod did not play by any means well, but Armstrong's thirty-one was full of good strokes.   Rhodes again got him out.   He bowled against him ten times on this tour and claimed his wicket eight times.   Ransford, a left-hander, shaped very well.   As he is only eighteen, he should have a future before him.   Our fielding was excellent, and not one chance was missed.   For a big match the attendance was miserably poor, scarcely 2,000 people being present.   Perhaps the weather had something to do with this, for, though the sun was not oppressively hot, there was a burning wind blowing.   That it can rain in other countries besides England was proved during the course of this match, for, after a violent duststorm on Friday night, about 9.30 the rain came down in torrents and continued for the best part of twenty-four hours.   Saturday was a blank so far as cricket was concerned.   There was more wet on Sunday and a heavy shower early on Monday morning, but the Melbourne cricket ground is well drained, and, with a strong wind helping, the pitch dried so quickly that play was resumed at 1.45.   The wicket was, naturally enough, very difficult indeed, and Rhodes had another opportunity of demonstrating how unplayable he is on rain-sodden turf.

What a difference rain does make in cricket!   On Friday Rhodes had taken one wicket for forty-nine runs ; on Monday he dismissed five men for another thirteen runs; and so Victoria were all out for 299. When we went in the wicket was as difficult as it could be, and our subsequent total of 248 was a brilliant achievement.   But while giving the batsmen every credit, one must admit that the bowling was not up to the mark, while the fielding was faulty. Harry Trott was of opinion that we would not get a hundred runs with the pitch in the condition it was. Now, a sticky wicket in Australia is a far different thing from an English sticky wicket. In England the ball takes any amount of turn, but it does not as a general rule get straight up in your face as it does in Australia. I got hit five times on the fingers of the left hand and once somewhere in the region of the neck by balls from Laver which came off the pitch with a whip and a fizz that made me wish for two pairs of gloves.

Saunders bowled some good balls, but not a few bad ones, though it is only fair to say that he was suffering from a chill, and was by no means himself.

Stumps were drawn for the day at the end of our innings, but there was more rain in the night, and the wicket next morning was in much the same condition as on the previous day.

Rhodes began to McAlister, and from the very first ball it was obvious that there would be some extraordinary cricket. The third and fourth balls of Rhodes' first over got rid of McAlister and Armstrong, and from the fifth Trott should have been caught at extra slip by Bosanquet. It was a one-handed catch, and for a second the ball seemed to have stuck.

It was hard luck for Rhodes to just miss the hat-trick, a feat he has never yet accomplished, though playing for Yorkshire *v.* Kent a season or two back he obtained the last two wickets with consecutive balls in Kent's first innings, and then dismissed E. W. Dillon with the first ball of the second innings.

Arnold's first two balls each took a wicket, and four
men were out for no runs.   I have but once before seen
that on a scoring-board—namely, on the Belmont ground
at Philadelphia, when J. B. King and P. H. Clark dismissed the first four men in my Eleven without any of us

THE SCORE-BOARD—VICTORIA SECOND INNINGS.

getting a run.   Had Bosanquet caught Trott I do not
believe our opponents would have made ten runs.

Baker, who made three, was missed by Strudwick off
Rhodes before he had scored, and Scott, who made one,
should have been stumped for a duck.   In fact, had
everything come off even ten might have been putting
the total too high !

Saunders was too ill to bat, and the innings, which
lasted forty-five minutes, was over.   This total of fifteen

is by far the lowest ever made in a first class match in Australia, and the third lowest in the world. Oxford University's twelve *v.* M.C.C. still stands as the absolute lowest, and the thirteen of Notts *v.* Yorkshire comes second.

Rhodes and Arnold bowled magnificently, but the batting was terribly feeble. Few—very few Australians —have any idea of playing on a bad wicket. Trumper, of course, is the finest batsman in the world, be the wicket good, moderate, or indifferent, and Duff, Noble, Hopkins, and Hill have very decided methods on bad wickets, but the majority are hopeless. They either slog blindly *at every ball* or play forward as if it were a cast-iron pitch. There is nothing of the " in medio tutissimus ibis " about them. *Rhodes took five wickets for six runs in six overs and a ball, and Arnold four wickets for eight runs.* The Yorkshireman's success on the Melbourne ground was astonishing.

In the first match against Victoria he took five wickets for twenty-six runs, and three wickets for fifty-eight runs. In the second test match he took seven for fifty-six runs and eight for sixty-eight runs, and in this last game six for sixty-two runs and five for six runs, making in all thirty-four wickets for 276 runs, or an average of eight runs a wicket ! In the first match the pitch was perfect ; in the second and third very difficult.

A shower just before we went in caused the ball to cut through, and we won easily by eight wickets. It was a brilliant victory, and a very welcome one, for we had not won a game since the second test match.

VICTORIA.

First Innings.		Second Innings.	
P. McAlister, b. Rhodes	139	c. Strudwick, b. Rhodes	0
C. E. McLeod, st. Strudwick, b. Bosanquet	23	c. and b. Arnold... ...	0
W. W. Armstrong, l.b.w., b. Rhodes ..	31	c. Strudwick, b. Rhodes	0
G. H. S. Trott, c. Arnold, b. Bosanquet	13	c. Arnold, b. Rhodes ..	9
V. Ransford, b. Arnold...	26	c. Rhodes, b. Arnold...	0
F. Laver, c. Foster, b. Rhodes	34	b. Rhodes	1
C. Baker, st. Strudwick, b. Arnold ...	14	st. Strudwick, b. Arnold	3
W. Scott, c. Arnold, b. Rhodes	2	not out	1
W. Carkeek, c. Hirst, b. Rhodes ...	2	c. Bosanquet, b. Arnold	0
H. Fry, c. Warner, b. Rhodes	0	c. Bosanquet, b. Rhodes	0
J. V. Saunders, not out...	0	absent	0
Extras	15	Extra	1
Total	299	Total	15

Bowling Analysis.
First Innings.

	O.	M.	R.	W.		O.	M.	R.	W.
Hirst	10	2	26	0	Rhodes	30	6	62	6
Arnold	26.3	9	61	2	Bosanquet ...	25	3	75	2
Braund	22	6	50	0	Hayward ...	4	1	10	0

Hirst bowled 2 wides and Arnold 1.

Second Innings.

	O.	M.	R.	W.		O.	M.	R.	W.
Rhodes	6.1	3	6	5	Arnold	6	2	8	4

ENGLAND.

First Innings.		Second Innings.	
Tyldesley, b. Saunders...	2	not out...	23
P. F. Warner, c. Saunders, b. McLeod	49	c. Trott, b. Fry	16
Braund, run out	6		
R. E. Foster, st. Carkeek, b. Laver ...	7	not out	1
Hayward, c. McAlister, b. Laver ...	77	run out	26
Knight, c. McAlister, b. Saunders ...	6		
Hirst, c. Laver, b. Saunders	21		
B. J. T. Bosanquet, c. Baker, b. Armstrong	13		
Arnold, not out	17		
Rhodes, b. Laver	5		
Strudwick, c. Ransford, b. Armstrong	13		
Extras	32	Extras	2
Total	248	Total (2 wkts.)	68

Bowling Analysis.
First Innings.

	O.	M.	R.	W.		O.	M.	R.	W.
Saunders... ...	15	3	39	3	Ransford ...	2	0	5	0
Laver	16	1	64	3	Fry	5	1	23	0
Trott	3	0	15	0	Armstrong ...	12.2	3	35	2
McLeod	9	0	35	1					

Saunders bowled 1 wide

Second Innings.

	O.	M.	R.	W.				O.	M.	R.	W.
McLeod	8	0	21	0	Laver	...	...	6	1	9	0
Fry	10	1	24	1	Ransford		...	3	0	12	0

Fry bowled 2 wides.

FALL OF WICKETS.

First Innings of Victoria.

1	2	3	4	5	6	7	8	9	10
65	122	147	205	281	287	290	297	297	297

Second Innings of Victoria.

1	2	3	4	5	6	7	8	9
0	0	0	0	5	12	14	15	15

First Innings of England.

1	2	3	4	5	6	7	8	9	10
6	33	49	102	114	149	185	214	227	248

Second Innings of England.

1	2
26	62

A VISIT TO THE MELBOURNE KENNELS.

CHAPTER XII

THE return with New South Wales was, next to
the all-important test matches, the most interesting game in the latter half of our programme. At
our first meeting at the end of November, it will be
recollected that we won by an innings and ten runs. At
that period the New South Wales batsmen had scarcely
struck form, but with Trumper, Duff, Noble, and
Gregory in the run-getting vein they were at this time,
it was felt that our opponents were very nearly as strong
as a combined Australian Eleven. The weather was
beautifully fine on the first day, but the pitch had, I
think, been slightly over-watered, for Cotter, a fast bowler
with an action very similar to Wilson's, of Worcestershire, made the ball get up very awkwardly and in a
manner altogether foreign to a Sydney wicket in dry
weather. On the other hand, it is not unusual for the
ball to kick a bit at the start of a match at Sydney; at
least, that is what Noble and Hopkins told me, and they
ought to know. In build Cotter is not unlike Jessop,
and as he ran up to the wicket to deliver the ball his
style reminded one forcibly of the Gloucestershire
Captain. From a fast rising ball I was caught at point,
and so badly did things go that five of us were out for

sixty-eight runs. Hirst played superbly for forty-four, but on Cotter going on again he tried to hook a short ball off his head, and was easily caught at short leg. Hirst makes heaps of runs by his famous pull, but it sometimes brings trouble with it. After Hirst had gone Bosanquet hit beautifully, and drove with great power on both sides of the wicket. He was batting an hour and five minutes, and his fifty-four was, up to this period, by far the best innings he had played in the big matches. Howell and Hopkins got some work on the ball from the off, but Bosanquet hit the breaking ball round on the on-side with fine power and pluck. Lilley was batting well when Bosanquet called him for an impossible run. Cotter took five wickets in twelve overs, and well deserved his success, for he certainly bowled very fast. His action is low, but his deliveries have anything but a low trajectory.

New South Wales had lost six wickets for 150 runs when time was called. George Hirst sent down one of his best swervers to C. Gregory, but Relf bowled very short, and Trumper hit him when and where he pleased. The Australian champion was in dazzling form until he hooked a shortish ball to mid-on. His forty-four runs were made in just under half an hour. Braund bowled Mackay with a very good leg-break, and Bosanquet got Noble caught at the wicket in his first over, and Gregory (who shaped indifferently) stumped. Rhodes had gone on at Hirst's end and should have had a wicket, for Gregory was twice missed off him, first by Hirst at mid-off and then by Relf at extra slip. The first was an easy chance, the second rather awkward, the ball coming rather fast and straight at the fields-man's face, but Relf had made so many really fine catches that one expected him to bring off this one.

Hopkins and Kelly made a useful stand after six wickets had gone for 114 runs, and their partnership continued into the second morning. They added ninety runs before Hopkins pulled a ball which came with the bowler's arm into his stumps. Hopkins got his fifty-two in a trifle over an hour, and hit nine fours. From first to last he shaped in thorough form, his only mistake being a difficult chance to Relf at extra slip off Rhodes. The innings eventually realised 232. Rhodes bowled grandly, and with ordinary luck would have obtained five or six wickets. The wicket after luncheon on the first day was perfect, but the Yorkshireman kept a fine length and made the ball come off the pitch with a great deal of life. The ball which beat Bowden was a beauty ; it pitched on the middle and leg stumps and hit the off. There are a few cricketers in England who will persist in saying that Rhodes cannot bowl on a "plumb" wicket. Let me assure them that they are quite wrong. There is only one sort of wicket on which Rhodes is easy to play, and that is the wicket on which any bowler in the world is simple—I mean the slow-paced, true pitch like Trent Bridge, Nottingham, or Melbourne as we saw it on the first day of the recent Victorian match. Hirst took three wickets for sixty-one, and bowled well without being particularly good. Bosanquet, as usual, was a mixture of greatness and mediocrity—but he is very useful. As Duff said : " Bos. is a nuisance ; you never know what he is going to do." The fielding was good, Rhodes, Knight, and Tyldesley especially so. Our second innings started badly, but, as a whole, it was very satisfactory, for though Foster, as well as myself, failed, Hayward got forty-six very well indeed, and Knight batted superbly and at a time of great stress. At six o'clock he was still undefeated with seventy-five to his credit, and the total 255 for six wickets. Hirst again got forty —a punishing and sound display. Once more did short leg catch him, this time off a slow half-volley, which the sturdy Yorkshireman quite mis-timed.

It was a good day's cricket, and left the game in a very interesting state. For a Saturday in Sydney the attendance of 10,000 was poor.

There had been some rain on Sunday, but the wicket was hard when the game was resumed on Monday morning, though there was considerable grass on it. Cotter was unable to bowl or field, as he had fallen on his shoulder in attempting to stop a hard drive at mid-off, and the wrench he sustained prevented him taking any part in the out cricket.

Bosanquet and Knight went on batting, and very valuable their partnership was, resulting in all in an addition of 143 runs. Bosanquet was first out—caught at mid-on from a skier. He made ninety-seven runs in sixty-five minutes, his driving being magnificent. Shortly after resuming his innings on the Monday morning he hit a ball up on the off-side, but there was a misunderstanding between Gregory and Trumper, and the chance was not taken. This was Bosanquet's one and only mistake, and this innings of his must rank as the best he has ever played. The ball was turning a bit —Howell especially got a good deal of work on from the off—but Bosanquet prefers the ball to turn into him than come straight on, and he banged this breaking ball to all quarters of the on-side. Noble could not

M. A. NOBLE.

Q

place his field for him. Three balls in succession would he flick round on the on-side ; the field would gather in that direction, and then the next ball or two would be sent rattling against the off-side boundary. Yes, Bosanquet, you surpassed yourself. I have seen you play a great deal, but you never in all your life batted quite so well as you did on Monday, February 15.

Knight's 104 was, in a totally different style, an equally good innings, and to his patience and judgment on the Saturday afternoon we owed much.

The cut is his great stroke—the genuine late cut behind point, and I do not know of a better exponent of this stroke. He plays it with great power and certainty, and with a wise discretion in picking the right ball. For a first-class batsman Knight is, I think, rather wanting in those on-side strokes which nearly all the great players of the day make so pointed a feature of their play ; but he is a very powerful off-driver, and all the skilful manœuvring of the field did not prevent his scoring freely by this stroke. It was essentially an off-side innings, and a very pleasing one to watch.

The New South Wales men were heavily handicapped by Cotter's absence, but their fielding was magnificent. Noble, Hopkins, Bowden, and Howell bowled well, but Bosanquet made every one appear to be bowling badly.

Trumper and Duff opened the second innings of New South Wales to the bowling of Hirst and Braund. Trumper did not shape in his usual form, and with the first ball of Braund's second over he was clean bowled. The ball worked in quickly from the leg-side and Trumper played back at it. Hirst was making the ball jump up every now and again, and from one of these rising deliveries Duff was caught at short-leg off his hand—32—2—18. Noble and Hopkins added nine runs, and then Lilley caught the N.S.W. captain splendidly, low down, with the left hand. The ball was a slow one, but it swerved a great deal, and Lilley, standing back, only just reached it. Hopkins and Gregory batted freely, though Hopkins was at first rather in trouble with Braund's leg-breaks. The 100 appeared after an hour and twenty minutes, the stroke which sent up three figures being a swinging leg-hit off Bosanquet, who had relieved Hirst. Twenty-two runs came from three overs of Bosanquet, but his fourth over saw Gregory spoon one to short-leg, and from that moment the Old Oxonian carried all before him. He bowled Hopkins and Mackay with the off-breaking leg-break, and had C. Gregory caught at short-leg off a full-pitch. Then Kelly was finely caught and bowled with one hand, and Cotter—who, despite his injured shoulder, pluckily came in—was beautifully caught by Knight at deep square-leg. Howell was last, but before he received a ball Bowden's wicket was thrown down by Hirst from mid-off, and we had won a brilliant victory by 278 runs. For Bosanquet the match was one long triumph, for he scored 168 runs and took eight wickets in twenty-five overs for ninety-six runs. One has to go back to the best days of W. G. Grace, A. G. Steel, Lohmann, and Barnes to find anything better than this.

Braund bowled well, and so did Hirst, while Rhodes kept the runs down and Bosanquet got the wickets. The pitch had worn somewhat, but a total of 300 should not have been out of the question for so powerful a batting side as N.S.W Much, of course, depended on Trumper, Duff, and Noble, for when they fail it is no unusual thing for their companions to follow suit.

Hopkins got over fifty each time, and deserved every run he made, for he used his feet cleverly and drove on both sides of the wicket with fine power. He is a very attractive batsman when he is going.

Our bowling was up to a high standard and, as usual, full of variety. Hirst was good, without being particularly so ; Braund bowled with more life and spin than he had done for some time ; and Rhodes in the first innings was in his finest form.

It is not given to every English team to defeat New South Wales—the champion State of Australia—twice in one and the same season. It was a great win, earned by all-round cricket of the best description, and our opponents were generous enough to say that they were out-played at every point.

ENGLAND.

First Innings.		Second Innings.	
P. F. Warner, c. Noble, b. Cotter	0	b. Bowden	8
Hayward, c. Kelly, b. Cotter	5	b. Cotter	46
Tyldesley, c. Trumper, b. Cotter	17	l.b.w., b. Cotter	28
R. E. Foster, l.b.w., b. Bowden	19	c. Bowden, b. Cotter	4
Braund, b. Hopkins	5	c. S. Gregory, b. Noble	32
Knight, b. Howell	23	c. Bowden, b. Howell..	104
Hirst, c. Noble, b. Cotter	44	c. Noble, b. Hopkins ..	40
B. J. T. Bosanquet, c. Howell, b. Hopkins	54	c. Howell, b. Noble	114
Lilley, run out	8	c. Howell, b. Bowden	2
Relf, c. Kelly, b. Cotter	1	c. Noble, b. Howell	21
Rhodes, not out	2	not out	49
Wide, 1 ; byes, 10 ; leg-bye, 1	12	Extras	13
Total	190	Total	461

Bowling Analysis.

First Innings.

	O.	M.	R.	W.		O.	M.	R.	W.
Cotter	14	3	44	5	Bowden	12	0	34	1
Hopkins	18	4	65	2	Howell	8	2	35	1

Hopkins bowled 1 wide.

Second Innings.

	O.	M.	R.	W.		O.	M.	R.	W.
Cotter	11	0	56	3	Noble	21	1	92	2
Bowden	39	6	135	2	Hopkins	26.1	5	85	2
Howell	23	3	80	1					

Noble bowled 1 wide and 1 no-ball and Hopkins 2 wides.

NEW SOUTH WALES.

First Innings.		Second Innings.	
C. Gregory, b. Hirst	1	c. Rhodes, b. Bosanquet	8
V. Trumper, c. Hayward, b. Hirst	44	b. Braund	5
M. A. Noble (capt.), c. Lilley, b. Bosanquet	36	c. Lilley, b. Hirst	11
J. R. Mackay, b. Braund	2	b. Bosanquet	9
S. E. Gregory, st. Lilley, b. Bosanquet	20	c. Rhodes, b. Bosanquet	24
R. A. Duff, run out	10	c. Relf, b. Hirst	18
A. J. Hopkins, b. Rhodes	52	b. Bosanquet	56
J. J. Kelly, not out	33	c. and b. Bosanquet	1
A. J. Bowden, b. Rhodes	0	run out	5
A. Cotter, b. Rhodes	16	c. Knight, b. Bosanquet	3
W. P. Howell, c. Tyldesley, b. Hirst	8	not out	0
Byes, 4 ; leg-byes, 3 ; wides, 3	10	Extra	1
Total	232	Total	141

Bowling Analysis.

First Innings.

	O.	M.	R.	W.		O.	M.	R.	W.
Hirst	16.3	3	61	3	Braund	10	0	30	1
Relf	4	0	30	0	Rhodes	19	7	50	3
Bosanquet	14	2	51	2					

Bosanquet bowled 1 and Rhodes 2 wides.

Second Innings.

	O.	M.	R.	W.		O.	M.	R.	W.
Hirst	11	0	37	2	Rhodes	10	3	20	0
Braund	10	2	38	1	Bosanquet	9	0	45	6

After the N.S.W. match it had been arranged that we should play a Western District Fifteen at Bathurst, and accordingly to Bathurst we had to go. The game, of course, ended in a draw—these two-day contests always do—but we met Marsh, the famous Aboriginal bowler, about whose delivery we had heard and read so much. Unlike Henry, the Queensland black, Marsh is sturdily built ; but, equally unlike Henry, his action

MR. SHERIDAN'S PICNIC PARTY ON SYDNEY HARBOUR.

is most unsatisfactory. Indeed, in my humble opinion, he throws three balls an over, and the other three would scarcely satisfy an English umpire. Marsh has once or twice, I believe, represented New South Wales, but in recent years Noble has taken up a firm attitude by refusing to play Marsh in any inter-State

MARSH, THE ABORIGINAL BOWLER.

game. Hence he is often urged by the Sydney barrackers to "put on Marsh."

Crockett and Curran, I am told, are the only two umpires out here who have had the courage to no-ball Marsh, and the former, rumour says, has stated that he will always call him unless his method undergoes a very radical alteration.

When he was in Australia two years ago Mr. MacLaren objected to Marsh's playing against his team on the ground that his fast bowling might injure some of his men ; but, whatever his pace then, there was no physical danger to be anticipated as we saw him at Bathurst, for he bowled (!) about the pace of Jack Hearne, with an occasional fast ball.

Some of my Team wished me to object to Marsh on the ground of his unfair delivery, but I dissented from them, holding—and, I think, rightly so—that the fairness or unfairness of his delivery was a question for the umpires.

As it happened, both umpires thought it wiser to pass his action, and their attitude probably saved a lot of unpleasantness and fuss. It was a holiday game, and they did not wish to spoil the pleasure of it—but I was rather surprised to hear one of them say that Marsh's action was absolutely above suspicion.

I shall probably never see Marsh again, so think not that I am in any way prejudiced against him, though he did knock down my middle stump.

The Western District XV. were a long way the strongest odds Team we have yet met on this tour, and had the best of things at the finish, though, as I have hinted, our cricket was a good deal lacking in energy. Full score:

BATHURST XV.

First Innings.

C. Gregory, not out	139
R. N. Hickson, c. Strudwick, b. Braund	4
G. Payne, b. Braund	14
Edwards, c. Strudwick, b. Relf	13
A. Diamond, c. Tyldesley, b. Braund	26
W. H. Lipscombe, b. Braund	0
A. J. Bowden, c. Foster, b. Hayward	15
E. Kenna, c. Strudwick, b. Bosanquet	18
R. L. Turner, c. Braund, b. Hayward	0
O. Smith, st. Strudwick, b. Bosanquet	5
Dr. Kenna, l.b.w., b. Bosanquet	0
Allman, st. Strudwick, b. Relf...	1
K. McPhillamy, run out	4
A. Sims, b. Relf	0
J. Marsh, c. Braund, b. Relf	0
Extras	9
Total	248

Second Innings : Hickson, st. Strudwick, b. Relf, 82 ; Edwards, b. Relf, 19 ; Payne, b. Bosanquet, 43 ; E. Kenna, not out, 2 ; extras, 5. *Total (for 3 wickets), 151.

* Innings declared closed.

Bowling Analysis.

First Innings.

	O.	M.	R.	W.			O.	M.	R.	W.
Fielder	17	2	40	0	Hirst		1	0	4	0
Relf...	14.4	8	25	4	Braund		23	3	77	4
Bosanquet ...	12	0	62	2	Hayward ...		7	1	31	2

Second Innings.

	R.	W.		R.	W.
Fielder	20	0	Hayward	25	0
Relf	38	2	Bosanquet	0	1
Braund	54	0			

ENGLAND XII.

First Innings.		Second Innings.	
Hirst, c. Diamond, b. Marsh	2	not out	13
Hayward, c. Allman, b. Kenna	59		
Tyldesley, c. Diamond, b. Allman ...	5	b. McPhillamy	18
Lilley, b. Allman	7	b. Marsh	16
Knight, c. E. Kenna, b. Marsh	19	b. Allman	0
P. F. Warner, b. Marsh	5		
Relf, l.b.w., b. Kenna	39	not out	28
R. E. Foster, not out	19	b. E. Kenna	30
B. J. T. Bosanquet, c. Edwards, b. Kenna	6		
Braund, c. Hickson, b. McPhillamy ...	1	b. E. Kenna	1
Fielder, b. Marsh	4		
Strudwick, b. Marsh	0		
Extras	10	Extras	9
Total	176	Total (5 wkts.)	115

Bowling Analysis.

First Innings.

	R.	W.		R.	W.
Marsh	55	5	McPhillamy	24	1
Allman	59	2	Bowden	6	0
Kenna	22	3			

Second Innings.

	R.	W.		R.	W.
Allman	26	1	E. Kenna	24	2
Marsh	36	1	Bowden	7	0
McPhillamy	13	1			

It would be impossible to write any frank account of the incidents of the tour without dealing with the question of umpires, which at one time looked like assuming a rather painful degree of importance. Perhaps there was no question connected with the tour which was more completely misrepresented in the Press reports, and I am glad, at any rate, to have this opportunity of giving the true story of everything that occurred. In looking back upon the discussion, which for a few days raged so furiously about my luckless head, it is at least some satisfaction to remember that the Australian Captain was throughout the whole proceedings entirely at one with me in all that I was fighting for. Indeed, it would be impossible for any two captains to work together with greater unanimity than that which fortunately characterised all the relations between Noble and myself.

In England, when the test matches are under discussion, it is the theory that the names of the leading umpires are put into a bag, and that the two drawn are selected for duty. This, I say, is the theory; but in practice things work out very differently. For this lucky-bag policy is qualified by a rule that either captain can object to any umpire after his name has been picked out; so that practically, if the process of objection is carried on beyond a single name, what it amounts to is that the two captains select the umpires on their own responsibility. I believe that, when the last Australian Team was touring in England (although the theory of the " bag " still survived), MacLaren and Darling practically selected the umpires in the exercise of their own judgment.

And now for Australia. When we got to Sydney for the first test match, we found that the Australian team was being selected by Clem Hill, Noble, and Johns.

This council of three was indeed dining at the Australia Hotel two days before the match for the express purpose of picking the team, and we ourselves were at the same hotel. I was in the hall when they came out from dinner, and Noble came up to me, and said, " Now, how about the umpires? Won't you choose them for yourself? " I replied, " No ; I want these test matches to be played out without the slightest possibility of trouble or criticism of any kind. We must have the best umpires." I added, " If we can choose one each, may I have Crockett?" Noble replied, " Of course ; and won't you choose the other, too ? " To

CROCKETT.

this I replied that Noble must choose the other himself, and he chose Jones.

At Melbourne precisely the same thing occurred, except that we then chose Crockett and Argall, and when it came to the third test match Noble proposed the same pair again. So far, so good. Everything had passed off most pleasantly, and a better pair of umpires it would be impossible to desire.   Crockett, in my opinion, is one of the best umpires in the world, and Argall was equally satisfactory.   After the New South Wales match, however, Noble came into our dressing-room and, alluding to the fourth test match, said, "Now what about the umpires next time?" I said that I did not think we could do better than stick to Crockett and Argall.   Noble replied, "How about Curran?"   I said that Curran was a very good umpire, but that he had never stood in a test match, and, having regard to the highly satisfactory umpiring that we had had up to then, I thought we had better stick to the old pair.   To this Noble heartily consented, and matters were left as though settled.   Two days later, however, I received a letter from the New South Wales Association saying that the Association had held a meeting to decide upon the umpires for the fourth test match ; and, understanding that I preferred Crockett, they had appointed Giltinan to stand at the other end.   In answer to this letter, I at once wrote as follows :

HOTEL AUSTRALIA, SYDNEY,
Feb. 16, 1904.

DEAR SIR,—Many thanks for your letter of to-day's date.   In the previous test matches which have been played this season, Mr. Noble and myself have invariably selected the umpires for the test match, the arrangement being that the names of all umpires in first-class cricket in Australia should be put in a hat, and two drawn from it, either captain having the right to object to any name. This is the custom adopted in the test matches in England, and it has been found to work admirably. Mr. Noble spoke to me at the conclusion of yesterday's

ARGALL.

match, and we both agreed that Crockett and Argall were the umpires we desired for the fourth test match. These two men umpired both at Melbourne and Adelaide, and gave every satisfaction. I object strongly to Mr. Giltinan being appointed umpire on the grounds of inexperience and the lack of necessary ability. I question the right of the Association to appoint either umpire for a test match, and, with due respect, I must decline to accept the Association's nominee. The question of umpires is solely for Mr. Noble and myself. I should be glad for a reply to this letter at your earliest convenience, as I am leaving for Bathurst on Thursday morning. Should there be any extra expense incurred in bringing Crockett and Argall to Sydney, the M.C.C. could meet it. My own desire, and Mr. Noble's also, is to have the two best umpires in Australia, and we both agree that Crockett and Argall are the best obtainable.

I am, yours truly,

P. F. WARNER,

Captain M.C.C. Team.

This letter, which seemed to me entirely moderate and just in tone, upset the Association extraordinarily. Their Chairman said it was " highly discourteous and in very bad form," and the Treasurer pronounced it " impolitic and impertinent." They immediately gave my letter away to the Press, and a storm of newspaper comment followed, echoes of which, I believe, reached the English newspapers, inevitably blown into exaggerated shapes by the ocean winds. In comment upon the course taken by the Association, I need only say that in England, if I write a private letter to the Committee of the M.C.C., they do not immediately hand it over to the first reporter they meet ; and that besides this, as affecting my general position, I maintain that

R

the New South Wales Association had no standing in the matter ; that custom ordained that the umpires should be appointed by the captains, or if not that, that they should be chosen by chance ; and that the Association was entirely stepping outside the limits of its own authority in interfering in the matter. I had no objection to Giltinan, except on the ground that he had not the experience necessary for a test match, and perhaps I may add that he had not the temperament either. In a match of this importance great judgment and calmness are required, and these qualities only accrue to an umpire at the cost of much experience. After many words the Association withdrew Giltinan as their candidate, but forwarded me a list of other umpires from whom they said the umpire to stand in the fourth test match must be picked from a bag in the presence of the Secretary of the Association—a proviso which certainly seemed to imply a sort of slur upon Noble and myself. Matters were thus rather at a deadlock, and a meeting of the Association was held to try to smooth things over. As the result of that meeting they wrote to Mr. Murdoch, asking him whether the method that Noble and I had adopted in choosing the umpires was the method obtaining in England. This was no doubt intended as a concession to the situation, and on Mr. Murdoch replying that our method was practically the English method, the Association consented that Crockett and Argall should be appointed after all. The whole thing thus blew over, and the situation remained precisely where it was at the start. In the meantime, however, much unnecessary annoyance had been caused, and I may say that nothing during the whole course of the tour gave me more personal anxiety than the worry arising out of these counter-arguments. Still, I was fighting for a principle, and I did not think it right to spare myself. I stoutly maintain that the umpires ought to be chosen by the captains, and particularly in a case of such unanimity as that which existed between Noble and myself during the whole of the tour.

CHAPTER XIII

THE FOURTH TEST MATCH

THE fourth test match, looked forward to by thousands in every quarter of the globe, began at Sydney on February 26, and was destined to be a memorable match in the annals of English cricket, for at twenty minutes to six on the afternoon of March 3, Hirst bowled down Cotter's wicket, and after many long years of waiting and disappointment, the prestige of English cricket was restored. I suppose every man has a great moment in his life, and this was certainly mine.

I had said before I started out on our campaign that, if we succeeded in bringing home the ashes, I should be content if I never made another run in first class cricket, and lo! the popularly-unexpected had happened, the croaking of the critics had been set at nought, and my own confidence in the soundest set of cricketers that ever took the field had been abundantly justified. The rubber was won: the "ashes" were in my cricket-bag: the hour of my *Nunc Dimittis* had arrived. As long as I live, whatever lies ahead of me, I shall look back to the evening of March 3, 1904, as the golden evening of my cricket career, an evening of memories never to be repeated, but never to be swept away.

The wicket was never quite easy on the first day. It was a little too slow to be exactly difficult, but the ball turned a good deal, and Trumble occasionally made one jump up. There had been a great deal of rain before Friday, but the wicket was covered on Thursday, and the pitch, to all appearances, was hard and true when the game started. Had the weather kept quite fine, batting first would, I think, have been a disadvantage; but the glass was falling, the sky unsettled looking, and

P. F. WARNER AND HAYWARD GOING IN.

a captain would have been taking an enormous risk in sending his opponents in.

The last English Captain in Australia found the Sydney ground a paradise for run-getting; not so myself, for in the seven innings I played there I only made double figures twice, *and no fewer than three ducks!* This time Noble bowled me with one well up, which, for want of a better term, I will say "flopped" in the air. Tyldesley was playing nicely when Gregory

caught him at extra cover from a hard hit. Hayward
was out rather unluckily, the ball bouncing off Kelly's
pads to short slip, and Foster was splendidly caught at
short leg from a hard hit. In getting his runs Foster
had shaped in quite his old form. Four wickets had
gone for sixty-six runs. But Braund was in a determined mood, and Knight batted perfectly. The bowling
was very good, Noble and Trumble especially taking a
lot of playing, but Knight's defence was impregnable,
and Braund, while stopping the good balls, occasionally
made a powerful drive, though the outfield was too dead
to allow the ball to travel quickly. Several runs were
smartly made, and things were going well for us when
Trumble caught Braund low down at slip with his left
hand. His thirty-nine was an invaluable innings.
Hirst made several fine strokes, and a few lucky ones,
before he dragged a ball into his wicket, and Bosanquet
fell to Hopkins with the last delivery of the day,
207—7—12. Not a bad score by any means, considering the wicket. Let me be quite understood. The
wicket was not really difficult ; it was a little too slow
for that ; but the ball was always turning, and one or
two deliveries kicked up rather awkwardly. Noble has,
I venture to think, never bowled better in his life. His
length was as accurate as Trumble's, and with that
difficult flight of his and that quick break back required
a lot of watching. So accurate a length did he and
Trumble bowl that they were very seldom hooked
round on the on-side. The fielding was splendid, and
no one better than Noble himself at point. Knight was
not out sixty-four—a great innings, and quite faultless,
with the exception of a hard chance of caught and
bowled to Trumble's right hand.

G. H. HIRST.

Our last three wickets added forty-two runs on the second morning, Lilley playing a bright innings, and scoring twenty-four out of twenty-nine. Knight carried out his bat for seventy, made in four hours and a quarter, and it would be difficult to over-estimate the value of his wonderful patience and skill. He hit six fours, and was as strong as ever in the off drive.

There had been no rain in the night, and the wicket was appreciably faster and truer—and, an important point this—the outfield was again at something like its normal pace.

Sixteen runs were scored by Trumper and Duff before lunch from Hirst and Braund, the Yorkshireman only just missing bowling both batsmen with his famous "swervers." Afterwards Braund had Trumper in difficulties, and at twenty-eight he beat him, the ball coming in quickly from leg and upsetting the wicket after hitting Trumper on the pad. It was a somewhat similar ball to the one with which Braund bowled the great batsman in the New South Wales match. Trumper played back, and the pace of the ball off the pitch beat him. Hill joined Duff, and between interruptions caused by rain runs came fairly quickly from Duff's bat. Rhodes bowled instead of Braund, but Duff got ten off his first over. Then Duff was very badly cut over by Hirst, and soon after was bowled by Arnold, who had gone on at Rhodes' end after the left-hander had sent down a couple of overs. Duff had batted very attractively, though he was once or twice rather lucky in his strokes on the leg side off Hirst. After Hirst had bowled twelve very good overs he gave way to Rhodes, who soon got McAlister splendidly caught at point, standing close up and rather behind the wicket, by Arnold. The ball came quickly off the bat, and Arnold caught it with his right hand fully extended. This was at seventy-two, and at ninety-seven Braund bowled Hopkins with a magnificent ball, and a minute or two later caught Hill at slip at the second attempt. Hill was at the wickets for an hour and a half, but did not shape as well as usual. In a bad light, against which there were several appeals, McLeod and Kelly played out time.

I have described the cricket, for clearness' sake, as though it had been running an uninterrupted course, but as a matter of fact there had been many interruptions. Rain—at one time heavy, at another a fine misty drizzle, very wetting if not very violent—had caused several cessations, and with the score at thirty-five for one wicket, there was an interval of eighty minutes, which unfortunately set the crowd off its balance. Indeed, the consequences of that delay might well lead one to believe that the big cricket of the world is becoming very serious. This is what might have happened that afternoon. I can imagine an official rushing to the telephone and ringing up the War Minister. Across the wire comes :

" Send troops."

" What for ? "

" International match now on. Crowd on hill armed to the teeth with umbrellas, bottles, melon skins, and rude language, advancing determinedly on wicket. Three policemen and groundman's dog doing good work. Umpires Crockett and Argall retreating to the mountains."

This is what might have been. This is what it will certainly come to : " A cable has been received stating that the English Cricket Team has left London for

Australia accompanied by complete Army Corps. General French is in command, and the opinion is freely expressed that this time, at any rate, the cricketers will be adequately protected. Several batteries of the new Maxim gun go out with the troops, and they are expected very effectually to sweep the hill on the Sydney ground whence in the past so many onslaughts on the players and umpires have issued."

Seriously, a portion of the cricket on the Saturday proceeded under police protection, for it was thought necessary to station several constables inside the fence, because it was feared that a section of the crowd would rush the ground. Bottles were thrown on to the cycle-track which runs round the ground, and soon the fringe of the playing area was littered with broken glass. The ground staff were sent out with sacks to clear this up, and then there was more bottle-throwing, yelling, and insulting remarks.

The trouble arose through the umpires thinking that the rain had not sufficiently stopped to allow of the game proceeding. Many quite unbiased persons thought that they ought to have ordered the game to proceed at least twenty minutes before they did; but my own opinion is that there was always a slight rain falling, and that Crockett and Argall were only acting in a scrupulously fair manner in the attitude they took up. Mind you, that is my own personal view; I do not say I am right, and it is no province of mine to defend the umpires. They are the sole judges of fair or unfair play, fitness of light, weather, &c. I never saw either Crockett or Argall during the wait which lasted an hour and twenty minutes; yet many of the crowd thought that it was my fault that play was not in pro-

gress. Coming after the umpire dispute, the ordinary
"larrikin" had it firmly screwed in the back of his
ignorant skull that I had "squared" the umpires!
Indeed, I received two anonymous letters to that effect
next morning! Then when play did start they yelled
and shouted at every ball—and there were 35,000 people
looking on. They chanted "Crock," "Crock," "Crock,"
advised the umpires to get ready their coffins, and inquired "How much did you pay them, Warner?" Then
they tried to balk Rhodes by shouting "One, two,
three!" in time with the Yorkshireman's stride up to
the wickets, though this probably disconcerted the batsman more than the bowler. Yes; they are a lovely
crowd at Sydney, and anyone who has taken part in a
test match there may consider himself thoroughly salted
and fit to play before an audience from the infernal
regions. As Albert Knight says: "The howling of the
crowd reminds me of the dog Cerberus barking at the
gates of Hell!" But some excuse may be found in that
the delay must have been very exasperating to people to
whom Saturday is their only chance of watching cricket.

To return to the course of the day's play, the wicket
after the first shower of rain—which occurred when
Trumper and Duff had scored twenty-one runs—and to
the end of the day was very fast indeed, the ball coming
off the pitch ike lightning. But though so fast it was
true, and our opponents are accustomed to these extra-
fast wickets. Perhaps you will think I am prejudiced;
then, if you do not believe me, ask any member of the
M.C.C. Team; and if you still think that they too are
unduly influenced, well, ask Noble, or Trumble, or
Trumper when you next see them. Braund bowled
better than I have ever seen him, keeping a beautiful

length just outside or on the leg stump, and making the ball nip quickly off the pitch, while his fast ball came about once an over, and pitched on the wicket, instead of that wildly erratic ball which he used to send down during the earlier part of the tour. Braund, indeed, had been an altogether different bowler during the past fortnight.

Arnold was very quick off the pitch, and occasionally kept low. He again got Clem Hill feeling for that off ball with the happiest results for us. Hirst did not get a wicket, but he bowled a dozen exceptionally good overs. He is not the bowler in Australia he is in England—his swerve is less pronounced—but he did not have the best of luck. Duff's cricket was very attractive, wristy, free, and powerful, and he would probably have made more runs had he not been badly cut over by Hirst.

On the third day, Monday, February 29th, not a ball could be bowled on account of the rain, and, indeed, no play was attempted until ten minutes past four on the Tuesday. Those who have not seen the extraordinary drying powers of the Sydney wicket will doubtless think that I have come under the spell of a De Rougemont when I tell you that, even after the deluge of the previous day, the wicket was quite hard on the top, except for a quarter of an inch of what I can call nothing else but slime. This Bulli soil is wonderful in its resistance to wet. You may put a piece of Bulli into a bucket of water for a week, and at the end of that time it will be practically as hard as when it went in and very little moisture will have permeated. This Bulli is like wood, and the groundman at Sydney compared it with a wood-paved street. The heaviest rain apparently cannot enter into its vitals. Deeper than an inch I defy the water to go. The pitch at two o'clock on this fourth day was under water ; the moment the rain stopped the water ran off. The wet does not run *through the Bulli ;* it runs off it on either side of the pitch, which is slightly higher than the rest of the ground.

When play was started Arnold and Rhodes took up the bowling, and in three-quarters of an hour the remaining five wickets fell for seventeen runs. It was a miserable display of batting, for the ball never turned, but simply cut through. Rhodes took three wickets and Arnold two. Kelly was caught at extra slip, McLeod clean bowled with a delivery which came with Rhodes' arm, Trumble caught at the wicket, Gregory at extra slip from a wretched stroke, and Cotter at third man from a mis-hit. Noble was not out six. Our bowling throughout this innings was better than I have ever seen it. Rhodes and Arnold were the most successful, but it would be difficult to say whether they bowled better than Braund and Hirst.

On that wicket eighty or ninety, instead of seventeen, would not have been an impossibility. *The ball, I repeat, did not turn.* It came quickly off the pitch, and occasionally "cocked" up a bit—at least Arnold did. Rhodes bowled McLeod with one that went with his arm—a not unusual ball of his on a "plumb" wicket— but he did not turn the ball back. Now, be a wicket ever so slightly sticky, Rhodes, more perhaps than any other living bowler, can make the ball break. Here he did nothing, and in this one finds convincing proof that the wicket was not difficult.

Arnold seemed to me to be bowling faster than usual,

and two or three deliveries of his went quickly with his arm and jumped a little. No—it was not the wicket that got Australia out; it was bad batting *and* good bowling. Mind you, the pitch *was not absolutely* "*plumb*"—the wet surface was drying every minute— and it is during the hour or two when it is drying that a batsman has to fear the Sydney wicket; but it was nothing like what one would imagine from the score.

The light roller was put on between the innings, and I altered the usual order, sending in Foster with Hayward instead of going in myself. My reasons were twofold. First, I thought Foster more likely to force the game than I was on that wicket; secondly, I had been quite out of luck going in No. 1 at Sydney, and Foster latterly had been equally unfortunate at No. 4. Therefore I decided that we should change places. They call me a lucky Captain; perhaps I am. Anyhow, the alteration was, in both cases, a complete success. The anxious hour was ahead of us, one in which it was anticipated we might easily have lost three or four wickets. But Foster and Hayward played superbly. The wicket was drying every moment. For the first ten minutes the ball more or less cut through; for the next half-hour it turned a good deal, though slowly; then for the last twenty minutes quickly. That first partnership of fifty runs was worth untold gold. Trumble ought to have been more difficult than he was, but he seemed a little off his length. The two batsmen had some luck—a stroke or two going between the wicket-keeper and slip—but they deserved their good fortune.

I have read somewhere, in the *Daily Express*, I think, that C. B. Fry considers that Hayward at his best is never worth more than thirteen runs on a bad wicket.

Mr. Fry should really not make these rash statements. Against Victoria at Melbourne, and now in this game, Hayward played a great game under conditions which gave the bowler every chance to distinguish himself. Next day Hayward continued to bat superbly; so watchful and strong, his defence was of the finest. Braund, too, was very good, and Hirst made some fine drives, but an occasional shower prevented the wicket from becoming *really* difficult until the last half-hour of the day's play. Up to half-past five we were going strongly, but in the last twenty minutes or so Hayward, Hirst, Bosanquet, and Lilley were dismissed.

And then came one of those incidents which seem inseparable from a tour in Australia. You will recollect the law laid down by the M.C.C. *re* the preparation of wickets. It runs like this :

" The ground shall not be rolled, covered, mown, watered, or beaten during a match, *except before the commencement of each innings and of each day's play.*"

Now the first condition under which Marylebone consented to send out a team to Australia was that *all matches should be played under M.C.C. rules of cricket.*

The Australians accepted this condition, and I, at all events, thought that that clause would avoid all trouble.

But trouble was about; for it seems that it is the custom in Australia to roll the wicket for ten minutes at the end of a day's play *if there has been rain at any time during that day.*

During the second test match at Melbourne I found the groundman at the close of the day's cricket (there had been rain during that day) preparing to roll the

THE FOURTH TEST MATCH.

Stand for the last wicket. Warner hits a four.

wicket, we being in possession of the wicket at the time
with five or six men out. I objected, but Noble and
Trumble urged that the custom had obtained all over
Australia for ten years, and that it was so much of a
custom as to be practically a law. I argued "that the
Australians had consented to play under M.C.C. rules,
and that there was nothing in those rules which allowed
of a wicket being rolled at
the end of a day's play."

But Noble and Trumble
were obdurate, so I con-
sented, under protest, to
the wicket being rolled.

COTTER.

Now let me clearly put
forward the facts as they
happened in this fourth
test match. At the end
of Wednesday's cricket,
when we had scored 154
for nine wickets, the
groundman brought out
the heavy roller. I told
him I wanted the light,
and he replied that Noble
had ordered the heavy
roller to be put on. I
claimed, however, that as Captain of the side in possession of the wicket it rested with me.

I had given way at Melbourne on the question
of the actual rolling, and *that the wicket was to be
rolled at the end of the day's play in the event of
rain during that day I distinctly understood;* but that
the Captain of the in side would not be allowed to

S 2

select the roller he desired never occurred to me for a moment.

Noble argued that the custom had grown up because by adopting it the element of luck was eliminated as far as possible. My answer to this was that however it might so act in certain cases—*e.g.*, for the purpose of keeping a wicket good—in this particular instance it tended in quite a contrary direction. Look at it from our point of view !

At the end of an innings a-piece we had gained a strong lead by superior cricket under conditions which did not unduly favour either side.

Then our second innings—that is to say, nine wickets of it—was played on a far from easy pitch, which the Australians proposed I should roll out into a good one for them. I told Noble that I could not imagine a case at cricket which would tend more *not* to eliminate the element of luck than this one. In the end I gained my point ; but the whole thing only showed how absolutely necessary it is to have all the conditions, customs, rules, &c., applying to test matches, or any other matches, in black and white before a ball is bowled. It would save an untold amount of worry and bother to a Captain.

The weather on the Wednesday night was beautifully fine, with a strong, drying wind, and no one would have recognised the wicket next morning. It was hard and dry—a good batsman's wicket. I did not have any roller on at all, though I noticed that one of the London evening papers remarked " that the wicket was still difficult : but Rhodes and Warner scored freely before the effect of the roller had worn off !" which is only another instance of the many inaccurate statements the cable was guilty of throughout this tour.

My reason for not having the roller on was that I thought that a double rolling might counterbalance anything that Rhodes and myself might put on for the last wicket. I believe my judgment was sound, as the result proved ; and, at any rate, when Rhodes and I went on batting, we added fifty-five runs on this good, true wicket. You could play forward or you could play back—just a nice easy pace—the only difficulty was that the ball sometimes came at different paces. The Australians were set 329 to win—a hard task against our bowlers, but not by any means an impossible one. Indeed, I know now that the Australians themselves thought that they had the best of chances ; and well they might, for after the heavy roller had been on the wicket rolled out better and faster than ever, and had they not the inimitable Trumper, the brilliant Duff, the versatile Hill, and the determined and skilful Noble on their side? But Arnold, Hirst, Braund, Rhodes, and Bosanquet never bowled better than they did on the afternoon of March 3rd, 1904, and they were backed up with splendid fielding, Lilley surpassing himself behind the stumps. Finally, we were all fired with the zeal of battle and urged on by that splendid enthusiasm which had carried us through many long months.

There was but ten minutes' batting before lunch, McAlister and Duff scoring 7 runs. After lunch Hirst bowled McAlister with a beautiful swerving ball, and though Hill and Duff made a short stand the bowling always seemed to be on top of the batting. Braund was bowling very well indeed, but as the batsmen stayed together Arnold was brought on, and in his first over clean bowled Duff. The ball was well pitched up and swerved from the leg stump on to the middle and off. Trumper made a fine stroke or two, but another " swerver " had him palpably l.b.w.

The Worcestershire professional did not take another wicket; but those who know what the moral effect of the cheap dismissal of Trumper and Duff means realise how great his share was in our final triumph.

Following my almost invariable custom, I put Bosanquet on to bowl a quarter of an hour before the tea interval, and in a couple of overs he had dismissed Hill and Gregory, so that at four o'clock five wickets were down for seventy-six runs.

Hopkins, McLeod, Trumble, and Kelly could not look at Bosanquet, who, at one time, had five wickets for twelve runs, and though Noble and Cotter made one last gallant effort twenty minutes before time, the match was over and England had won by 157 runs.

Beyond everything else the feature of the cricket was Bosanquet's bowling. Except when Rhodes and Arnold put Victoria out for fifteen, nothing more startling was done with the ball during the tour.

Unkind people have said ere this that I " ran " Bosanquet into this Team because he was a friend of mine, but on his day he rivalled Hirst and Braund as an all-round cricketer, and I repeat that when he gets a length he is, on hard wickets, about the most difficult bowler there is. The Sydney wicket suited him better than any other, for whatever may have been the experience of former tours, we at any rate always found the Sydney wicket the fastest; and the faster the wicket the better he bowls.

Certain critics in England have suggested that we

THE FOURTH TEST MATCH.

Hill and Trumper batting, Braund bowling.

owed our success more to good fortune than to skill.   I
protest that is a most unfair and ungenerous suggestion. We won the rubber
fairly and squarely by
superior cricket, and our
victory could be attributed
in no way to fluke or
chance. On the contrary,
no match has ever been
more distinctly won on
sheer merit. We played
over the Australians in
every department of the
game, except, perhaps
fielding, in which the
honours were pretty well
divided. In batting and
bowling we showed to
great advantage, and that
on the form of the five
days' play the stronger side
won the match even the
most ardent Australian
barracker could not deny.
What luck there was went
to our opponents, for in
their second innings the
wicket was a great deal
easier than at any time
during the game.

B. J. T. BOSANQUET.

*If the pitch had not been dry and in good condition
Rhodes and Arnold would certainly have been the first
bowlers, as it was Hirst and Braund began.*

At the conclusion of the match we had a great reception from the spectators, who cheered as heartily as if it had been at Lords or the Oval.

Next day I received between fifty and sixty telegrams from every part of the world—from the West Indies—from South Africa—from America—from New Zealand—in fact the sun did not set in the Cable offices which flashed their messages of congratulations and good wishes.

And so we brought back the prize for which we had striven so hard, and won—I know I can say it—so deservedly.

ENGLAND.

First Innings.		Second Innings.	
P. F. Warner, b. Noble	0	not out	31
Hayward, c. McAlister, b. Trumble ...	18	l.b.w., b. Trumble ...	52
Tyldesley, c. Gregory, b. Noble	16	b. Cotter	5
R. E. Foster, c. McAlister, b. Noble	19	c. Noble, b. Hopkins...	27
Knight, not out	70	c. McAlister, b. Cotter	9
Braund, c. Trumble, b. Noble	39	c. McLeod, b. Hopkins	19
Hirst, b. Noble	25	c. Kelly, b. McLeod ...	18
B. J. T. Bosanquet, b. Hopkins	12	c. Hill, b. McLeod ...	7
Arnold, l.b.w., b. Hopkins	0	c. Kelly, b. Noble ...	0
Lilley, c. Hopkins, b. Trumble	24	b. McLeod	6
Rhodes, st. Kelly, b. Noble	10	c. McAlister, b. Cotter	29
Extras	16	Extras	7
Total	249	Total	210

Bowling Analysis.

First Innings.

	O.	M.	R.	W.		O.	M.	R.	W.
Cotter	14	1	44	0	Hopkins	8	3	22	1
Noble	41.1	10	100	7	McLeod	8	5	9	0
Trumble ...	43	20	58	2					

Noble bowled 1 no-ball and Cotter and Hopkins 1 wide each.

Second Innings.

	O.	M.	R.	W.		O.	M.	R.	W.
Cotter	18.3	3	41	3	Noble	19	8	40	1
McLeod	20	5	42	3	Trumble	28	10	49	1
Hopkins	14	5	31	2					

AUSTRALIA.

First Innings.		Second Innings.	
V. Trumper, b. Braund	7	l.b.w., b. Arnold ...	12
R. A. Duff, b. Arnold	47	b. Arnold	19
C. Hill, c. Braund, b. Arnold	33	st. Lilley, b. Bosanquet	26
P. McAlister, c. Arnold, b. Rhodes ...	2	b. Hirst	1
A. J. Hopkins, b. Braund	9	st. Lilley, b. Bosanquet	0
C. McLeod, b. Rhodes...	18	c. Lilley, b. Bosanquet	6
J. J. Kelly, c. Foster, b. Arnold... ...	5	c. Foster, b. Bosanquet	10
M. A. Noble, not out	6	not out	53
S. E. Gregory, c. Foster, b. Rhodes ...	2	l.b.w., b. Bosanquet ...	0
H. Trumble, c. Lilley, b. Rhodes ...	0	st. Lilley, b. Bosanquet	0
A. Cotter, c. Tyldesley, b. Arnold ...	0	b. Hirst	34
Extras	2	Extras	10
Total 131		Total 171	

Bowling Analysis.

First Innings.

	O.	M.	R.	W.			O.	M.	R.	W.
Hirst	13	1	36	0	Bosanquet ...		2	1	5	0
Braund	11	2	27	2	Arnold		14.3	5	28	4
Rhodes	11	3	33	4						

Arnold bowled 1 wide.

Second Innings.

	O.	M.	R.	W.			O.	M.	R.	W.
Hirst	12.5	2	32	2	Rhodes		11	7	12	0
Braund	16	3	24	0	Bosanquet ...		15	1	51	6
Arnold	12	3	42	2						

FALL OF WICKETS.

First Innings of England.

1	2	3	4	5	6	7	8	9	10
4	34	42	66	155	185	207	208	237	249

Second Innings of England.

1	2	3	4	5	6	7	8	9	10
49	49	57	73	106	120	138	141	155	210

First Innings of Australia.

1	2	3	4	5	6	7	8	9	10
28	61	72	97	101	116	124	126	130	131

Second Innings of Australia.

1	2	3	4	5	6	7	8	9	10
7	35	59	76	76	76	86	90	114	171

CHAPTER XIV

THE FIFTH TEST MATCH

TO arrange two test matches in succession, with a single day between each, as it happened, was absurd. It was not the fault of M.C.C., for the moment we landed at Adelaide every effort was made on our part to alter the date of the fifth test ; but Major Wardill's invariable reply was that it was too late. Hurrying away from Sydney at eight o'clock in the evening of March 3, we did not reach Melbourne until one o'clock next day, and what with the excitement and strain of the Sydney game, and the fatigues of an Australian railway journey, we were a bit slack and worn out when the fifth test match commenced on Saturday, March 5. It was just as well for us that the rubber had been won, for the strain of a deciding match would, in the circumstances, have been intolerable.

Now, the laws of cricket say that a wicket may be covered before the commencement of a match. That, to my mind, is a most unfair rule, for, in the event of rain, it gives an overwhelming advantage to the side which wins the toss. If you are to cover a wicket at all it should be covered throughout and not only before a match. In England this practice of covering a wicket is never adopted—at least I have not heard of it. The law says you are perfectly within your right in so doing, but with us, at any rate, it has fallen so much into disuse that five cricketers out of six think it is against the rules.

I have a notion that there was a certain Lancashire *v.* Yorkshire match, in which two wickets were prepared : one had been covered and the other had been left to take its chance of the weather. Lord Hawke refused to play on the protected wicket, and the match was fought out on the wicket which had not been protected. There had been rain, and the result was a sticky wicket throughout—that is, equal conditions for both sides.

Just before this match the weather (at Melbourne) had been fine, and a beautiful wicket had been prepared. Up to eight o'clock on the morning of the first day there had been no wet, but between eight and ten it rained heavily. The moment the groundman saw the rain coming he covered the wicket up, and at twelve o'clock it was in perfect condition—just the right pace; indeed, a regular Trent Bridge wicket. But the outfield was damp and very slippery, and so was the ball. Now, if the weather had kept fine, this covering of the pitch would not have mattered so greatly; but it rained again on Sunday, as it always did when we were in Melbourne, and we played both our innings on a difficult wicket. If the wicket had not been covered at all, the match would have been fought under equal conditions—a difficult wicket for both sides, but equal conditions all the same. But this covering the pitch for only one side made the conditions absurdly unequal.

I am the first to admit that we won the second test match by winning the toss. But the conditions there were different. There was no rain immediately before the match. The game started on a wicket which had not been protected—and it was just the Australians' bad luck that rain should have come on the second day.

Many of the rules of cricket require, as it seems to me, serious consideration, and none more so than this one dealing with the preparation of wickets.

And now to the match itself. We played the same side as at Sydney, but the Australians substituted Gehrs for Gregory. Duff was clean bowled by Braund when thirteen runs had been made, but Trumper, who was once again in his best form, and Hill scored quickly

BRAUND CATCHES HILL AT SLIP.

until Rhodes, going on in place of Braund, got the left-hander easily caught at slip. At lunch Noble was in with Trumper, but soon after resuming he was easily caught at extra-slip. This was at 142, and two runs later Trumper was finely caught and bowled with the left hand. He had been batting one hour and fifty minutes and gave no actual chance, though he made a couple of dangerous hits in the slips off Arnold's bowling. He hit ten fours, all of them beautifully timed strokes, one in particular off Arnold being a grand forcing hit on the on-side. The rumours that had been going the round that Trumper was in

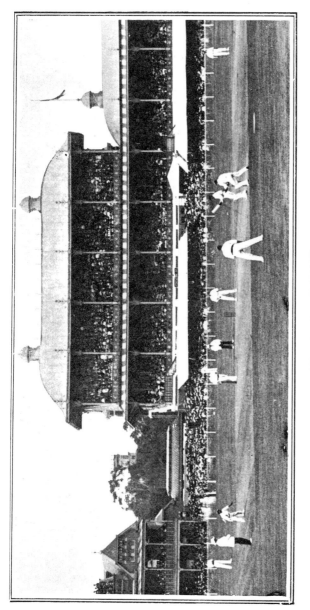

THE FIFTH TEST MATCH.

Braund bowling to Hopkins.

bad health were at once dispelled by this brilliant innings.

Hopkins and McAlister made a good stand for the sixth wicket, but Braund was bowling very well, and our opponents once more showed that there was a decided tail to their eleven. Braund took eight wickets in twenty-nine overs for eighty-one runs, and considering that the pitch was never quite fast enough to really suit him, his performance was an even finer one than it reads. He kept a most accurate length, and bowled his leg break very well. Next to Braund, Hirst was the best bowler, though he did not take a wicket. When he went on for the third time at 200 he made the new ball swerve, but his luck was cruel indeed, for over and over again he just missed the wicket. He bowled so well that he might easily have had two or three wickets. There were some fine catches made—one especially by Foster at mid-off from a hard low drive—but the ground fielding was not up to the mark.

The twenty minutes which remained were disastrous to us, for in answer to the Australians' 247—quite a poor total on that wicket—we lost Hayward and Arnold for four runs. Hayward played a ball on to his foot, whence it rolled into the wicket, and Arnold was splendidly caught by Kelly on the leg side.

There was no play on Monday until 4.15. The wicket was wet but not really difficult, and 120 runs instead of sixty-one should have been quite within our power. Noble did not make the ball turn; he kept a good length, and Cotter at the other end did most of the damage. He bowled very fast, and two or three times in an over the batsman had to duck his head to avoid the ball.

T

The pitch was not soft enough yet to be sticky; it was wet on the top, and the ball did not turn. The difficulty about it was that Cotter bumped very awkwardly. It was what one may call an unpleasant wicket. Cotter is very active and well built, and he kept his foothold in the most wonderful way.

Rhodes and myself were out to poor strokes off long hops—Rhodes caught at point off the first ball of the day, and I at extra slip, who was standing very deep.

Tyldesley and Hirst were magnificently caught on the off-side—the former at cover from a hard, clean hit, and the Yorkshireman at mid-off. Foster gave a difficult chance to Trumble off Noble before scoring, but subsequently played well, and made one fine square-leg hit off Noble into the crowd.

Braund was caught at long-on and Bosanquet at short leg. It was a poor display of batting.

In the twenty-five minutes which remained the Australians lost McAlister, McLeod, and Cotter for thirteen runs. Rhodes began with a very bad over, nearly every ball being short-pitched, and McAlister scored nine runs off him. Getting to the other end, McAlister was caught at extra slip, and then Braund, who had gone on bowling fast instead of Rhodes, saw McLeod finely caught by Bosanquet, who ran from third slip behind the wicket and took a mis-hit in great style. Immediately Cotter came in I put on Hirst, who with his second ball clean bowled the N.S.W. colt.

In spite of the rain which fell early on Tuesday morning, the umpires pronounced the wicket fit to play on at 12.15, when the Australians resumed their second innings. The pitch was now thoroughly soaked, and promised to be a regular "glue-pot" in an hour or two. At the moment of commencing it was a little too slow to be very difficult, but it was, even then, not easy. Trumper, who wanted ten to complete a thousand runs for the season's first-class cricket, joined Kelly, who was not out four, but the Australian champion was clean bowled by the first delivery of the day. It was one of Hirst's very best, for the ball swerved in the air, and, pitching a couple of inches outside the off stump, hit the top of the middle stump. Trumper played back, but the break and the pace the ball left the pitch beat him. He had not made a duck for over a year, this was the first time indeed in eighty innings ! Hill followed and Rhodes bowled at the other end. But the Yorkshireman for some reason or other could not keep a length, and runs were knocked freely off him, and at thirty-three Arnold was deputed to bowl. Kelly hooked his first and fifth balls to the boundary, and had made twenty-four when the total was forty-two. Without adding to his score he hit the slowest and softest of long-hops back to the bowler and was easily caught. He hit five fours and played better than in any previous innings against us. Seven runs later Hill hit a full pitch hard to me at short mid-on. Noble then joined Duff and runs came quickly, Arnold bowling much below his true form. At seventy-six Rhodes went on again, and off his second ball Noble was rather badly missed at extra slip by Relf, who was fielding for Hayward, the Surrey professional being in bed with an attack of tonsilitis. Braund bowled a couple of overs (slow) before lunch instead of Hirst, and with the total at ninety-two the adjournment took place. The wicket dried during luncheon, and was very difficult when the game was continued. Noble was beautifully stumped in Rhodes' first over, the ball turning very quickly. Hopkins was evidently bent on forcing the hitting, but before he had scored he lifted one from Rhodes high on the on-side. Bosanquet was fielding at mid-on rather wide and square, and he ran for the catch and got it well into his hands. He appeared to have caught the ball when it dropped to the ground. It was a fine attempt, and would have been a finer catch, for there was a strongish wind blowing, and the ball "wobbled" about very awkwardly in the air. Duff, when twenty-seven, hit one hard back to Rhodes, which the bowler failed to hold, but shortly after he skied one to mid-on, and was easily caught. Duff batted exactly an hour, and hit five fours. Gehrs was caught and bowled, and Trumble caught at mid-off, running behind the bowler, Hopkins carrying out his bat for a plucky, if lucky, twenty-five. Hirst again bowled admirably, and with more success this time, but the other bowlers fell far below their usual standard.

Had Rhodes bowled in his true form Australia should not have made more than ninety or one hundred. But Rhodes experienced for the first time on this tour an off-day. He had a little bad luck, but he never bowled a really good length, and it was his comrade, George Hirst, who did the best work.

Hirst, like Cotter, is one of the few fast bowlers who can keep his feet and length on a sticky wicket, though I am sure Australian wickets are easier to get a foothold on than English ones. The wet does not seem to go so far into the earth.

The Australians' second total of 133 left us with 320 runs to make on an impossible wicket. All the morning the wicket had been gradually becoming more difficult, and from after luncheon it was very bad. We went

A. R. GEHRS.

C. McLEOD.

J. J. KELLY.

H. TRUMBLE.

in about four o'clock, and by half-past five we were out for 101. Cotter and Noble began, but after the fast bowler had sent down five overs for twenty-five runs and two wickets he gave way to Trumble, who up to the fall of our ninth wicket had taken six wickets for eleven runs! Then there came a heavy shower, and after it, with the wicket wet and easy on the top, Rhodes and Arnold added forty runs and somewhat spoiled Trumble's analysis. But in the end he had seven wickets for twenty-eight runs *and* a hat trick.

The pitch before the shower was impossible, the ball breaking from two inches to a foot, and getting up perfectly straight. Trumble, indeed, was unplayable. C. B. Fry doubts whether he was so, as he did not clean bowl one of his seven wickets. Mr. Fry has never seen a sticky Melbourne wicket, or he would know that the ball there jumps up so high that it is very unusual to find a batsman bowled out.

Recollect the second test match at Melbourne. Then, on a sticky wicket, we got the Australians out for 122 and 111, and not once was the wicket hit in either innings, while only two men on our side were bowled out when the wicket was sticky, both of them with yorkers.

I should much have liked to have seen what methods the late Arthur Shrewsbury, F. S. Jackson, C. B. Fry, or A. C. MacLaren would have adopted under the prevailing conditions. It was no use playing steadily, to be caught close in on the on-side ; and if one jumped out to drive, unless one got right to the very pitch of the ball, there was every chance of being caught at long-on or wide long-on, or deep square leg. Those who hit and trusted to fortune were the most successful, and Foster, in particular, played a superb innings. He was finally caught by Trumper with one hand—a magnificent long-field catch.

It is said that Hugh Trumble has played his last big match. If that is so, he could not have had a more splendid wind-up to what has been a great career. And so Australia beat us by 218 runs. The toss meant the match, but after the rain had come and ruined the wicket they played the better cricket. Therefore they deserved their victory, but coming so soon after the stress and anxiety of the Sydney game, there was something of an anti-climax about the match.

Tom Hayward's absence through illness in our second innings did not make the difference between victory and defeat, but he had batted so splendidly and consistently on all sorts of wickets that, had he been able to take his place, we should assuredly have made a better fight.

AUSTRALIA.

First Innings.		Second Innings.	
R. A. Duff, b. Braund	9	c. Warner, b. Rhodes...	31
V. Trumper, c. and b. Braund	88	b. Hirst...	0
C. Hill, c. Braund, b. Rhodes	16	c. Warner, b. Hirst ...	16
M. A. Noble, c. Foster, b. Arnold ...	29	st. Lilley, b. Rhodes ...	19
P. McAlister, st. Lilley, b. Braund ...	36	c. Foster, b. Arnold ...	9
A. R. Gehrs, c. and b. Braund	3	c. and b. Hirst	5
A. J. Hopkins, c. Knight, b. Braund...	32	not out	25
C. E. McLeod, c. Rhodes, b. Braund...	8	c. Bosanquet, b. Braund	0
H. Trumble, c. Foster, b. Braund ..	6	c. Arnold, b. Hirst ...	0
J. J. Kelly, not out	6	b. Hirst	0
A. Cotter, b. Braund	6	c. and b. Arnold	24
Extras	8	Extras	4
Total	247	Total	133

Bowling Analysis.
First Innings.

	O.	M.	R.	W.		O.	M.	R	W.
Hirst ...	19	6	44	0	Arnold ...	18	4	46	1
Braund	29.1	6	81	8	Bosanquet ..	4	0	27	0
Rhodes	12	1	41	1					

Second Innings.

	O.	M.	R.	W.				O.	M.	R.	W.
Rhodes	15	2	52	2	Braund	...	...	4	1	6	1
Arnold	8	3	23	2	Hirst	...	...	15.1	4	48	5

ENGLAND.

First Innings.		Second Innings.	
Hayward, b. Noble	0	absent, ill	0
Rhodes, c. Gehrs, b. Cotter...	3	not out	16
Arnold, c. Kelly, b. Noble	0	c. Duff. b. Trumble ...	19
P. F. Warner, c. McAlister, b. Cotter.	1	c. and b. Trumble ...	11
Tyldesley, c. Gehrs, b. Noble	10	c. Hopkins, b. Cotter...	15
R. E. Foster, b. Cotter	18	c. Trumper, b. Trumble	30
Hirst, c. Trumper, b. Cotter	0	c. McAlister, b. Trumble	1
Braund, c. Hopkins, b. Noble	5	c. McAlister, b. Cotter	0
Knight, b. Cotter	0	c. Kelly, b. Trumble ...	0
B. J. T. Bosanquet, c. Noble, b. Cotter	16	c. Gehrs, b. Trumble ...	4
Lilley, not out	6	l.b.w., b. Trumble ...	0
Extras	2	Extras	5
Total	61	Total	101

Bowling Analysis.

First Innings.

	O.	M.	R.	W.				O.	M.	R.	W.
Noble	15	8	19	4	McLeod ...	...		1	1	0	0
Cotter	15.3	2	40	6							

Noble bowled 1 no-ball.

Second Innings.

	O.	M.	R.	W.				O.	M.	R.	W.
Cotter	5	2	25	2	Trumble ...	...		6.5	0	28	7
Noble	6	2	19	0	McLeod ...	...		5	0	24	0

TEST MATCH RESULTS.

		1st Inn.	2nd Inn.	Totl.
Dec. 11, 12, 14, 15, 16, 17 ...	ENGLAND	577	194†	771
Sydney	* AUSTRALIA	285	485	770

England won by 5 wickets. † Five wickets down.

Jan. 1, 2, 4, 5	* ENGLAND	315	103	418
Melbourne	AUSTRALIA	122	111	233

England won by 185 runs.

Jan. 15, 16, 18, 19, 20... ...	ENGLAND	245	278	523
Adelaide...	* AUSTRALIA	388	351	739

Australia won by 216 runs.

* Denotes the side winning the toss and batting first.

Feb. 26, 27, Mar. 1, 2, 3 ...	* ENGLAND	249	210	459
Sydney	AUSTRALIA	131	171	302

England won by 157 runs.

Mar. 5, 7, 8	ENGLAND	61	101	162
Melbourne	* AUSTRALIA.. ...	247	133	380

Australia won by 218 runs.

* Denotes the side winning the toss and batting first.

AGGREGATES.

England scored 2,333 runs for 92 wickets ; average 25·35.
Australia scored 2,324 runs for 100 wickets ; average, 23·24.
Highest English score, 577 ; Australian, 485.
Lowest English score, 61 ; Australian, 111.

The result of the five test matches was therefore : England three wins, Australia two. But the second and fifth games—both of which were played at Melbourne —were decided by the weather ; so that the rubber, so far as a test of the abilities of the respective teams, was confined to three matches. Of these three, England won on both occasions on the Sydney ground, and Australia at Adelaide. It may be interesting, at this point, to take a brief review of the campaign.

In the first test at Sydney the Australians won the toss, and, after losing Trumper, Hill, and Duff for twelve runs, ran up a total of 285, Noble playing a magnificent innings of 133.

The wicket on the first day was perfect, but Hirst, Arnold, and Bosanquet bowled so well, and our fielding was so exceptionally smart, that when stumps were drawn Australia had lost seven wickets for 259 runs. That night it rained heavily, and next morning Rhodes soon dismissed the remaining Australians. Up to lunch time the pitch was very difficult ; but it rapidly improved during the afternoon, and after four o'clock was once more a good wicket. When the wicket was sticky

Tyldesley batted as well as he has ever done in his life. On the third day record after record was smashed. Foster played the innings of his life ; Braund got 102 ; Foster and Relf added 115 for the ninth wicket ; and Foster and Rhodes 130 for the last. The total was 577.

The Australians, in a minority of 292, might well have quailed before the task in front of them, but, true to their traditions, they played a magnificent up-hill game, and ran up a total of 485, Trumper making a wonderful 185 not out, Duff eighty-four, Hill fifty-one, and Gregory forty-three. We eventually won by five wickets ; Hayward, ninety-one, and Hirst, sixty not out, playing grandly at a crisis.

In this first game the luck was, if anything, against us, for the rain which fell at the close of the first day's play made the wicket difficult for a time, and we had to tide over an awkward hour or two. In the last innings, the wicket, quite naturally after all the great scoring which had gone before, showed signs of crumbling.

The second match at Melbourne was ruined by the weather, and winning the toss meant winning the match. On the first day we made 221 for two wickets. The batting was slow indeed, but then the Australian bowling was very fine, and the fielding even finer. Then the rain came, and the rest of the match was fought out on a sticky wicket. Rhodes took fifteen wickets for 124 runs, and would have had an even better analysis if our catching had been even fair. As it was, catch after catch was dropped in the most inexplicable way. The batting honours of this match were carried off by Tyldesley, ninety-seven and sixty-two, and Trumper, seventy-four and thirty-five, both of whom displayed the greatest possible skill on the damaged pitch. The first day's play had put us in a strong position, and, in spite of our mistakes in the field, we won easily by 185 runs. The weather smiled on the side which batted first, wept on their antagonists; but we too had some ill-fortune to contend against, for Foster was compelled to retire through illness in the middle of the match, and Bosanquet and Arnold were unable to play on account of minor injuries.

The Adelaide Oval is supposed to be a veritable death-trap for English cricketers, for not since 1892, when W. G. Grace was in command of Lord Sheffield's team, has England won a test match there.

Once again was history true to her teaching, for on a perfect wicket from start to finish Australia won by 218 runs. Poor batting lost us the match, only Hayward, Hirst, and myself doing ourselves justice. In the two innings we made 510 runs from the bat, and of this number Hayward, Hirst, and myself scored 316. The four great Australian batsmen, Trumper, Duff, Hill, and Noble, all came off—Trumper, with 113 and fifty-nine, particularly·so—while in the second innings S. E. Gregory came along at a most opportune time with a brilliant 112. Our bowling and fielding were excellent, Bosanquet being the most successful, with seven wickets for 160 runs, and had our batting been on the same level with our out-cricket we should have made a close fight.

Hopkins and Trumble bowled best for Australia, whose fielding was tip-top.

We were fairly and squarely beaten.

The fourth match at Sydney was greatly interfered with by rain. I won the toss, and on the first day we made 207 for seven wickets. The wicket gave the

CLEMENT HILL.

bowlers some help, and with a very dead outfield we did not do at all badly. Trumble and Noble bowled magnificently. Next day the innings closed for 249, Knight seventy not out, a fine defensive display when things were going against us. The Australians then lost five men for 114—the wicket being now harder and faster than on the first day. There were several light showers during the afternoon, but the ball cut through very quickly, and it was a great performance on the part of our bowlers to dismiss the Australians so cheaply. On the third day there was no cricket, and on the fourth the Australians were all out for 131, and we lost Foster for fifty runs. A splendid innings by Hayward on a far from easy pitch and a most useful last-wicket stand by Rhodes and myself on the sixth morning, when the wicket had quite recovered, left our opponents 328 to get. During this last innings the wicket was a great deal better than at any previous time, and many people thought the Australians would get the runs. But Arnold, Hirst, and Bosanquet all did excellent work, especially Bosanquet, who actually took six wickets for fifty-one runs, and we won easily by 157 runs.

The rubber having been lost and won, the final game at Melbourne was something of an anti-climax, and, like the second, was spoilt by rain. The Australians won the toss, and when the pitch was in good order scored 247, Braund, eight wickets for eighty-one runs, bowling magnificently. We then lost Hayward and Arnold for four runs. Had the weather kept fine we had so far little the worst of the position, and the match would have been a keen one. As it happened, there was a great deal of rain, and for the remainder of the game the wicket was difficult.

The bowlers had a good time, Hirst on our side and Trumble and Cotter for the Australians particularly distinguishing themselves.

This last game, like the second, may be struck out of the list, for the toss in each case decided the match.

Judging, then, by the three real tests we were, on the whole, the better side. Our batting throughout was sounder, for we were not dependent on four or five men.

Australia, on the other hand, relied almost entirely on Trumper, Duff, Hill, and Noble. Hopkins is a decidedly fine bat, but he was out of luck in the test matches, when there was a most decided tail to the team. Trumper I consider the finest batsman in the world, and Noble was not far below him when the wickets were hard. Duff is a brilliant, versatile player, but Hill seemed to me to have fallen off. He has developed a weak stroke in the slips, where Arnold and Hirst frequently got him caught.

Hayward played magnificently, and was most reliable; but we had no one batsman standing out head and shoulders above his comrades. Foster was a little disappointing after his wonderful innings in the first test match, but ill-health probably had something to do with this.

Our bowling was the stronger. We had variety; they, until Cotter came into the team, had none. Their attack suffered in the second and third matches from Noble's injury, and Saunders was quite out of form and was dropped early in the season. Howell was much the same as ever, always a good length and always doing a little; but he is not the bowler he was five or six years ago.

Cotter will certainly be seen in England next year; he is a fast bowler of decided promise.

The most improved bowler on the Australian side is Hopkins, but Trumble and Noble are not quite the bowlers they were.

It was our bowling, indeed, more than anything else which won us the rubber, and here we were exceptionally strong. There was a man for every type of wicket, and each fresh bowler as he went on was a real change and no makeshift.

The Australians fielded better than we did. Except in the second test at Melbourne, our catching was quite as good as theirs, but in ground work, throwing and returning the ball they were our superiors. Foster and Braund made a splendid pair of slips, and Tyldesley, Relf, and Rhodes were very good.

Some of the reports cabled to England might lead people to suppose that the Australians had in this respect fallen away from their high standard. I can only say that I did not see it, and many of the catches reported as missed had no existence in point of fact. Gregory and Noble were superb, as were Trumper, Duff, Hopkins, Gehrs, McAlister, and Laver.

Kelly still retains his form, and Lilley, on our side, was both safe and brilliant.

The Australians are not just now so strong all round as they were in the years 1896-1902. In Trumper, Duff, Hill, and Noble they have a formidable quartette—probably the four finest batsmen who have played for Australia at one and the same time; but their bowling has gone off. There is no Jones, and Trumble and Noble have fallen away somewhat. Their fielding is as good as ever, and so are their determination and know-

U

ledge of the game. It is in bowling that they must bestir themselves. Here Cotter has given high promise, and, as there is a powerful reserve of young batsmen coming on, England will require her strongest team to defeat her old rivals when next they visit us in 1905.

ENGLAND.—BATTING AVERAGES.

	Arnold.	Bosanquet.	Braund.	Fielder.	Foster.	Hayward.	Hirst.	Knight.	Lilley.	Relf.	Rhodes.	Tyldesley.	Warner.
First ...	27	2	102	—	287	15	0	—	4	31	*40	53	0
	—	*1	0		19	91	*60	—	—	—	—	9	8
Second	—	—	20	1	*49 ret.	58	7	2	4	*3	2	97	68
			3	4	abs.	0	4	0	0	*10	9	62	3
Third...	*23	10	13	6	21	20	58	—	28		9	0	48
	1	10	25	*14	16	67	44	—	0		8	10	79
Fourth	0	12	39	—	19	18	25	*70	24		10	16	0
	0	7	19	—	27	52	18	9	6		29	5	*31
Fifth ...	0	16	5	—	18	0	0	0	*6		3	10	1
	19	4	0	—	30	abs.	1	0	0		*16	15	11
Totals..	70	62	226	25	486	321	217	81	72	44	126	277	249

Strudwick did not take part in any Test game.

	Matches.	Inn.	Times Not Out.	Total Runs.	Most in an Inns.	Aver.
Foster, R. E. ...	5	9	1	486	287	60·75
Relf ...	2	3	2	44	31	44·00
Hayward ...	5	9	0	321	91	35·66
Tyldesley ...	5	10	0	277	97	27·70
Warner, P. F. (capt.) ...	5	10	1	249	79	27·66
Hirst ...	5	10	1	217	60*	24·11
Braund...	5	10	0	226	102	22·60
Rhodes ...	5	9	2	126	40*	18·00
Knight...	3	6	1	81	70*	16·20
Arnold...	4	7	1	70	27	11·66
Lilley ...	5	9	1	72	28	9·00
Bosanquet, B. J. T. ...	4	8	1	62	16	8·85
Fielder...	2	4	1	25	14*	8·33

* Signifies not out.

Braund—First match (Sydney), December 11   102
Foster, R. E.—First match (Sydney), December 11   287

"SPECTACLES."

Arnold—Fourth match (Sydney), February 26.
Knight--Fifth match (Melbourne), March 5.

ENGLAND.—BOWLING AVERAGES.

	Inns.	Overs.	Mdns.	Runs.	Wkts.	Aver.
Rhodes...	10	172	36	488	31	15.74
Bosanquet, B. J. T.	7	106.1	7	403	16	25.18
Arnold	8	158.3	32	475	18	26.38
Braund...	9	120.3	30	359	13	27.61
Hirst	10	163.2	29	451	15	30.06
Relf	4	22	5	79	1	79.00
Fielder	2	31	11	84	1	84.00

CATCHES BY THE ENGLISHMEN.

Foster caught eight, Braund caught eight, Relf caught five, Hirst caught four, Bosanquet caught four, Arnold caught four, Tyldesley caught three, Rhodes caught three, Warner caught two, Hayward caught one, Knight caught one.

Strudwick made three catches when fielding substitute for Foster in the second match.

Lilley behind the wicket caught six and stumped nine batsmen in the series.

AUSTRALIA.—BATTING AVERAGES

	Armstrong.	Cotter.	Duff.	Gregory, S. E.	Hill.	Hopkins.	Howell.	Kelly.	McAlister.	McLeod.	Noble.	Saunders.	Trumble.	Trumper.
First..	46	—	3	23	5	39	5	10	—	—	133	*11	—	1
	*27	—	84	43	51	20	4	13	—	—	22	2	—	*185
Second	1	—	10	1	5	18	0	8	—	—	0	*2	2	74
	0	—	8	0	20	7	3	7	—	—	*31	0	0	35
Third .	10	—	79	8	88	0	*3	1	—	8	59	—	4	113
	39	—	14	112	16	7	*1	13	—	2	65	—	9	59
Fourth	—	0	47	2	35	9	—	5	2	18	*6	—	0	7
	—	34	19	0	26	0	—	10	1	6	*53	—	0	12
Fifth..	—	6	9	—	16	32	—	*6	36	8	29	—	6	88
	—	0	31	—	16	*25	—	24	9	0	19	—	0	0
Totals.	123	40	304	189	278	157	16	97	48	42	417	15	21	574

F. Laver (4 and 6) played on December 11.

* Signifies not out.

	Matches.	Inns.	Times Not Out.	Runs.	Most in an Inns.	Aver.
Trumper V. (N.S.W.)	5	10	1	574	185*	63·77
Noble, M. A. (N.S.W.) (capt.)	5	10	3	417	133	59·57
Duff, R. A. (N.S.W.)	5	10	0	304	84	30·40
Hill, C. (S.A.)	5	10	0	276	88	27·60
Gregory, S. E. (N.S.W.) ...	4	8	0	189	112	23·62
Armstrong, W. W. (V.) ...	3	6	0	125	48	20·83
Hopkins, A. J. (N.S.W.) ...	5	10	1	157	39	17·44
McAlister, P. (V.)	2	4	0	48	36	12·00
Kelly, J. J. (N.S.W.)	5	10	1	97	24	10·77
Cotter, A. (N.S.W.)	2	4	0	40	34	10·00
Saunders, J. V. (V.)	2	4	2	15	11*	7·50
McLeod, C. E. (V.)	3	6	0	42	18	7·00
Laver, F. (V.)	1	2	0	10	6	5·00
Howell, W. P. (N.S.W.) ...	3	6	2	16	5	4·00
Gehrs, A. R. (S.A.)	1	2	0	8	5	4·00
Trumble, H. (V.)	4	8	0	21	9	2·62

CENTURIES FOR (4).

Gregory, S. E.—Third match (Adelaide), January 15 112
Noble, M. A.—First match (Sydney), December 11 133
Trumper, V.—First match (Sydney), December 11 ... ... *185
Trumper, V.—Third match (Adelaide), January 15 113

* Signifies not out.

" SPECTACLES."

Trumble, H.—Fourth match, February 26.

———

AUSTRALIA.—BOWLING AVERAGES.

	Inns.	Overs.	Mdns.	Runs.	Wkts.	Aver.
Cotter, A.	4	52.5	6	150	11	13·63
Trumble, H.	7	199.4	60	398	24	16·58
Noble, M. A.	8	136.1	41	330	16	20·62
Howell, W. P.	6	137.5	51	296	14	21·14
Hopkins, A. J.	7	107.1	26	295	11	26·81
McLeod, C. E.	6	83	21	177	5	35·40
Saunders, J. V.	4	79.1	14	270	6	45·00
Armstrong, W. W.	5	84	20	158	2	79·00
Laver, F.	2	53	16	153	1	153·00
Trumper, V.	3	12	1	21	0	—
Gregory, S. E.	1	2	0	8	0	—

CHAPTER XV

WE had a great send-off from Melbourne on Thursday afternoon, March 10. First of all the officials and several members of the Melbourne Club, together with nearly all of the Australian Eleven, assembled at Menzies Hotel just before the time for our starting for Adelaide, and Mr. Roderick Murchison, the President of the Melbourne Club, in the course of a very charming speech, said that for keenness, earnestness, and singleness of purpose the M.C.C. Team surpassed all its predecessors, and that we had won the rubber fairly and squarely. He congratulated us on taking home "the ashes," and incidentally remarked that losing the rubber would do Australian cricket no harm, for defeat would act as an incentive to strengthen any weak points in their armour.

From Menzies we hastened to the station, which was thronged with people, all eager to wish us good luck and congratulate us on our success. The Australian cricketers are ever hard fighters, but they know well how to take a defeat, and nothing could have been more genuine than their congratulations.

Noble was there, and Duff, and Hill, and Hopkins, and just at the last Hugh Trumble, towering head and shoulders above the crowd, arrived to wish us *bon voyage* and all good luck, and to be himself congratulated on the triumphal ending to his great cricket career. Our send-off was, indeed, so hearty, and the expressions of goodwill so spontaneous and so genuine, as to accentuate the desire of nearly all of us to at some not very distant

HIRST IN THE SMOKING ROOM AT MENZIES.

date revisit Melbourne, and to meet again those who had shown us so much kindness.

It was a splendid send-off, and proved conclusively that the initial venture of the Marylebone Club had been a big success. I was very sorry to leave, for I had grown very fond of Australia and the Australians, who had everywhere welcomed us with open arms. And so it

P. F. WARNER.

was that, with the echoes of the good wishes of our Melbourne friends ringing in our ears, we took our seats in the Adelaide express with our noses pointed homewards.

The last match of a tour is apt to be a tame affair. The original object has either been attained or not, and there is, as a rule, a very natural wish to put aside bat and ball, and to return to England as quickly as one may. Not so, however, this final game of ours against South Australia, for we were all keen to win, as South Australia was the only State we had not beaten. It will be remembered that in the opening match of the tour we had victory assured when we were compelled to abandon the game.

Hayward was still too ill to play, and as I left out Arnold and Lilley, Strudwick and Fielder once again came into the side.

Adelaide, as usual, gave us beautiful weather; sunshine and warmth during the day, and a cool breeze at night, and after the damp and wet of Sydney and Melbourne the change was much appreciated.

The wicket was of the usual Adelaide type—fast, but very true, and the ball never getting up above the stumps. Hill won the toss, and we did well to dismiss them for 259. Gehrs played very well for 63. He was strong in his back play, and treated anything like a loose ball in no uncertain way. He is almost certain to be in the next Australian eleven for England, as in addition to his batting he is another Gregory at extra-cover.

Jennings and Claxton also shaped in good form, and Newland, the wicket-keeper, coming in after seven wickets had fallen for 191 runs, played a vigorous and plucky innings of fifty. These three men have, like

Gehrs, a capital chance of visiting England next summer.

No one did anything out of the common in the bowling line. Hirst was, on the whole, a long way the best, and Relf for a time kept a most excellent length. Bosanquet until hit about by Newland had a good analysis, but he got Claxton caught at the wicket off a ball which must have pitched three times, and which was so wide that the batsman ran almost to point to reach it. Strudwick followed, and Claxton, just touching the ball, our wicket-keeper brought off a wonderful catch. It was, I feel certain, the worst delivery that has ever got a wicket in first-class cricket, but I can recollect one almost as bad with which Bosanquet got Abel out at Lord's in a Middlesex and Surrey match two or three years ago. Curiously enough he very nearly had Trumper caught off much the same sort of ball in the third test match.

We in our turn failed badly. The hundred went up with only three men out, but then on a perfect wicket came a collapse. Braund, Bosanquet, and myself contributed 102 between us; the other eight forty-six! The bowling was good; the batting very poor. Most of the team do not seem to care for the Adelaide wicket. They say that the bright glaring light makes it difficult to follow the ball off the pitch. The light is certainly very strong, much more so than at Sydney or Melbourne. I myself prefer the Adelaide Oval to any other ground in Australia, but the fierce light beating down on the brown, almost grassless pitch renders it undoubtedly hard to watch the ball off the ground on first going in. The remedy is to sit in the sunlight for four or five minutes before the commencement of one's innings.

ANOTHER VIEW OF THE ADELAIDE OVAL.

Claxton, a right-hand medium-paced round-the-wicket bowler, who made the ball go with his arm, had a fine analysis, and H. J. Hill, a younger brother of Clem, has an easy, natural left-handed action, and kept a most accurate length.   There is one ball of his, however, which is, I think, open to question.   Young Hill seems about as active and safe a field as his brother was three or four years back, and as he is too a very fair bat, he is by no means unlikely to add lustre to the family name.

If we had failed in batting, South Australia were even less successful in their second innings, for in an hour and a half Braund and Hirst dismissed them for seventy-seven.   Braund took eight wickets for forty three runs. Rather freely hit at first, the moment he got a wicket he simply ran through the side.   He kept a fine length with his leg breaks, and his fast ball was very deadly.   Braund thus wound up in great style, and, in fact, ever since he took Victor Trumper's wicket in the second New South Wales match, he bowled as well as he ever did in his life.   Up to that period he had been singularly unsuccessful in the first class matches for one of his abilities.

Hirst at the other end did fine service.   He was on for an hour and ten minutes, and did not send down one bad ball.   During the day nineteen wickets fell for 222 runs on a batsman's pitch !

It is the fashion nowadays to say that the batting was poor, whenever bowlers succeed on hard wickets.   The batting may have been so or it may not, but it is quite certain that the bowling on both sides was exceedingly good.

Next day we knocked off the 180 odd runs we required to win for one wicket.   Foster and myself put on 117 for the opening partnership, and then Tyldesley came in, and by most brilliant cricket scored fifty in twenty-eight minutes. Foster was seventy-three not out at the finish —a free, wristy, and faultless innings. It was the first time he had got going at Adelaide, and the few spectators were delighted with his style.

Thus ended a tour for which many had prophesied

SOME FAMOUS CRICKETERS AS FOOTBALLERS.

failure, but which was little short of a triumphal march from start to finish.

By way of a final flourish, and just to show, as it were, that cricket was not our only game, we wound up the season with an Association football match, which we won by 6 goals to love. Foster, of course, was a tower of strength, and carried everything before him, while the vigour of Hirst appalled his adversaries, who fell back to right and left before his triumphal charge, so that he fairly cleft a passage before him whenever he got the ball. Lilley also was very good at back, but some of the rest of the Team were decidedly new to the game, and caused some amusement by their exposition of its intricacies.

SOUTH AUSTRALIA.

First Innings.		Second Innings.	
A. R. Gehrs, b. Hirst	63	st. Strudwick, b. Braund	30
F. T. Hack, b. Bosanquet	13	c. Relf, b. Hirst	5
C. Hill, c. Strudwick, b. Hirst	22	c. Fielder, b. Braund ..	7
C. B. Jennings, c. Strudwick, b. Relf	32	l.b.w., b. Braund ...	0
N. H. Claxton, c. Strudwick, b. Bosanquet	40	b. Hirst	1
J. H. Pellew, b. Relf	4	b. Braund	13
A. E. H. Evans, c. and b. Braund ...	29	b. Braund	0
H. J. Hill, b. Bosanquet	0	c. Strudwick, b. Braund	10
P. M. Newland, b. Fielder	50	c. Tyldesley, b. Braund	8
J. F. Travers, run out	0	not out	1
P. H. Coombe, not out	0	b. Braund ..:	1
Leg-byes, 5 ; no-ball, 1	6	Leg-bye, 1	1
Total	259	Total	77

Bowling Analysis.

First Innings.

	O.	M.	R.	W.			O.	M.	R.	W.
Hirst	18	3	40	2	Rhodes		5	0	18	0
Fielder	11	3	40	1	Braund		9.2	1	38	1
Bosanquet ...	17	1	70	3	Relf...		17	6	47	2

Hirst bowled 1 no-ball.

Second Innings.

	O.	M.	R.	W.			O.	M.	R.	W.
Hirst	11	4	22	2	Bosanquet	...	4	0	11	0
Braund	14.4	2	43	8						

ENGLAND.

First Innings.

P. F. Warner, c. H. J. Hill, b. Pellew	50
R. E. Foster, c. Hack, b. Claxton	2
B. J. T. Bosanquet, c. C. Hill, b. Coombe	22
Tyldesley, b. H. J. Hill	12
Knight, c. Jennings, b. Claxton	18
Braund, c. Travers, b. Claxton	30
Hirst, c. Evans, b. Claxton	1
Relf, c. Newland, b. Claxton	3
Rhodes, b. H. J. Hill	4
Fielder, not out	5
Strudwick, c. Pellew, b. H. J. Hill..	1
Byes	6
Total	154

Second Innings : Foster, not out, 73 ; Warner, c. Evans, b. Claxton, 54 ; Tyldesley, not out, 50 ; byes, 7. Total (for one wicket), 184.

Bowling Analysis.

First Innings.

	O.	M.	R.	W.		O.	M.	R.	W.
Claxton	27	7	56	5	Hill, H. J. ...	19.4	8	27	3
Travers	9	4	20	0	Evans	2	0	4	0
Coombe	6	1	22	1	Pellew	6	1	19	1

Second Innings.

	O.	M.	R.	W.		O.	M.	R.	W.
Claxton	12	1	58	1	Pellew	1	0	8	0
Travers	7	1	34	0	Gehrs	2	0	16	0
Hill, H. J. ...	6	0	18	0	Hack	1.3	0	10	0
Evans	3	0	10	0					

Umpires : P. Argall and G. A. Watson.

COMING OFF THE FIELD FOR THE LAST TIME.

CHAPTER XVI

AUSTRALIAN WICKETS

ÆRE PERENNIORA

TO give a proper description of the Australian wicket would require the technical knowledge of an Apted, combined with the pen of a Fry, but I shall endeavour to give some idea of the character of the wickets on which so much depended, and on which was fought out many a hard struggle. I can only take the wickets as we found them, and if previous tourists take exception to my remarks, let them remember that we experienced an exceptional summer, one of the wettest on record in Australia, following on a protracted period of drought. The idea underlying this chapter is that it may be of assistance to the world of cricket in understanding something of the conditions under which cricket is played " down under."

Australia is the Groundman's Paradise. He who has experienced in England the difficulty of preparing from the best of material, and following on much attention during the spring, a wicket which will not only be good, but which will remain so during the course of a match, can have no conception of the excellence of wickets in Australia, an excellence which is obtained after comparatively slight preparation from the most unpromising material. Take Adelaide. If Apted, "the Batsman's friend," were, for example, engaged there, and told that a match between England and Australia would take place in three weeks' time, his first remark, after a preliminary inspection, would probably be "where's the pitch?" He would be told to prepare one as near the middle as possible, and would probably leave for England by the next boat, considering he had been asked to attempt the impossible. Let me explain why this should be.

In England, in the centre of a ground, a portion some thirty yards square is always specially prepared and receives the most careful treatment with roller and mowing-machine for months before the commencement of the season. Walk over the Adelaide ground a fortnight or three weeks prior to the time fixed for the first match, and you will not be able to find any portion which will give the impression of being specially prepared or at all suitable for a wicket. The grass is rank and grows unevenly, and it looks as if even fielding would be impossible on such turf. (As a fact, fielding at Adelaide, at the best of times, is a matter of considerable difficulty, and demands a fair amount of courage.) Checkett, the groundman, nothing daunted, takes a hose-pipe and saturates a spot about twenty-five yards long by three wide. The roller is then applied, and by the use of these two agents, Apted, if he remained, would be astounded to witness the evolution of a wicket which will be the equal of any in the world. It will last for four or five days without showing appreciable signs of wear, and, if necessary, in about a fortnight's time, a further application of water and roller, and perhaps a little top dressing, will once more render it fit for any match ever played, and the despair of the poor bowler.

I have selected Adelaide as an example of what can be done, by the simplest means, in the way of preparing a good wicket from bad material, for this reason. The Adelaide Ground, owing to lack of money, is not nearly so well kept up as the grounds at Melbourne and Sydney, on both of which the turf is in much better condition, and the fielding ground excellent; also, both at Melbourne and Sydney, the wicket is prepared from soil brought from a distance, and of a different nature to that forming the rest of the ground. This method is also adopted at a few of the smaller towns in New South Wales, but the methods employed at Adelaide may be taken as fairly typical of those in general use throughout Australia. You will see at Adelaide old practice wickets which have crumbled practically to dust, and are useless for purposes of practice. A very little work with water and roller will convert one of these into as perfect a wicket as can be desired for an afternoon's practice. Of course, it will not last very long, but is quite good enough for a day or two.

At Melbourne, the soil is brought from a place called Merri Creek, and is applied in the form of a top-dressing. A wicket there generally requires about a month's preparation. When we first played at Melbourne v. Victoria, in the early part of the tour, a few yards from the wicket which we were using was a patch of ground some twenty-five yards by ten yards, raised some two inches above the ordinary level of the ground, and covered with a luxuriant growth of vivid green grass. Someone said, "What is that?" and was told that it

was the wicket for the test match. In about six weeks'
time we returned to find this converted into a most
perfect wicket, brown in colour, shiny as any shirt-front,

A SNAPSHOT AT ADELAIDE.

and with hardly a blade of grass showing, and the
whole, if anything, lower than the surrounding turf.
Once more water and roller had done their work,
and once more did batsmen smile, while wondering
withal at the marvellous change that had been wrought.

Sydney obtains the soil for those world-famed wickets from the Bulli Range, and the soil is known as " Bulli." This is put down to a depth of some six inches over the central portion of the ground and rolled into a compact mass, water again doing its share. A description of this wonderful soil, and wickets prepared from it, will be found in the chapter devoted to the fourth test match. I will merely say here that if a wicket were prepared of " Bulli" soil, absolutely *bare of grass*, it is my opinion that no amount of rain would ever affect it sufficiently to enable the bowler to derive any appreciable assistance from it, so great is its power of resisting water. It is only the roots of the grass which break up the surface sufficiently to enable rain to penetrate even to the slight depth it does. Fine wickets these are for Australia, and for batsmen ; also, curiously enough, not disliked by bowlers, but no wickets for English cricket, or for three day matches.

It is a curious fact that the Sydney wicket, as we found it, always possessed more " life " than any other in Australia, and the bowler could always make the ball " spin " off the pitch, and occasionally, at the beginning of a day, " get up " to an appreciable extent. This was especially noticeable with a new ball. In spite of this the Sydney wicket is the easiest to bat on I have ever known. Nowhere else does the ball ever seem to come so true, or to hit the middle of the bat so easily. To be well-set at Sydney is the dream of every batsman, and once experienced is a sensation never to be forgotten. Melbourne and Adelaide are less in favour of the bowler, but runs never come so easily on either ground as they do at Sydney.

Paradoxical as this may sound, it was none the less

the experience of most of us. It is impossible to explain why this should be ; perhaps it is merely due to the extra pace of the ground, and the ease with which boundaries seem to be made. Batsmen do not seem to take nearly so long to get set at Sydney as elsewhere, and apparently get the pace of the wicket quicker.

The Sydney wicket is unique in one way ; when there has been any rain, the *heavy* roller is nearly always the one to be employed. A little reflection will show why this should be the rule at Sydney, and nowhere else. In the ordinary way rain penetrates the wicket and sinks through into the soil beneath. If the heavy roller then be applied it has the effect of bringing the underlying moisture to the top, and thus prevents the wicket from drying quickly. Rain does not penetrate the " Bulli " soil, and therefore there is no water to be brought up to the surface. Only the top of the wicket is soft, and the more this is rolled the sooner will the surface be once more rendered hard and true, the roller having the effect of squeezing out the water. If the wicket has been in any way fit for play at the close of a day's play, a fine night and the roller in the morning can be absolutely relied upon to produce a *plumb* wicket. Some of the grounds in Australia have the most extraordinary recuperative powers. We had a striking example of this at West Maitland. When we arrived at 10.30 on the morning of the match, a heavy thunderstorm had just broken over the ground, and one or two of the team who had a look at the wicket reported that it was absolutely under water. An hour later we were hurriedly summoned to the ground. Foster won the toss and put them in. The wicket, less than an hour and a half after the storm—turned out to be *hard* and *fast*, and showed absolutely no traces of the recent rain !

The sub-soil on most grounds is sandy, and this is probably the reason of the rapidity with which they recover from the effects of rain. Melbourne is the only ground that remains affected for any considerable time after rain, and then only at the lower side of the ground, which of course is only natural. There is a difference of nine feet in the level of the ground at the upper and lower extremes, and of course the water drains down to the lower side, and collects there. The wicket at Melbourne can be the easiest pace possible, and can also be the worst in the world, when rain has done its work. We never played at Adelaide on a wet wicket, but were told that it is worse than Melbourne. This hardly seems possible, and from what we saw of the wicket the day after the close of the South Australian match—finished in a shower of rain, which continued for some hours—I should say that it takes about half the time to recover that Melbourne does.

CHAPTER XVII

A S a pendant to the history of the tour, something,
I think, ought to be said of the honour paid to us
by the M.C.C. in inviting the members of the Team to a
banquet at the Trocadero on Friday, April 22. The
occasion was naturally a delightful one to us all, and
though there were many faces that we missed around the
crowded tables, more particularly those of W. G. Grace,
C. B. Fry, G. L. Jessop, Lord Hawke, F. S. Jackson,
and A. C. MacLaren, the company of 200 cricketers
assembled included many of the names best known and
honoured at Lord's and upon all cricket grounds.

The Chair was taken by Lord Alverstone, the Lord
Chief Justice of England. I myself was awarded the
place of honour on his right hand, with Hayward on his
left, while Lord Lichfield, and Mr. A. G. Steel, K.C.,
were close by. And looking round the room, one saw
on every side faces that reminded one of great reputations and well-fought fights. Opposite the Chairman
sat Mr. F. E. Lacey, Secretary of the M.C.C., himself for
years holder of the record score in county cricket. Not
far off was Mr. A. E. Stoddart, whose praise is in all
pavilions ; Mr. F. R. Spofforth, the hero of that greatest

of all test matches in August, 1882 ; Mr. F. G. J. Ford, whose unequalled left hand hitting is now too rarely seen in first-class cricket ; Mr. H. D. G. Leveson-Gower, best of friends when the Team is in a tight corner ; Mr. A. J. Webbe, under whom I had my first taste of county cricket ; Mr. Frank Marchant (and where shall Kent find another so fearless hitter ?) ; Mr. G. J. Mordaunt, who gave me my Blue at Oxford ; Mr. H. W. Bainbridge, whose name will always be associated with the rise of Warwickshire into the front rank ; Mr. G. McGregor ; Dr. Russell Bencraft ; Mr. G. Brann ; Mr. A. W. Ridley ; Mr. F. H. E. Cunliffe ; Mr. G. J. V. Weigall ; and so many other cricketers who have helped to make history that it is impossible to go through the muster-roll and do them adequate justice. Wherever one looked, one met the form of a giant of the cricket world, and it was not surprising that one felt humble in the midst of such an assemblage. There were also present in the room Viscount Barrington, Lord Lilford, Hon. R. H. Lyttelton, Col. H. B. Kingscote, C.B., Sir G. Newnes, Sir A. Conan Doyle, Sir Francis Evans, Bart., M.P., Rev. A. Carter, Dr. Wharton Hood, Major W. E. Hardy, W. H. Blyth, F. S. W. Cornwallis, G. C. Cobb, C. E. Cobb, L. C. Docker, C. Heseltine, T. A. Higson, G. F. Higgins, H. J. Henley, R. Leigh Ibbs, Middleton Kemp, R. L. Knight, A. M. Latham, E. H. Leaf, F. W. Leaf, H. M. Leaf, Geo. Marsham, C. H. B. Marsham, E. C. Mordaunt, J. A. Murdoch, R. H. Mallett, D. R. Onslow, W. B. Pattisson, E. Preston, S. S. Pawling, H. Perkins, R. Kennerley Rumford, A. W. Ridley, A. F. Somerset, G. Hillyard Swinstead, H. R. Bromley Davenport, R. V. Turnham, M. Turner, F. W. Westray, T. Westray, J. T. Watson, A. D. Whatman,

A. H. Wood, H. O. Whitby, Sir James Blyth, and many others.

The clever and artistic Menu card, designed by Mr. G. H. Swinstead, himself no slight cricketer, is here reproduced. It inevitably loses something by reduction, but fortunately not enough to allow its excellences from escaping notice. After the usual loyal toasts, Lord Alverstone proposed the health of the Team in a fine and eloquent speech, of which the following brief report can give but a vague idea.

He said " May I be permitted to intervene for a few minutes at this most pleasant of gatherings of cricketers old and new, past and present, for I see that some of the giants of the game have come here this evening. I intervene because I do not think you would be satisfied if, however feebly it were done, a few words were not spoken by me on such a subject as the one we all love. For fifty years or more I have followed it, and there are all kinds of topics on which I might descant, but my observations must be short and to the purpose. I am not going to say that the Team that has just returned and which we are honouring to-night was the finest team that could be collected in Great Britain, because you would not believe me if I did. But they have more than justified the choice of the Selection Committee."

Continuing, after a burst of applause, Lord Alverstone asked of the company, Why were they all so glad to congratulate the Team, and what had they learnt? That the real secret of the success was that they were, as the artist had depicted, an all-round team. Every man had worked for the good of his side and not for himself. Look at the first test match at Sydney. If the Team

THE MENU CARD. APRIL 22, 1904.

were excited in Australia, and he heard since that they were, we in the London streets were even more so, and eagerly devoured the news brought us in the morning. On entering the Temple at half-past nine he had himself found the halfpenny papers commanding a rapid sale.   That was R. E. Foster's match, with his grand two hundred and eighty-seven, but that of itself would have been of little service without that one hundred and two from Braund or Relf's thirty-one and Rhodes' forty.   They had met gallant opponents, and the one hundred and eighty-five from the bat of Trumper would not readily be forgotten.   He said that the first chance which Laver had failed to accept from Hirst might have greatly changed the course of the game, and then referred to the brilliant bowling in the later test games of Rhodes with fifteen wickets for 104 and of Bosanquet, who sometimes bowled as good as it was possible to do and sometimes as badly.   He was, however, the bowler who wins matches.   In turn he made reference to the other members of the side, of the excellence of Lilley, and the possible hard luck of Strudwick in getting no chance of keeping in a representative match.   He was especially gratified at the success, because the Team had been sent out under the auspices of the M.C.C.   Everyone who had studied English cricket knew full well that we could not hope to get a fully representative side, and this time there were five or six amateurs who were asked, but could not, through business, family ties, &c., accept.   It was in the highest degree important that the selection should rest with the M.C.C., a body independent of any county interest and far more representative than any other club in the world. As regards the loss sustained, that was scarcely germane, and they did not grieve because the financial result had not been profitable. Like Stoddart's team in 1894–5, they had won three out of five test games, but they had also beaten New South Wales twice. He paid a hearty tribute to the Captain, whose anxieties had first begun when he collected the laggards, who, like Tom Hayward, had feared to face the Bay of Biscay. His duties were not confined to the field, for he had entered into their life and happiness off as well as on, and had made friends wherever he went. He had shown infinite tact and discretion, and, beyond anything which tended to an amicable agreement, there had been nothing to mar the pleasure of the tour. He heartily congratulated the M.C.C. Captain because he and his Team had always played the game and maintained in the highest degree the honour of the Old Country, creating fresh bonds of union by the many friends made.

The toast was received in a way we are none of us likely to forget, with "musical honours," full bumpers, and the most genial expressions of good feeling all round the tables. It was with no ordinary sentiment of gratitude that I rose to reply, and I know that what I could say fell far short of the obligations of the occasion. I had to do my best, however, and did it in the following words :—

"Lord Alverstone, my Lords, and Gentlemen—A few weeks ago I saw a cartoon in *Punch*, where I was depicted as a Lion to whom the Kangaroo was handing over 'The Ashes.' I am afraid I am a lion without a mane. As Lord Alverstone will tell you, in the law one usually starts by denying everything, but I do not see how, standing before you here, I can well deny that I am maneless. I am proud—very proud and happy—that a kindly fate made me Captain of the first Team which went forth to fight under the banner of the M.C.C.— the premier cricket club of the world. I heard Mr. MacLaren was going to be here to-night. I wish he were.

"A great many people have tried to make out that Mr. MacLaren and I are bitter enemies and are at daggers drawn. I assure you that is not true. Mr. MacLaren and I are friends. We missed him in Australia, and the Australian public missed him, because anyone who has studied the cricket records there must admit that Mr. MacLaren has been the prince of batsmen on Australian wickets. I missed him very much on many occasions, not only for his magnificent abilities as a cricketer but also for his judgment, and I hope that anyone who ever thought that he and myself were enemies will drive it from their minds for ever. You have heard, I daresay, a good deal about 'barracking' from the cables, but I am inclined to think the matter has been rather exaggerated, and in the case of the first test match there was some excuse for it. Trumper was going in all his glory—and a great many of you here know how his charming style and fascinating brilliancy lay hold of a crowd. Hill, the rock on whom many an English team has split, was in with him, and despite the long lead we had established on the first innings it looked as if the tide was turning in favour of the Australians. Hill was at this point given out—he *was* out. Of that I have no doubt from the evidence. I am not for a moment approving the scene which followed, though when one thinks of the frenzy of enthusiasm to which the grand uphill fight of their men had raised the crowd there were, as I think Lord Alverstone might agree, extenuating circumstances. As far as I am concerned, and I believe I voice the feelings of the whole Team, I have torn the pages from the book of memory and forgotten it for ever. Indeed, the splendid reception we received on every cricket ground in Australia—and when we won the rubber the crowd cheered as heartily as if it had been at Lord's or the Oval—has entirely obliterated the matter.

"As you all know, the Team are to meet the Rest of England at Lord's on May 9. I could have wished that it had been June 16—but I am assured that date was impossible owing to the numerous county fixtures. Now I rather think too much is made of county cricket. No one is fonder of county cricket than I am, but after all it is only a means to an end—the improvement of cricket generally. It seems to me that some of those great games which were played ten or fifteen years ago, and which had no points or percentage about them, were the ideal games, and I would like to see some sacrifice made for once in a way for a team which, after all, has worked hard for the honour of English cricket. Test matches in this country ought, I think, to be played to a finish. Mr. Chamberlain has advised us to think 'Imperially'; I, too, would urge you to think Imperially, and when the Australians next visit us to give up something for these great international contests. After all, England v. Australia is the greatest cricket match in the world, and it really seems absurd that the Australians should come 12,000 miles across the long seas, play five test games, and bring only one to a conclusion, as happened in the summer of 1899.

"Gentlemen, we pride ourselves on our pluck in a tight

corner. I can assure you the Australians are as good as, if not better than, we are in an uphill fight. Take that first test match at Sydney. You will recollect that at the end of the first innings we led by 292 runs. Every cricketer knows what the moral effect of such a lead is, and yet the Australians started their second innings in a manner which suggested they were winning easily. In the end they set us 190 odd runs to get ; and, by Jove, they nearly beat us !

" In Noble, their Captain, they possess the finest all-round cricketer in the world on Australian wickets. In England, Hirst is probably his equal—but in Australia Hirst will, I think, be the first to admit that Noble stands alone.

" But Noble is not only a great cricketer, but a great captain, and a great sportsman ; and I wish to say here that these test matches were played in the best and purest spirit. Before the first test match I said I wanted the game played in this spirit, and whichever side was beaten, they would admit themselves beaten and not put it down to bad luck, or to the umpiring, or to the hundred and one reasons so often brought forward by beaten sides.

" Before we left England we were somewhat severely criticised. But I am sure this criticism did us good. For our detractors said we could neither bat nor bowl, so we set out to show them that we could. The Great Napoleon had said that the only attribute he envied our race was that we never knew when we were beaten, and, if I may say so, the splendid success which we achieved was due to this quality.

" A great deal had been said about my selection as Captain. I do not say whether I am a good captain or

Y

not—if one accepts a position like mine one must expect to be criticised—but I graduated in a good school under Mr. Webbe, Mr. Stoddart—and I can assure Mr. Stoddart that his name is held in great respect in Australia—and Mr. MacGregor, and I should be a very stupid boy if I had not acquired some knowledge of the game.

" I tried to convert that strip of twenty-two yards into a battlefield on which no quarter was to be given ; and, if we were to go down, we were to do so fighting to the very last ball.

" I am proud—very proud indeed—but with my pride there is a feeling of great humbleness, for I could have done nothing myself without the loyalty and support of my Team. Lord Roberts has said of the South African Army that they were heroes on the field of battle and gentlemen off it—and I can say the same of this Team.

" Lord Alverstone alluded to Strudwick, and certainly it was hard luck for him to have no chance in a test match. But with Lilley in such peerless form it was impossible to leave him out: and the future is with Strudwick after all. The time will come when he will be quite *blasé* with the experience of keeping wicket in a score of ' tests.'

" Finally, there was one member of the party who took no share in our work on the field, but I am not sure that in some ways he was not the most valuable member of the combination, I mean Mr. Murdoch. He had a great deal of work to do of the sort which tries the temper, but he was always tactful and resourceful, and I personally cannot thank him enough.

" I am indeed proud that I should have been the Captain of the first M.C.C. Team for Australia, and it will ever be a splendid consolation to me to know that I

J. A. MURDOCH.

did not altogether fail to justify the confidence which you placed in me."

And so ended the last lap in the long story of the tour, a tour that I shall ever look back upon as a time which, though of course it was not without its anxieties and even its annoyances, was nevertheless, as a whole, a time of unclouded satisfaction and good-fellowship. And so, my good comrades on so many battlefields, I wish you a hearty and a grateful good-bye. When next we meet, we shall—many of us—be on opposite sides : we shall be fighting against each other, instead of against a common enemy ; the fortune of war will have changed. But one thing will never change. I shall never forget the unswerving pluck with which you fought every inch of the way ; I shall never forget the pride of being your leader. I have led great men into battle, and we have come out of the fray victorious. And now I lay down the staff of office with gratitude and pride.

APPENDIX

APPENDIX

STATISTICS OF THE TOUR, ETC.

FIRST-CLASS MATCHES ONLY.

BATTING AVERAGES.

	Matches.	Inns.	Times not Out.	Total Runs.	Most in an Inns.	Aver.
Foster, R. E.	11	18	3	7co	287	46˙66
Hayward	10	16	0	651	157	40˙68
Tyldesley	11	19	2	580	97	34˙11
Hirst	11	17	1	518	92	32˙37
Warner, P. F. (capt.)	11	19	1	559	79	31˙05
Knight	7	11	1	279	104	27˙9
Bosanquet, B. J. T.	10	15	1	371	114	26˙5
Braund	10	16	0	393	102	24˙56
Rhodes	11	15	6	188	49*	20˙83
Relf	7	9	2	119	31	17˙00
Lilley	8	13	2	176	91*	16˙00
Arnold	7	10	3	108	27	15˙42
Fielder	4	5	2	30	14*	10˙00
Strudwick	3	2	0	14	13	7˙00

* Signifies not out.

BOWLING AVERAGES.

	Overs.	Mdns.	Runs.	Wkts.	Aver.
Rhodes	357.3	92	906	62	14˙61
Braund	235	46	625	29	21˙55
Arnold	267.2	57	748	34	22˙00
Bosanquet, B. J. T.	245.4	19	889	35	25˙40
Fielder	86	28	187	7	26˙71
Hirst	324.5	73	812	30	27˙06
Relf	113.4	37	274	9	30˙44
Hayward	4	1	10	0	—

SUMMARY OF RUNS.

The M.C.C.'s team scored 4,883 runs for 161 wickets, average 30·32 per wicket.

The Australians scored 4,163 runs for 216 wickets, average 21·49 per wicket.

N.B.—First-class matches are the five Test games and the fixtures with South·Australia, Victoria, and New South Wales.

ALL MATCHES.—BATTING AVERAGES.

	Inns.	Times not Out.	Total runs.	Most in an Inns.	Aver.
Hayward	25	1	1181	157	49·20
Foster, R. E.	28	5	1053	287	45·78
Tyldesley	27	2	926	127	37·04
Bosanquet, B. J. T.	24	3	711	124*	33·85
Knight...	25	2	766	109	33·3c
Hirst	26	2	775	92	32·29
Rhodes	24	10	411	49*	29·35
Warner, P. F.	29	1	805	79	28·75
Braund	25	2	620	102	26·95
Lilley	22	4	432	102*	24·00
Relf	19	3	298	39	18·62
Arnold	16	3	192	34	14·76
Strudwick	11	0	142	42	12·90
Fielder	15	4	88	23	8·00

The following also batted : G. S. Whitfeld, 12, 5, 0 ; G. Drummond, 8, 1, 0.

* Signifies not out.

BOWLING AVERAGES.

	Overs.	Mdns.	Runs.	Wkts.	Aver.
Rhodes...	486.3	130	1181	76	15·53
Braund...	414.3	78	1161	72	16·12
Arnold	387.1	111	954	53	18·00
Fielder	247.1	64	605	33	18·33
Relf	242.5	83	539	28	19·25
Hirst	428.1	105	1007	45	22·37
Bosanquet, B. J. T.	337.4	29	1317	53	24·84

The following is the complete record of the twenty matches played by the M.C.C. Team :—

Won, 10.

At Melbourne, v. Victoria, November 13, 14, 16.—England, 443 for 8 (innings closed) ; Victoria, 162 and 210. Won by an innings and 71 runs.

At Sydney, v. New South Wales, November 20, 21, 23. England, 319 ; New South Wales, 108 and 201. Won by an innings and 10 runs.

At Brisbane, *v.* Queensland, November 27, 28, and 30.—England, 215 and 119 for 4 ; Queensland, 242 and 91. Won by 6 wickets.

At Sydney, *v.* Australia (No. 1), December 11, 12, 14, 15, 16, 17.— England, 577 and 194 for 5 ; Australia, 285 and 485. England won by 5 wickets.

At Melbourne, *v.* Victorian Juniors (18), December.—England, 416 ; Juniors, 124 and 193. England won by an innings and 99 runs.

At Melbourne, *v.* Australia (No. 2), January 1, 2, 4, 5.—England, 315 and 103; Australia, 122 and 111. Won by 185 runs.

At Melbourne, *v.* Victoria, February 5, 8, and 9.—England, 248 and 68 for 2 ; Victoria, 299 and 15. Won by 8 wickets.

At Sydney, *v.* New South Wales, February 12, 13, 15. England, 190 and 461 ; New South Wales, 232 and 141. Won by 278 runs.

At Sydney, *v.* Australia (No. 4), February 26, 27, 29, March 1, 2, 3.— England, 249 and 210. Australia, 131 and 171. England won by 157 runs.

At Adelaide, *v.* South Australia, March 12, 14, 15.—England, 154 and 184 for 1 ; South Australia, 259 and 77. Won by 9 wickets.

Lost, 2.

At Adelaide, *v.* Australia (No. 3), January 15, 16, 18, 19, 20.—England, 245 and 278; Australia, 288 and 351. Lost by 216 runs.

At Melbourne, *v.* Australia (No. 5), March 5, 7, 8.—England, 61 and 101 ; Australia, 247 and 131. Lost by 218 runs.

Drawn, 8.

At Adelaide, *v.* South Australia, November, 7, 9, 10, 11.—England, 483 for 8 (innings closed) ; South Australia, 172 and 343 for 7.

At Maitland, *v.* Maitland District (18), December 2, 3.—England, 453 ; Maitland, 284 and 241 for 6.

At Newcastle, *v.* Newcastle (15), December 4, 5.—England, 306 and 381 for 8 ; Newcastle, 203.

At Bendigo, *v.* Bendigo (18), December 26, 28.—England, 273 for 5 (innings closed) ; Bendigo, 94 and 64 for 7.

At Ballarat, *v.* Ballarat (18), January 8, 9.—England, 326 and 226 ; Ballarat, 197.

At Hobart, *v.* Tasmania, January 25 and 26.—England, 185 and 354 for 4 (innings closed) ; Tasmania, 191 and 63 for 1.

At Launceston, *v.* Tasmania, January 29 and 30.—England, 353 ; Tasmania, 141 and 259 for 2.

At Bathurst, *v.* Western District (15), February 19, 20.—England, 176 and 115 for 5 ; Western District, 248 and 151 for 3 (innings closed).

Played 20—Won 10, Lost 2, Drawn 8.

SOME TEST MATCH STATISTICS.

Fifty runs and over each innings of a match.

Trumper, V., for Australia, Adelaide, 1904—113 and 59—172.
Tyldesley, J. T., for England, Melbourne, Jan., 1904—97 and 62—159.
Noble, M. A., for Australia, Adelaide, 1904—59 and 65–124.

Batsmen who aggregated 100 runs for a test match without scoring the century in either innings.

Tyldesley, J. T., for England, Melbourne, Jan., 1904—97 and 62 – 159.
Warner, P. F., for England, Adelaide, 1904—48 and 79—127.
Noble, M. A., for Australia, Adelaide, 1904—59 and 65—124.
Trumper, V., for Australia, Melbourne, Jan., 1904—74 and 35—109.
Hayward, T., for England, Sydney, 1903—15 and 91—106.
Hill, C., for Australia, Adelaide, 1904- 88 and 16—104.
Hirst, G. H., for England, Adelaide, 1904—58 and 44—102.

LONG PARTNERSHIPS IN THE TEST MATCHES.

First Wicket.

148—Hayward and Warner, at Adelaide, Jan., 1904.
129—Duff and Trumper, at Adelaide, Jan., 1904.
122—Hayward and Warner, at Melbourne, Jan., 1904.

Second Wicket.

143—Hill and Trumper, at Adelaide, Jan., 1904.

Fourth Wicket.

162—Gregory and Noble, at Adelaide, Jan., 1904.
106—Armstrong and Noble, at Sydney, Dec., 1903.

Fifth Wicket.

192—Braund and Foster, at Sydney, Dec., 1903.

Ninth Wicket.

115—Foster and Relf, at Sydney, Dec., 1903.

Tenth Wicket.

130—Foster and Rhodes, at Sydney, Dec., 1903.

Individual Scores of 50 and over.

287—Foster, R. E., for Eng'and, Sydney, 1903.
185*—Trumper, V., for Australia, Sydney, 1903.
133—Noble, M. A., for Australia, Sydney, 1903.
113- Trumper, V., for Australia, Adelaide, 1904.
102—Braund, L. C., for England, Sydney, 1903.
97—Tyldesley, J. T., for England, Melbourne, Jan., 1904.
91—Hayward, T., for England, Sydney, 1903.
88—Hill, C., for Australia, Adelaide, 1904.
88—Trumper, V., for Australia, Melbourne, March, 1904.
84—Duff, R. A., for Australia, Sydney, 1903.
79—Duff, R. A., for Australia, Adelaide, 1904.
79—Warner, P. F., for England, Adelaide, 1904.
74—Trumper, V., for Australia, Melbourne, Jan., 1904.
70*—Knight, A. E., for England, Sydney, 1904.

* Signifies not out.

68—Warner, P. F., for England, Melbourne, Jan., 1904.
67—Hayward, T., for England, Adelaide, 1904.
65—Noble, M. A., for Australia, Adelaide, 1904.
62—Tyldesley, J. T., for England, Melbourne, Jan., 1904.
60*—Hirst, G. H., for England, Sydney, 1903.
59—Noble, M. A., for Australia, Adelaide, 1904.
59—Trumper, V., for Australia, Adelaide, 1904.
58—Hayward, T., for England, Melbourne, Jan., 1904.
58—Hirst, G. H., for England, Adelaide, 1904.
53*—Noble, M. A., for Australia, Sydney, 1904.
53—Tyldesley, J. T., for England, Sydney, 1903.
52—Hayward, T., for England, Sydney, 1904.
51—Hill, C., for Australia, Sydney, 1903.

NOTABLE PERFORMANCES WITH THE BALL IN THE TEST MATCHES.

Ten wickets and over in a match.

15 for 124—Rhodes, W. R., for England, Melbourne, January, 1904.

Seven wickets and over in an innings.

8 for 68—Rhodes, W. R., for England, Melbourne, January, 1904.
8 for 81—Braund, L. C., for England, Melbourne, March, 1904.
7 for 28—Trumble, H., for Australia, Melbourne, March, 1904.
7 for 56—Rhodes, W. R., for England, Melbourne, January, 1904.
7 for 100—Noble, M. A., for Australia, Sydney, 1904.

"Hat Trick."—Trumble, H., for Australia, Melbourne, March, 1904.
The Melbourne bowler is the only man who has performed the hat trick a second time in Tests. Strangely enough, his first example was recorded in the last innings of the final Test at Melbourne during the last tour of the Englishmen there.

SUNDRY RECORDS.

Fifty Extras and over in a Match.—53, Sydney, December, 1903.

Catches.—Braund, 9 ; Foster, Noble, 7 each ; McAlister, Trumper, 6 each ; Howell, Relf, Rhodes, Trumble, 5 each; Arnold, Duff, Hirst, 4 each ; Bosanquet, Gehrs, Gregory, Hill, Hopkins, Tyldesley, 3 each ; Armstrong, Fielder, McLeod, Warner, 2 each ; Hayward, Knight, Laver, 1 each.

Sundries.—England gave Australia 71 byes, 9 wides, 5 no balls—85 ; Australia gave England 62 byes, 12 wides, 3 no balls—77.

Big Aggregates.—1,541 for 35 wickets at Sydney, 1903 ; 1,262 for 40 wickets at Adelaide, 1904.

* Signifies not out.

Big Innings.—577, England, Sydney, 1903; 485, Australia, Sydney, 1903.

Wicket Keeping.—Lilley caught 8, stumped 9—17; Kelly caught 6, stumped 5—11.

———

England won three of the games, and Australia two, the aggregate records standing:—England, 2,333 runs for ninety-two wickets, average 25·35 ; Australia, 2,424 runs for 100 wickets, average 24·24. It will be noticed that all ten innings were completed by Australia.

———

ENGLISH CENTURIES.

Bosanquet, B. I. T.—*v.* Tasmania (Hobart), January 25 ... ... *124
Bosanquet, B. J. T.—*v.* N.S.W. (return), February 12 114
Braund—*v.* Australia (1), December 11 102
Foster, R. E.—*v.* XV. of Newcastle, December 4 105
Foster, R. E.—*v.* Australia (1), December 11 287
Hayward—*v.* South Australia, November 7 157
Hayward—*v.* XVIII. of Bendigo, December 26... 115
Hayward—*v.* XI. of Northern Tasmania, January 29 134
Knight—*v.* XVII. of Ballarat, January 8 109
Knight—*v.* New South Wales (return), February 12 104
Lilley—*v.* XVIII. of Northern District, December 2 ... ... *102
Tyldesley—*v.* XVIII. of Northern District, December 2 101
Tyldesley—*v.* XV. of Newcastle, December 4 127

———

AUSTRALIAN CENTURIES.

Gregory, C.—for XV. of Bathurst (N.S.W.), February 19 138
Gregory, S. E.—for Australia (3), January 15 112
Hill, C.—for South Australia, November 7... 116
McAlister, P.—for Victoria (return), February 5 139
Noble, M. A.—for Australia (1), December 11 133
Savigny, J. H.—for XI. of Northern Tasmania, January 29 .. ... *164
Trumper, V.—for Australia (1), December 11 ... ... *185
Trumper, V.—for Australia (3), January 15 113
Waddy, Rev. P. S.—for XVIII. of Northern District, December 2... 102

* Signifies not out.

TRUMPER'S CENTURIES AGAINST ENGLISH BOWLING.

1899—135 (not out) *v.* England, at Lord's.
1899—104 *v.* Gloucestershire, at Bristol.
1899—300 (not out) *v.* Sussex, at Brighton.
1902—128 *v.* Cambridge University, at Cambridge.
1902—127 *v.* Eleven Players of England, at Harrogate.
1902—125 *v.* Gloucestershire, at Cheltenham.
1902—121 *v.* Oxford University, at Oxford.
1902—120 *v.* South of England, at Hastings.
1902—119 *v.* Essex, at Leyton.
1902—113 *v.* England's XI., at Bradford.
1902—109 *v.* Essex, at Leyton.
1902—105 *v.* M.C.C., at Lord's.
1902—104 *v.* England, at Manchester.
1902—101 *v.* Surrey, at Oval.
1903—185 (not out) England, at Sydney.
1904—113 *v.* England, at Adelaide.

————

TEST MATCH RECORDS.

IN AUSTRALIA.

Highest Australian innings, 586—Sydney, 1894.
Highest English innings, 577—Sydney, 1903.
Lowest Australian innings, 42– Sydney, 1888.
Lowest English innings, 45—Sydney, 1887.
Highest scorer (Australia), 201—S. E. Gregory, 1894.
Highest scorer (England), 287—R. E. Foster, 1903.

IN ENGLAND.

Highest Australian innings, 551—Oval, 1884.
Highest English innings, 576—Oval, 1899.
Lowest Australian innings, 36—Birmingham, 1902.
Lowest English innings, 53—Lord's, 1888.
Highest scorer (Australia), 211—W. L. Murdoch, 1884.
Highest scorer (England), 170—W. G. Grace, 1886.

CENTURIES.

1877—Melbourne	C. Bannerman	165
1880—Oval	W. G. Grace	152
	W. L. Murdoch	153*
1882—Melbourne	T. Horan	124
Sydney	P. S. McDonnell	147
Melbourne	G. Ulyett	149
1883—Sydney	A. G. Steel	135*
1884—Lord's	A. G. Steel	148
Oval	P. S. McDonnell	103
	W. L. Murdoch	211
	H. J. H. Scott	102
	W. W. Read	117

* Signifies not out.

1884—Adelaide	P. S. McDonnell	124
	W. Barnes	134
1885—Melbourne	J. Briggs	121
Sydney	G. J. Bonnor	128
Melbourne	A. Shrewsbury	105*
1886—Lord's	A. Shrewsbury	164
Oval	W. G. Grace	170
1892—Sydney	... J. J. Lyons	134
	R. Abel	132*
Adelaide	A. E. Stoddart	134
1893—Lord's	A. Shrewsbury	106
	H. Graham	107
Oval	F. S. Jackson	103
Manchester	... W. Gunn	102*
1894—Sydney	S. E. Gregory	201
	A. Ward	117
1895—Melbourne	A. E. Stoddart	173
Adelaide	F. A. Iredale	140
Sydney	... H. Graham	105
Melbourne	A. C. MacLaren	120
	J. T. Brown	140
1896—Lord's	... S. E. Gregory	103
Manchester	K. S. Ranjitsinhji	154*
	F. A. Iredale	108
Lord's	... G. H. S. Trott	143
1897—Sydney	A. C. MacLaren	109
	K. S. Ranjitsinhji	175
	J. Darling	178
1898—Melbourne	C. McLeod	112
Adelaide	... J. Darling	178
	A. C. MacLaren	124
Melbourne	... C. Hill	188
Sydney	... J. Darling	160
1899—Manchester	T. Hayward	130
Oval	T. Hayward	137
	F. S. Jackson	118
	S. E. Gregory	117
Lord's	... C. Hill	135
	V. Trumper	135*
1902—Sydney	A. C. MacLaren	116
Melbourne	... R. A. Duff	104
Adelaide	L. C. Braund	102
Birmingham	J. T. Tyldesley	138
Sheffield	... C. Hill	119
Manchester	F. S. Jackson	128
	V. Trumper	104
Oval	G. L. Jessop	104
1903—Sydney	R. E. Foster	287
	M. A. Noble	133
	V. Trumper	185*
	L. C. Braund	102
1904—Adelaide	V. Trumper	113
	S. E. Gregory	112

* Signifies not out.

TEST MATCH BOWLING RECORDS.

1879 ... Melbourne	Spofforth	13 wkts. for 110
1882 ... Oval	Spofforth	14 wkts. for 90
1883 ... Melbourne	Palmer ...	10 wkts. for 126
1883 ... Melbourne	Bates	13 wkts. for 102
1883 ... Sydney	Spofforth	11 wkts. for 117
1886 ... Lord's	Briggs	11 wkts. for 74
1886 ... Oval	Lohmann	12 wkts. for 104
1887 ... Sydney	Lohmann	10 wkts. for 87
1887 ... Sydney	Turner... ...	12 wkts. for 87
1887 ... Sydney	Peel	10 wkts. for 58
1887 ... Sydney	Lohmann	9 wkts. for 52
1888 .. Lord's	Peel	8 wkts. for 50
1888 ... Lord's	Turner	10 wkts. for 63
1888 ... Lord's	Ferris	8 wkts. for 45
1888 ... Manchester	Peel	11 wkts. for 68
1890 ... Oval	Martin...	10 wkts. for 102
1890 ... Oval	Ferris	9 wkts. for 74
1892 ... Sydney	Lohmann	10 wkts. for 142
1892 ... Sydney	Giffen	10 wkts. for 160
1892 ... Adelaide	Briggs	12 wkts. for 136
1893 ... Oval	Briggs	10 wkts. for 148
1893 ... Manchester	Richardson... ...	10 wkts. for 156
1896 ... Lord's	Richardson	11 wkts. for 173
1896 ... Manchester	Richardson... ...	13 wkts. for 244
1896 ... Oval	Trumble	12 wkts. for 89
1896 ... Oval ... ...;	Peel	8 wkts. for 53
1898 ... Sydney	Richardson... ...	10 wkts. for 204
1898 ... Lord's	Jones	10 wkts. for 164
1902 ... Melbourne	Barnes...	13 wkts. for 163
1902 ... Melbourne	Noble	13 wkts. for 77
1902 ... Birmingham...	Rhodes	8 wkts. for 26
1902 ... Sheffield	Noble	11 wkts. for 103
1902 ... Manchester	Lockwood	11 wkts. for 76
1902 ... Manchester	Trumble	10 wkts for 128
1902 ... Oval	Trumble	12 wkts. for 173
1904 ... Melbourne	Rhodes	15 wkts. for 124

FIRST WICKET PARTNERSHIPS IN ALL TEST MATCHES.

The following is a complete list of the occasions on which a hundred has been made for the first wicket in the Test matches between England and Australia :

T. Hayward and F. S. Jackson, Oval, August, 1899..	185
W. G. Grace and W. H. Scotton, Oval, August, 1886	170
T. Hayward and A. C. MacLaren, Sydney, December, 1901	154
W. G. Grace and A. E. Stoddart, Oval, August, 1893	149
T. Hayward and A. C. MacLaren, Adelaide, January, 1902	149
T. Hayward and P. F. Warner, Adelaide, January, 1904	148
R. A. Duff and V. Trumper, Manchester, July, 1902	135
R. A. Duff and V. Trumper, Adelaide, January, 1904	129
R. G. Barlow and G. Ulyett, Sydney, February, 1882	122
T. Hayward and P. F. Warner, Melbourne, January, 1904	122
C. E. McLeod and J. Worrall, Oval, August, 1899	116
A. C. MacLaren and E. Wainwright, Sydney, February, 1898 ...	111

FULL LIST OF TEST MATCHES.

ENGLAND V. AUSTRALIA.

Matches played, 71—England, 31 ; Australia, 28 ; drawn, 12.

— ——

ENGLISH TEAMS IN AUSTRALIA.

FIRST TEAM : 1862.

II. H. Stephenson (capt.), Surrey.
C. Lawrence, Surrey.
W. Caffyn, Surrey.
G. Griffith, Surrey.
W. Mortlock, Surrey.
W. Mudie, Surrey.

T. Sewell, Surrey.
G. Bennett, Kent.
T. Hearne, Middlesex.
G. Wells, Sussex.
R. Iddison, Yorkshire.
E. Stevenson, Yorkshire.

SECOND TEAM : 1864.

G. Parr (capt.), Notts.
A. Clarke, Notts.
J. Jackson, Notts.
G. Tarrant, Cambridgeshire.
Mr. E. M. Grace, Gloucestershire.
G. Anderson, Yorkshire.

R. C. Tinley, Notts.
W. Caffyn, Surrey.
J. Caesar, Surrey.
R. Carpenter, Cambridgeshire.
T. Lockyer, Surrey.
T. Hayward, Cambridgeshire.

THIRD TEAM : 1873.

Mr. W. G. Grace (capt.), Gloucester-
shire.
Mr. G. F. Grace, Gloucestershire.
Mr. J. A. Bush, Gloucestershire.
Mr. W. R. Gilbert, Gloucestershire.
R. Humphrey, Surrey.
H. Jupp, Surrey.

Mr. F. H. Boult, Surrey.
J. Southerton, Surrey.
M. McIntyre, Notts.
W. Oscroft, Notts.
Andrew Greenwood, Yorkshire.
James Lilywhite, Sussex.

FOURTH TEAM : 1876.

James Lilywhite (capt.), Sussex.
H. Charlwood, Sussex.
A. Greenwood, Yorkshire.
T. Armitage, Yorkshire.
T. Emmett, Yorkshire.
A. Hill, Yorkshire.

G. Ulyett, Yorkshire.
H. Jupp, Surrey.
J. Southerton, Surrey.
E. Pooley, Surrey.
A. Shaw, Notts.
J. Selby, Notts.

FIFTH TEAM : 1878.

Lord Harris (capt.), Kent.
Mr. C. A. Absolom, Kent.
Mr. F. A. Mackinnon, Kent.
Mr. F. Penn, Kent.
Mr. A. N. Hornby, Lancashire.
Mr. V. K. Royle, Lancashire.
Mr. S. S. Schultz, Lancashire.

Mr. A. P. Lucas, Surrey.
Mr. A. J. Webbe, Middlesex.
Mr. H. C. Maul, Warwickshire.
Mr. L. Hone, Ireland.
G. Ulyett, Yorkshire.
T. Emmett, Yorkshire.

SIXTH TEAM : 1881.

A. Shaw (capt.), Notts.
A. Shrewsbury, Notts.
J. Selby, Notts.
W. Scotton, Notts.
W. Bates, Yorkshire.
E. Peate, Yorkshire.

T. Emmett, Yorkshire.
G. Ulyett, Yorkshire.
R. C. Barlow, Lancashire.
R. Pilling, Lancashire.
W. Midwinter, Gloucestershire.
J. Lilywhite, Sussex.

SEVENTH TEAM : 1882.

Hon. Ivo Bligh (capt.), Kent.
Mr. E. F. S. Tylecote, Kent.
Mr. C. T. Studd, Middlesex.
Mr. C. F. H. Leslie, Middlesex.
Mr. G. B. Studd, Middlesex.
Mr. W. W. Read, Surrey.

Mr. G. F. Vernon, Middlesex.
Mr. A. G. Steel, Lancashire.
W. Barnes, Notts.
F. Morley, Notts.
W. Bates, Yorkshire.
R. G. Barlow, Lancashire.

EIGHTH TEAM : 1884.

A. Shaw (capt.), Notts.
W. Barnes, Notts.
W. Scotton, Notts.
W. Attewell, Notts.
W. Flowers, Notts.
A. Shrewsbury, Notts.
R. Peel, Yorkshire.

G. Ulyett, Yorkshire.
J. Hunter, Yorkshire.
W. Bates, Yorkshire.
J. Lilywhite, Sussex.
J. M. Read, Surrey.
J. Briggs, Lancashire.

NINTH TEAM : 1886.

A. Shrewsbury (capt.), Notts.
W. Barnes, Notts.
W. Gunn, Notts.
W. Scotton, Notts.
A. Shaw, Notts.
W. Flowers, Notts.
M. Sherwin, Notts.

G. Lohmann, Surrey
J. M. Read, Surrey.
J. Briggs, Lancashire.
R. G. Barlow, Lancashire.
J. Lilywhite, Sussex.
W. Bates, Yorkshire.

TENTH TEAM : 1887.

Hon. M. B. Hawke (capt.), York-
shire.
W. Bates, Yorkshire.
R. Peel, Yorkshire.
J. T. Rawlin, Yorkshire.
W. Attewell, Notts.
Mr. A. E. Newton, Somerset.

Mr. G. F. Vernon, Middlesex.
Mr. A. E. Stoddart, Middlesex.
Mr. T. C. O'Brien, Middlesex.
Mr. W. W. Read, Surrey.
Mr. M. P. Bowden, Surrey.
J. Beaumont, Surrey.

ELEVENTH TEAM : 1887.

Mr. C. A. Smith (capt.), Sussex.
Mr. W. Newham, Sussex.
Mr. G. Brann, Sussex.
J. Lilywhite, Sussex.
G. Lohmann, Surrey.
J. M. Read, Surrey.
J. Briggs, Lancashire.

R. Pilling, Lancashire.
G. Ulyett, Yorkshire.
J. M. Preston, Yorkshire.
A. Shrewsbury, Notts.
A. D. Pougher, Leicestershire.
Mr. L. C. Docker, Warwickshire.

TWELFTH TEAM : 1891.

Mr. W. G. Grace (capt.), Gloucestershire.
Mr. A. E. Stoddart, Middlesex.
Mr. G. McGregor, Cambridge University.
Mr. O. G. Radcliffe, Gloucestershire.
Mr. H. Philipson, Northumberland.

G. Lohmann, Surrey.
J. M. Read, Surrey.
J. W. Sharpe, Surrey.
W. Attewell, Notts.
R. Peel, Yorkshire.
J. Briggs, Lancashire.
G. Bean, Sussex.
R. Abel, Surrey.

THIRTEENTH TEAM : 1894.

Mr. A. E. Stoddart (capt.), Middlesex.
Mr. A. C. MacLaren, Lancashire.
Mr. F. G. J. Ford, Middlesex.
Mr. L. H. Gay, Somerset.
Mr. H. Philipson, Middlesex.
T. Richardson, Surrey.

W. Brockwell, Surrey.
W. Lockwood, Surrey.
A. Ward, Lancashire.
J. Briggs, Lancashire.
R. Peel, Yorkshire.
J. T. Brown, Yorkshire.
W. A. Humphreys, Sussex.

FOURTEENTH TEAM : 1897.

Mr. A. E. Stoddart (capt.), Middlesex.
Mr. A. C. MacLaren, Lancashire.
Mr. N. F. Druce, Surrey.
K. S. Ranjitsinhji, Sussex.
Mr. J. R. Mason, Kent.
T. Hayward, Surrey.

T. Richardson, Surrey.
J. T. Hearne, Middlesex.
E. Wainwright, Yorkshire.
G. H. Hirst, Yorkshire.
J. Briggs, Lancashire.
W. Storer, Derbyshire.
J. H. Board, Gloucestershire.

FIFTEENTH TEAM : 1901.

Mr. A. C. MacLaren (capt.), Lancashire.
Mr. G. L. Jessop, Gloucestershire.
Mr. A. O. Jones, Notts.
Mr. H. Garnett, Lancashire.
Mr. C. McGahey, Essex.
Mr. C. Robson, Hants.
T. Hayward, Surrey.

J. T. Tyldesley, Lancashire.
W. G. Quaife, Warwickshire.
A. A. Lilley, Warwickshire.
L. C. Braund, Somerset.
J. Gunn, Notts.
C. Blythe, Kent.
S. F. Barnes, Lancashire.

SIXTEENTH TEAM : 1903.

Mr. P. F. Warner (capt.), Middlesex.
Mr. B. J. T. Bosanquet, Middlesex.
Mr. R. E. Foster, Worcestershire.
T. Hayward, Surrey.
G. H. Hirst, Yorkshire.
W. R. Rhodes, Yorkshire.
J. T. Tyldesley, Lancashire.

E. Arnold, Worcestershire.
A. E. Relf, Sussex.
A. A. Lilley, Warwickshire.
L. C. Braund, Somerset.
A. E. Knight, Leicestershire.
H. Strudwick, Surrey.
A. Fielder, Kent.

THE END

R. CLAY AND SONS, LTD., BREAD STREET HILL, E.C., AND BUNGAY, SUFFOLK.